THE THIRD ADVENT

Grégoire de Kalbermatten

daisyamerica LLC

Published by daisyamerica of New York

Library of Congress catalog-in-Publication Data has been applied for.

ISBN: 1-932406-07-7

First U.S. Edition 2003

10 9 8 7 6 5 4 3 2 1

Typeset and printed in the United States of America by King Printing, 181 Industrial Avenu
Lowell, MA 01852

TABLE OF CONTENTS

THE THIRD ADVENT

To the One who is both the Difficult River and the Far Shore, the Unchanging Essence and the Creator, Salutations again and again.

— Devi Mahatmyam

The All Powerful. Adi Shakti, the Goddess, who is the source of all Powers, who is beyond all the Powers, who is the pure Power of Sadashiva, of God Almighty, who alone gives Moksha or Self-realization, who destroys the demons to protect and save Her children from negativity.

— Shri Mataji Nirmala Devi

ACKNOWLEDGEMENTS

In August 1975, at Hurst Green in England, I met an extraordinary spiritual personality, Shri Mataji Nirmala Devi, and in a book entitled *The Advent*, which was privately published in New Delhi in 1979, I presented an account of this experience. In essence, *The Third Advent* pursues a reflection that has developed over the years since this first meeting. Frankly, I never considered myself equipped with any merit in the spiritual field but the experiences I went through and the perspectives opened by the teachings of this Master were simply too exciting; great news must be shared and explored further. I do not pretend to capture or reflect here the essence of the life or message of this Master, but the knowledge I am trying to share draws its meaning from this encounter. For me, it was the piece of the puzzle that revealed the whole design.

I've tried to relate to our common experience, this most peculiar condition of being both matter and consciousness. My approach treads the familiar paths of history, psychology and philosophy and I realize that the same subject could elsewhere be equally approached from the angle of medicine and the sciences.

There is an element of futility in putting into words a reality that constantly escapes description. Hence, in essence, this writing is unfinished and it merely stops at a point where the reader may come on board, pick up some interesting clues and continue her or his own journey. It is said that an accident on the path of a prepared mind leads to discovery and for this reason the ultimate value of this book is dependent on the curiosity of the reader.

I would like to record my deep appreciation to my friends Alan Wherry and James Kosakow for their work in copyediting and for their insights regarding the structure of this manuscript. Thanks too, to Irene Bose for her support, to Richard Payment for designing the jacket, to Ciaran McLaughlin, Linda Taylor and Ken Williams, for copyediting, to Uttam Bera for last minute work on the manuscript and to Siddhartha Chinai of King Printing for his support, help and professionalism. I also thank Professor Maurizio Zollo for his advice and encouragement. I am greatly indebted to Dan Costian, Flore Descieux, Geoffrey Godfrey, Gwen Verrez and Majid Golpour for their work and contributions to this subject.

The Author

INTRODUCTION

Even a casual read of today's newspapers reveals that the world we live in is in a bad state. We are beset with problems that seem beyond our abilities to solve: increasing levels of depression and stress, rising unemployment in the so-called developed countries and corporate malpractice. Only the climate is warming; solidarity is out of fashion, while the hearts of the societies in the North seem to have grown cold. On the other hand, poverty in the developing South is on the rise. The last 20 years have seen the gap between rich and poor increase at an alarming rate, both internally, within each of the 'developed countries' and externally, when these countries are compared to those in the Third World. There is today enough food on the planet to feed everyone, but alas, no political will to make it happen. Meanwhile we consume non-renewable natural resources at an ever-increasing rate, and on top of all this, we face the continued threat of terrorism and wars.

Where will solace come from? Many feel that the great religions of the world have failed to persuade their followers to behave as their founders said they should. Indeed, within them there is dissension and corruption on a scale that has caused many to question their very authority. On the other hand, there is an ongoing rise in religious fanaticism of every kind, and those who lead it appear to be bent on creating mayhem and misery. Politics does not seem to help. In many countries, people have lost faith in the political process to a point where fewer and fewer bother to vote in each successive election. Our interests are represented less and less by our political and governmental institutions, and are often at odds with the prerogatives of the corporate world.

Even with the material progress we have made, the individual often feels left behind. We are bombarded with data faster than we can absorb it. Our awareness and judgment have suffered. In modern democracies, we seem to have settled for an inequitable socio-economic system, a loss of ethics, a culture of escapism and trivia promoted and supported by the entertainment industry.

The Third Advent follows a trail of past teachings and prophecies and unveils a possible solution for our collective survival and regeneration. It describes an extraordinary encounter with a most enigmatic and endearing spiritual master, Shri Mataji Nirmala Devi. It presents Self-realization, introduced en masse by this holy personality, as the chief hypothesis leading to an evolutionary breakthrough, the awakening of our inner system, and ultimately our transformation into the beings we were designed to become.

The implications of this discovery in terms of the history of consciousness are far reaching and intriguing. *The Third Advent* describes the workings of the system inbuilt within each one of us: centers and channels of subtle energies whose powers are released by the awakening of a residual force known as Kundalini - which, when released, connects us to a universal power. Through Kundalini awakening, Self-realization occurs, and the human microcosmic computer becomes wired to the cosmic program. At that point data starts to flow in our nervous system and is felt as vibrations. We feel then the state of our own inner system and the systems of others. When

1

we are then linked to the cosmic program by vibratory awareness, we discover true reality and can perceive directly the most sacred, secret and beautiful core of our being. We connect with the whole, the first model of which the human system is a reflection. This awakening marks the entry into a higher state of consciousness and power, a state in which we understand better, enjoy more and become more effective in all aspects of our lives.

In our current condition, we have blockages in our energy centers, caused by our past actions, experiences and conditioning. The blockages inhibit the flow of the spiritual energy through the centers. Each center has specific qualities associated with it, and when the kundalini is unable to flow, the qualities of the centers recede, and in their place we find the problems associated with the improper functioning of the centers. *The Third Advent* discusses the specific problems of our inner system, the effects of blockages on the centers and the consequences on individual personality and on the world we live in. It discusses what we and our world can become when these blockages are cleared, and suggests the human qualities that would manifest with the activation of a fully functioning inner system. We become innocent, imaginative, satisfied, secure, collective, confident and real. As we change, so does our world.

The personality and destiny of each human being depends on the quality of the relationship between his spiritual instrument and God, the cosmic archetype. The manifestation of our hidden spiritual powers is essential for our collective survival. They work for the individual and the collective alike. This opens a path to a truly humanistic way of life in which we will find our satisfaction in what we are, and not in what we have.

At this stage of our evolution, *homo sapiens* can become *homo spiritualis* and in so doing, develop a new vibratory category of perception, which will, in turn, guide us into a new cognitive kingdom. *Homo spiritualis* will then enter into a new web of relationships with the cosmos, with nature, with all living beings including himself. Through vibratory awareness a collective consciousness develops for the common good of the community as well as the needs and aspirations of others.

Spiritual knowledge is essential, so we must make sense of it, we must know ourselves. In the process, we would not only survive, but we would feel for the first time an indescribable connection and sense of security and peace, a happiness and bliss which is our birthright. The question that we raise is therefore: can we achieve the purpose of our own design and of our collective destiny?

PART ONE

THE TWILIGHT ZONE

The owl of Minerva takes its flight at dusk.

         – Georg Wilhelm Friedrich Hegel

        The twilight is the time of day when things are not quite what they seem to be. I see a rope but it may be a snake; shade swallows forms. At the time of confusion, when the protective walls of certainties are being lowered and options start dancing before the puzzled mind, we need to sharpen our awareness. This is also the time when the potential for discovery may bear its promises for, as Meister Eckhart reminded us, it is in darkness that one finds the light, and from a spiritual point of view, these times seem dark enough.

1. THE STORY OF THE RUNNING DEER

I went to the woods because I wished to live deliberately, to front only the essential facts of life, and see if I could not learn what it had to teach, and not, when I come to die, discover that I had not lived.

– Henry David Thoreau, Walden

THE MESSAGE OF JOACHIM

Strange is our situation here upon earth. Each of us comes for a short visit, not knowing why, yet sometimes seeming to divine a purpose.

– Albert Einstein

Little over half a century since the madness of two world wars, violence and conflict again threaten to engulf our civilization. Images of natural disasters and catastrophes that moviemakers have used to provide for our entertainment are now returning as live events on our TV screens. Natural catastrophes such as forest fires, typhoons, hurricanes, and volcanic eruptions have steadily intensified in the 1990s. Their costs are rising - and this is happening in a context of climate change. How many of us, especially in the West, know that Mongolia's herdsmen lost about six million cattle in a succession of droughts and harsh winters in 2000 and 2001, and of those who do, can we begin to realize what it meant to these people? In the so-called rich countries, the economic mirage of the 1990s has left behind empty wallets, depleted pension funds and investment portfolios.

It was hoped in the minds of its authors, that the fateful 9/11 attacks on the great towers of New York City would launch a potentially titanic clash between the Christian and Muslim worlds; new nonsense along old fault lines. But is there a way out from the sheer stupidity of the killing fields? Understandably, our governments want to eradicate terrorism but can we ever hope to restore peace and stability in the world without first ensuring solidarity and justice for all? Surely the youth in parts of the Third World, many of whom live lives of poverty and frustration, must be given alternatives to the fundamentalist option. Preachers of hate from Algeria to the Philippines provide illusory meaning to the marginal lives of vulnerable groups, and neither cruise missiles, flying drones nor other gadgets of military technology can bring about the solution. A great storm is gathering, and hatred is on the rise.

The defense of civilization requires a more comprehensive concept and it begins with philosophy and wisdom. How can a more effective defense shield be built to protect civilization, enlarge our concept of security and indeed bring security to the hearts of all men? It can only be achieved through compassion and love but saying so sounds like the ravings of a utopian dreamer.

Were there ever any warnings about the pitfalls of these times and is there a method to chart a new course for our collective ship? Do we know of any paths that have been chartered towards this utopian destination?

About 1191 A.D., Joachim di Fiore broke away from the distracting duties of administration in the abbey of Corazzo, Sicily, to retire to the mountains in pursuit of a contemplative life. An Italian mystic and theologian, he developed a Trinitarian philosophy of history. According to this doctrine, history develops in three ages of increasing spirituality. The first two Ages correspond to the Old and New Testaments, to the cycles of Yahweh the Father and Christ the Son. The Third Age, that of the Holy Spirit, would come only after arduous pilgrimage and great tribulations for mankind. The truly original vision of Joachim concerns the Third Age and the 'pattern of threes'. Joachim was a poet and an artist, fascinated by the notion of the Trinity. He saw the three Persons built into the time structure in a process of increasing human perfectibility. His spritual experience is reflected in several of his illuminations, indeed, his lyricism flowed in his book of drawings and figures, the *Liber Figurarum*. His vision of the fulfillment of history is represented by trees that flower and which bear luxuriant fruits at the top. Joachim prophesized the advent of a new order of spiritual men and women who would bring about the culmination of history and the blessings of the Holy Spirit through the power of their meditation.

Joachim had been on a pilgrimage to the Holy Land that clearly had a profound effect on his conversion to religious life; he then founded the monastic order of San Giovanni in Fiore. In his lifetime, Joachim was acclaimed as a prophet gifted with visionary insights, and his ideas were widely popular for they provided complementary information to the esoteric Prophecy of John contained in the *Book of Revelation, the Apocalypse.* Man must wrestle with the letter of the scriptures to pierce through to the inner core of real spiritual understanding of the Spirit.

The Holy Spirit is a mysterious entity in Christian lore: Counselor, Comforter and Redeemer. The Third Person of the Holy Trinity is to reveal the knowledge of the Third Age and hides behind the humble symbol of the dove. Despite the fact that the Fourth Lateran Council condemned Joachim´s teachings in 1215, he influenced a number of friars, monks and sects down to the sixteenth century. Joachim has always retained a double reputation, both as a saint and as a heretic. The Roman Catholic Church saw his writings as highly dangerous.

The time referred to in his prophecy is around now. Astrologers usually consider the age of Pisces, corresponding to the Second Age, as being approximately from the birth of Christ to around the present time. The Aquarian Age, which starts now and runs for about 2000 years, would then logically correspond to the Third Age of the Joachite prophecy. If this is so, might we not assume that the message of *The Third Advent*, contained in the Joachite prophecy, anticipates the strivings of the modern seekers of truth, who, he predicted, would approach the city of the Spirit through trials and tribulations, and finally through circumstances of apocalyptic turmoil?

We certainly recognize the word "tribulations". Despite the glossy living depicted in our magazines that show and encourage a veritable paradise dedicated to consumption, our lives have become oddly difficult. Too many of us are only just functioning in society, like lemons squeezed hard with hardly any juice left, and a growing number of us struggle on the margins of poverty. Many have lost or are in the process of losing jobs, or for a considerable number of those who are employed, pressure in the work place is intolerably heavy. At the same time, there is a trail of evidence that suggests that the Joachite prophecy directly addresses the post war generation of aging baby boomers.

I, for one, have gone through some bewildering experiences and extraordinary encounters in my life that lead me to the conviction that Joachim was an authentic seer. His geometric figures and kaleidoscopic images tell us little, however, of the relevance of his message for our daily lives and we must probe further to grasp the stunning magnitude of the possibilities now opening for the human race. Here and now, in the midst of all the many troubles that surround the precarious opening of the third millennium, I believe that many of us are searching for something beyond the commonplace. Can we decipher the Joachite prophecy and grasp its meaning?

In our legends and myths, when rulers were good, then people, animals and nature were said to be happy and blessed. But when the rulers were bad or worse, then their subjects and the whole world suffered. Much of this second proposition seems true again today. Revolutions and elections come and go, politicians rise and fall; yet for many, there is little real improvement regardless of who is in power, and people have become despondent and cynical about our capacity to improve this state of affairs. Perhaps it is time to try another approach.

This book asserts that we need to change ourselves before we can change our surroundings, and that we have now reached a state of evolution wherein we are capable of doing just that.

INTO THE WOODS

The next morning was a midsummer's morning as fair and fresh as could be dreamed: blue sky and never a cloud, and the sun dancing on the water. Now they rode away amid songs of farewell and good speed, with their hearts ready for more adventure, and with knowledge of the road they must follow over the misty mountain to the land beyond.

– J.R.R. Tolkien, The Hobbit

We love adventures and life is the biggest of them all. I wish to share with you a story of India, which comes down from ages long gone by. It is the story of a deer and it goes like this: the deer is crazy for the scent of musk and is running in the woods, day in and day out, trying to find the source of the scent that so attracts him. Little does he know that a gland in his own belly emits the scent. He will run forever and the message of the story is that we should first look inside.

When I go to the movies, it sometimes occurs to me that maybe I simply failed to grow up. In the movies, I am still a child in my lurking belief that there is something real about them. I like moving about in the world of what we call in French '*le merveilleux*,' a world of wonders. In the towns of the European Middle Ages, they used to put on plays on stages erected in the central Town Square. Heaven was usually represented on the right side of the stage, while hell's cave, with a good fire burning inside, was on the left. I guess that in the cold of winter, the actors felt some advantage in being closer to hell, but most often the plots saw the actors torn between the two, seeking the first and avoiding the latter. Overall, not much has changed since then, although modern scriptwriters love to make hell look like heaven and vice versa. But I am not masochistic and I look for hunches or glimpses that are helpful, that make me happy, or better still, that make me laugh. Contrary to a widely held belief, I expect that heaven is a place where people are having fun.

There is no story without heroes and villains. It strengthens my belief in the usefulness of storytelling that there is hardly any story which does not involve the interaction of good and evil. Fiction follows real life and fantasy is serious business. In the fantasies I pay to watch, I enjoy movies with a happy ending, for this is what I wish for myself, as do most of us.

Film producers make movies which they assume will be of interest to a broad cross-section of the public. They attempt to film what people will pay to see. So, while movies are often fiction, they are also about reality, the reality of those who watch them, and their aspirations and desires. Attendance figures and movie ratings tell us about the likes, yearnings and tastes of the general public, and the tastes of successive generations of moviegoers tell us where they want to be led in their fantasies. Analyzing the marketing of dreams by moviemakers is not unlike psychoanalysis; both decipher the fantasies of our unconscious.

What is it that modern men and women are dreaming of? Of course we have love stories, suitably moving or desperate, stories of love lost; love found; love we make and unmake in a constantly repeating dance. Then there are variations. Romeo may nowadays fall in love with the waiter or with his mother-in-law, especially if she is Catherine Deneuve. However, not much new has been staged since Shakespeare. As indicated before, I personally prefer happy endings when people who love each other end up re-united and enjoying each other's company. Then we have propaganda movies thinly disguised as action stories full of increasingly spectacular special effects with the heroes marching through smoke, flames and explosions while pumping bullets into the enemy.

We have nightmares also: a long list of disaster movies and sinister horror movies, which ought to make us wonder about the content of our collective subconscious. They could well tell us something of reality, but which reality? Is it not as if some uncanny demons might want to attract our attention to their own dimension, to haunt it and then in some way to possess it? Whether they give the floor to the perverse or the cruel, whether they propose pleasure in inflicting pain or receiving it, such movies push gory, dark or twisted images into our consciousness. In some ways, they make us feel the Devil is an exhibitionist. He wants us to know about his whereabouts.

Then there are science fiction/fantasy movies. Let us dwell on this specific genre for a moment. This is how Joachim would have entertained us and if he were alive today, he might conceivably have been a movie producer. The reader, like the moviegoer for that matter, is made to remember that magic is within reality and that there is just a thickness of the movie screen between one world and another. Movies about magic and other dimensions are the modern successors of ancient legends, epic tales and sagas. This is where the new technological possibilities of computerized animation make some of their greatest contributions.

A consistent theme of a growing number of movies of the last decades of the Second Age concerns the existence of another reality. They speak about the intrusion of another dimension into our own or we are told that what we believe to be our reality is not, in fact, quite what we think it is. It is suggested to us that the sometimes boring and tedious everyday routines from which we try to escape when we buy a movie ticket have in fact a number of secret escape routes. Sometimes science fiction takes us directly into another preferably futuristic and separate universe, e.g. movies such as *Star Wars* or *Star Trek*; and quite often the future interrupts the present as in *Close Encounters of the Third Kind* or in those movies where another universe invites itself into our home, e.g. *E.T.* or *Gremlins*. Alternatively, quite by accident, we achieve the longed for evasion from everyday reality. We are sucked into another world, into the movie or the TV screen, into a book such as *The Never-ending Story*.

We are trading place and period. We are walking through an ordinary wardrobe that sends us to C.S. Lewis' *The Chronicles of Narnia* or playing with a pinball machine and finding ourselves engaged in a galactic fight thousands of miles above the earth. Whether they come to us or whether we are going to them, we interact with other planes of existence. Many times, as in the Harry Potter saga, the wizards are already here, incognito and unrecognized by the dull, dreary and foolish world of us, Muggles.

What is it really that we are dreaming about? What are such stories telling us? The popularity of these films tells us that we want to be able to dream about evasion or invasion, to yearn for the other side and to look for the beyond. The huge insight in *The Matrix* is the recognition that the everyday life we live in is not, in fact, the real one - which is quite a Buddhist view. The scripts spell out in so many forms that the beyond and the other side exist, hidden behind what we can see. This message is feeding the multi-billion dollar industry of the dream market.

It would seem a great waste that we could all be walking along a corridor of dreams that leads nowhere. Of course, it may be so; however, I find it more captivating to credit these numerous storytellers with true insights. That is, like many psychoanalysts, I would see dreams as a gate to some sort of new reality. In addition, this is precisely the inner code encrypted within the fiction message: there is a gate between the two worlds and the game is about finding it.

We are dreaming about finding that gate. Some movies are successful at making the story quite personal. Neo in *The Matrix* is The One and in the movie, *Unbreakable*, Bruce Willis, a regular guy, discovers that he possesses hidden powers. Yet another plot is about finding out that the other dimension is within us or within our grasp. The One is the one who cracks the code, the leader who can open access to the other side for the rest of the tribe who will then indeed be able to fulfill all their dreams. The story is about finding the place of that musk gland under the belly of the galloping deer. It is (did you notice?) a very old story.

Movies or books are often about another reality. We yearn for the other side but what if the other world truly exists? This is the theme of such movies, but how do we get there? The ancient scriptures or seers, such as Joachim, tell us that the other side, whilst hidden, is just here among us.

Therefore, the movie screen sends us back to ourselves and sitting there in the cinema, I recognize a little boy who looks like me. When I was that little boy I really wanted to be The One. I think that all of us do. Boys have heroic aspirations as to whether they will free the princess in a dark dungeon, play Cowboys and Indians or rehearse Middle Earth role-playing and resurrect the strangely prophetic world of Tolkien. They love to cross the gate of mysteries on a good treasure hunt. Little boys often do not grow up and when they are adults they go on playing - an ambassador, a writer, a seducer or maybe the CEO. They are chasing other roles indeed; yet in a sense, boys always want to be The One, not realizing how banal an aspiration it actually is. Girls have their dreams too, that may be different but equally powerful. Men and women are competitive. They run in the woods, smelling, chasing after this maddening musk. However, what is interesting in the story of the running deer is that the source of the scent really does exist. As I unfold this tale I hope to persuade you that there is a past to these endeavors: we have a history of these attempts at crossing the boundaries between the worlds.

WALKING THROUGH THE MOVIE SCREEN

The story is about you.

— Horace

Some dreams are helpful, some are disturbing and the disturbing dreams suck our strength, our faith, and our beliefs, and do not do anything for us: they spit us out, tired and empty. We find this too in movies that have nothing sensible to say, or we can find ourselves living other people's dreams, dreams that are nightmares.

The dreams that are helpful are those that give us clues. In a little-noticed film, *Last Action Hero,* the magic ticket takes the child through the screen. In many ways, I suggest the theme of these movies is also the theme of our lives: what if the world beyond does exist? What if it exists also in the here and now? Is there any secret passage, any wardrobe to get through, any access code? Are there any rules in the searching game? Moreover, what of the people who played before, and did they have any luck? Is there a key to the inner lock? As with many children who grow into adults, I stopped wanting to be The One. The change happened gradually, mostly, I think, because I did not want to play alone. It is more fun to play in a team. In *Once Upon a Time in the West*, Charles Bronson enters and exits alone. Noble perhaps, but boring too. Friendship is important to most of us. I soon found out that I was not the only one wanting to be The One and when many other people also want to be The One, we run into problems because only one person can be it.

Hence comes a point, which occurs in movies too, where the story moves from the solitary One to the collective We. Now, further in our symbolic story, some movies rephrase the question: "Can we crack the access code?" But, outside of the movie hall, who are those who are still looking for the access code? It is a scattered crowd and most of those who come out claiming that they have found the key have tended to make fools of themselves.

I bet Joachim would love to speak to those code seekers, the potential carriers of his Third Age. I did not myself meet them but I believe they exist. They would need to consult. I suppose they have met many messengers and deciphered many codes. As for me, I did encounter many preachers and at times they helped. Mostly, their pretensions were a waste of time. In *Entrapment*, Sean Connery and Catherine Zeta-Jones unlock the gate to penetrate the secret computer chamber by simultaneously turning two keys. The effectiveness of the synchronicity of collective action is a proposition that has always fascinated me ever since I discovered it in Arthur C. Clarke's science fiction novel, *Childhood's End*. Maybe the gate to the shining stars will open only when we, all together, turn the secret keys at the same moment. The plot thickens indeed and this is a plausible twist.

Let me make a proposal. The approach could be inspired by archeology, as we cannot rely only on movies. Instead of digging for stones, we could exhume ideas, intuitions and prophecies. This would help us to recognize the key and the code when we see it. By the way, we should not be narrow-minded and think that this quest is a recent invention of some astute producers in order to keep us entertained. Novelties always work better when they connect secretly with a very old script. Man's curiosity is ancient indeed, but before chasing these myths and dreams on the screen, we should look for them in our reality. We wrote learned treatises about it, many of these in the Sanskrit language, and many of which were never translated. We told stories about our dreams of knowledge, and Plato and Aristotle caught the tail end. Mankind is curious, always on the move, and satisfying one's curiosity is always rewarding. If we can conceive of reincarnation, we can even imagine that we have been our own predecessors. So, we would not be newcomers to this treasure hunting: we only need to rediscover the signals and symbols that we had buried then, to enable ourselves to find the trail back into the future. We might have been guiding each other and ourselves, through the generations and the ages.

For instance, once upon a time we felt that we had found Him who really was The One. Many thousands of years ago, cowherds in India danced around a magic flute player in the villages of Gokul and Vrindavan. They called the flute player Govinda, or Krishna. He was magnetic and fascinating, almighty and yet a tender friend. He showed to the bewildered eyes of his bowman disciple, Arjuna, the majesty of the Father, or, in Joachite terms, He revealed himself as the Master of the First Age. Then, The One came in another form, closer to western shores; the master of the Second Age took his birth in Bethlehem. He became human in order to lead us through the narrow gate at the entrance of our brains. Can anyone remember when he entered Jerusalem on the back of a donkey? How excited the crowd was! There was so much joy and dust with all the dancing, shouting and singing. Charlton Heston looked at Him in *Ben Hur* when they took Him away to His trial and then everything went wrong and we could not fix it anymore. Indiana Jones did not keep the Grail and there is no trace left of Percival's errands.

The great Nazarene Master left this earth promising that more clues would come after Him. Indeed, he promised that after Him would follow the Holy Ghost, but we are still waiting for this manifestation. In the meantime, in the land where He lived, conflicts are still raging. Armored vehicles of the Israeli army, parked in the Square of the Nativity in Bethlehem, remind us that the age of the Son is not quite finished yet.

The fresco of history is so rich and so moving, a tapestry of light, music and blood. It constantly weaves itself to retell the same story, which seems to be the story of human seeking. Pharaoh Akhenaton came down the road of Amarna in a chariot, en route to rituals for the sun God Aton. Were the code seekers walking behind? But the priests of Amon would have the last word. Priests usually do. Even if you are Pharaoh, priests do not like you to have ideas of your own. Soon the name of Akhenaton and his god were eradicated and their temples torn down. No point in withdrawing as an Anchorite monk in the Sinai dust or conquering a world with Muslim swords for the reign of Allah. Pain was distributed all around. Think about those who fought near Constantine XII, the last Basileus of the Byzantine Empire, when he fell before the gate of Constantinople, or those who were there in the retinue of the Inca, Atahualpa, so scared when he tried to escape from those wretched Spaniards. And can we possibly grasp what happened to the victims of the Holocaust?

Europeans conquered the New World because perhaps, as the Mormons pretend, the keys were buried there. All the while, keepers of phony keys were competing with and killing each other. These religious wars are still going strong today. Code seekers may have had long conversations with Goethe and Schiller about art and ethics in Weimar, trying to restore sense to the great game, but they were not always lucky and might have been among the Wehrmacht troopers who lost more than their marbles in trying to enact their Fuehrer's nightmare, in the same country just a few years later.

Many code seekers are and were women. Are they the sisters who buried the braves at Wounded Knee? Women have to face the dire consequences of men's silly and dangerous plays; however, they often have stronger instincts for the trail of lost treasure. We have ignored their skills and qualities and have paid a heavy price for it.

We have lived many lives in between, some happy ones, some difficult. It is easy to get confused and frankly, I do not know what code seekers look like today. We have walked so many miles together but on parallel roads. Today, they are sitting somewhere in this movie hall with me; maybe if we compare notes, if we search together, we will have a greater chance to walk through the screen and find ourselves in the real story. It is time we all came together; if we do not, we will not be able to turn our keys simultaneously.

Let us imagine, just for a while, that you are a code seeker. Have you been thinking about finding the passage through the screen? You may already have walked down the alleys of the great dream bazaar and found them overflowing with products and sets of keys of dubious quality. Perhaps, deep down, you have kept the courage of hope; hope that the key will be entrusted to you. Whether you choose to turn it in the lock or not, is yet another story, but turning the key is not a fantasy, it is a serious matter.

Many storytellers have wished to reach through the screen, and to draw the reader in, from the theater, into the story.

Let me draw you in. If you come you will oblige me greatly. You will oblige yourself also, but this you do not know yet; the risk for you, however, is small.

I am going to review a number of suggestions. It is for you to figure out whether you see a code or not. The movie I invite you to enter into is a vast fresco, with the world as a backdrop. There will be lots of twists and turns, plenty of dramatic episodes and a profound ongoing love story. The script is a mixture of old scriptures, Hator, Hegel and employment statistics. If we shake the mix a bit, we may locate the basic underlying structure of the drama. I had a friend who was a bartender and a disc jockey. He claimed to have learnt much by mixing tastes and sounds. The key to success is to find the binding unity in diversity, the combination that brings taste and harmony together.

In the disorder of events, whether within world history or within our daily lives, there may be a sequence, and its significance to us reveals the continuous thread of revelation. To navigate this passage, bewilderment is more helpful than cleverness. Can we invite the code seekers to this play? Obviously I must write because playing alone is not my idea of fun. The reader is only requested to invest the few hours it takes to read these lines. Whatever we invest, the returns will be proportionate. Between the unreal world - that is visible - and the real world - which is not - the screen is very thin indeed. The other side may not quite be within our sight yet, but that does not mean it does not exist. It does not mean that it is not accessible. The gate, the lock and the key belong to us, always have and always will. When to use them is our choice, the choice that leads to freedom.

2. TRAFFIC JAM ON COGNITION ALLEY

The unexamined life isn't worth living.
 – Socrates

THE CRYSTAL IN THE SNOW FLAKE

The first taste I remember, in my short and fairly insignificant existence, is the taste of snow through my woolen gloves. I am perhaps six years old and running quietly away from our snowed-in chalet in Verbier. The snow wraps in cozy softness all shapes and features of the landscape and snowflakes fall from the sky like liquid candies. I am completely fascinated by the butterfly dance of the thick snowflakes and the vibrant intensity of this winter's white silence.

I followed the charm and the shiver of this dance, and later, the police found my sister and I in the next village and brought us back home. There is something magical about the snowflake, as there is magic in life, and that magic hooked me.

Since then, I have been running after the magic. The police no longer found me and brought me home but I did not find myself either, or the magic. I had more serious business on my hands and soon discovered that I needed to play monkey games with the monkeys. That is, I had to become an adult. In so doing, I had to make these adults believe that I was one of them; I had to be able to mix and to fit in. It was a little difficult at first because I had to pretend that magic does not exist. Adults do not believe in magic; they believe instead in their own self-importance and the endless forms of this belief largely fill the agenda of the 'do's and don'ts' of a growing kid. I did what I had to do, graduated in law and political science, and wrote articles in a local newspaper. I did my army service and worked in a bank. One morning, I looked at myself in a mirror and decided that I was adult enough, by which I meant that I needed time for myself. I did not mean adult in the sense contained in the words 'adult magazine', but rather in the sense of lost innocence. I had tried hard to fit in with them and in the process lost something of myself.

Are we not all compelled to sacrifice some of our own poetry in order to respond to the peer pressure of these seriously rational adult colleagues? I gained credibility, however, for not many people around me suspected that I was still looking for the snowflake magic. What saddened me was that many who had also been clearly looking for the magic had already seemed to have given up or just gone astray.

When you look for the unknown, the trouble is that it is elusive by nature, and you may well be in for a few surprises along the way. I had long discussions during mountain treks with friends. One of them was a Dominican, a Professor of Theology at the Angelicum University in Rome. He was usually respectful of my grasp of Thomist ontology but I can still recall his expression of pain and disbelief when he realized I was proposing to walk on paths that had not been chartered in the dogma of his canonical books. He felt that I was challenging his faith and that every one of us was obliged to conform to a script where all imagination was outlawed. He was one of those people who has prepared for themselves a tight cage with the thin pages of the Holy Scriptures. Alas, his fear turned out to be stronger than his friendship. Perhaps adventure and magic scare many people who would, in theory, like to venture outside the garden of certainties, but are afraid of unpalatable encounters. They do have a point because there are many astute false prophets out there, waiting for the naïve and the uninformed to make a wrong move.

However, does it not make sense to try to capture the crystal in the snowflake, to find the secret passage to the other side of the screen, or to understand the real meaning of all the hours we hurriedly spend as we move towards the appointed hour of our death? Can all this be possibly called: looking for God? If so, it is a very traditional pastime. Our ancestors built cathedrals for Him, chiseled towards the sky, from which vantage point He was supposed to look down. The annals of this quest are written in the art and culture of all the world's civilizations and it is amazing that we are still looking for this encounter of another kind, after so many millennia of searching.

There are many ways to deal with the unknown. Atheists and modern rationalists think themselves knowledgeable enough to declare that God does not exist. Others do not see why they would wish to search for God, because the image they made of Him had already been consigned to the past, part of their old baggage that was long ago consigned to the attic. Comforted by their traditions, many others claim to believe in God, and they own this belief as they would own a piece of family furniture. Dusty but stylish, antique furniture provides a sense of respectability and social continuity. Those who pretend to have found God do not seem to know any better than the rest of us, nor does that supposed knowledge appear to make any difference to the way they behave in the everyday world. This is why, understandably, many do not engage in such pursuits and find the search for God perfectly pointless.

THE PITFALLS OF FICTION

In the early 1970s I visited many groups and tested many formulae that offered variations on the theme of the great quest. For instance, I found myself at a conference on Atlantis where the chain-smoking speaker, after a fumbling talk, had us lined against a wall to find out who would be the best medium. It wasn't me; I was found too resisting. He picked a frightened looking girl and persuaded her to channel messages from Atlantis to Calvinist Geneva. The poor thing was already hearing voices and had come to the conference in the vain hope of getting some relief. Drinking a beer with her after the program, I advised her to forget Atlantis and to see a counselor. I then came across a group of hypnotists who were allowing people to search for their past lives' incarnations under hypnosis. Sadly, I could not be hypnotized no matter how hard I tried. My memory would not really travel beyond the snowflake. I could not remember the intra-uterine bliss of my mother's womb, a memory that seemed to be standard procedure for the other members of the group who were more adept as time-travelling practitioners. One young man, a farm worker, had apparently been a Greek general in the armies of Alexander the Great, while a girl remembered drowning in a nineteen century ship bound for the USA. Curiously, nobody was revealed as having been an accountant, a nurse or a laborer. Everybody claimed a heroic, bizarre or exotic past. But it seemed to me that, waking up from such fantasies, the Greek hero and the Mayflower pilgrim did not really have any better a grip on, or grasp of, their lives than the average man or woman in the street. The young farm worker actually turned out to be the heir to a rural estate, which he eventually donated to a 'guru' somewhere down the path.

Even more spectacular was the craze of some European and American youths for a fat little boy who had come from India to the West as the redeemer of the new age. I came to know of this when one of them greeted me on the bank of the River Limmat in Zurich by the unusual words: "I salute the light in you." After a grey day of accounting in the office of the Union Bank of Switzerland, I found this approach rather cool and wondered whether he could offer me some other refreshing experiences. People flocking to the ensuing program seemed so sweet and so convinced that I decided to join them and to look for myself as to what the promises of the East might bring. I had to listen to a few courses of mumbo-jumbo metaphysics that had the appeal of exoticism and the advantage of being delivered by a very pretty girl. I readily overlooked the thinness of the philosophy and enjoyed the company of kind, albeit not always very bright people. Finally the day of my initiation came and I was brought, accompanied by whispers, respect and mystery to a suburban villa where a shaven-headed Indian guru, a prominent follower of the little fat boy, was to transmit to me his precious knowledge. I found the experience of initiation quite unremarkable, with the exception that this gentleman rather ferociously pressed my eyeballs. He told me I would see the inner light and, indeed, I did. Press your eyeballs and you will too.

Later on, in a larger gathering which took place at the Alexandra Palace in London, 'the Perfect Master', as the little boy was then called, appeared with his happy family. He lectured us in a high-pitched voice on the merits of his perfect knowledge. One moustached brother, we were told, was Jesus Christ and he smiled eerily to confirm the fact. Another brother, more bulky and seemingly less subtle, led the orchestra of devotees, sweating profusely as he conducted. He was supposed to be Shiva. We went in a procession to bow before 'the Perfect Master' and were thrown at his feet by the security people when the blessed moment came to face him. He avoided my gaze, and by that time I had had more than enough. But I remained puzzled as to how over ten thousand people in this vast hall could be so completely absorbed in the teachings of this very peculiar holy family. When the fat little boy came of age and married an American girlfriend, the world was simply told that she was Durga, the Divine Mother. This triggered some sort of cosmic fight with the earlier Divine mother who, of course, had been the mother of the boy. Even Walt Disney could not have invented such a ready-made pantheon, and I confess that I did feel sorry for so many youngsters who did not seem to mind being so thoroughly fooled. On many occasions, I felt quite foolish myself, of course, because I did not understand why a legitimate curiosity would land me in often bizarre and freaky situations.

The 1970s were a strange decade. The world became cynical after the optimism of the 60s and many people understandably chose to laugh at the silliness of the new age culture. I personally found it depressing to find that so many naïve seekers, time and again, found themselves betrayed. I could detail a long list of explorations, of my efforts to discover whether anyone had any real clues at all. These explorations went on and in a converted English nunnery a community of J.R.R. Tolkien's devotees were reviving *The Lord of the Rings*. They were attempting to discover the real location of Middle Earth by distributing elfish names to the features of the local surroundings. As part of the services on offer, massage of one's private parts was available, that was said to stimulate the chakra system. It was given during role-playing sessions that had nothing at all to do with Tolkien's saga, and for a fee, of course. This group may have felt uncomfortable with the reality of the twentieth century, but their brand of fiction had no appeal for me. I was of the opinion that sex was a rather straightforward and natural thing and did not need such mystical wrappings.

In fact, it was dismaying to find out how many so-called gurus or pseudo-spiritual leaders were using their teacher status to get free sex from their followers. It was a scam and a shame. Many of these types ruled over the minds of their devotees and in the process built up substantial bank accounts. It seemed to me that if the name of the game is to get power, money and sex, then fine, let's come out with it and say so. It is a very common game and I am grateful to those who get straight to it without ado or hypocrisy, without needing to build a spiritual fraud to camouflage their drives and desires. Later on, with added press coverage unveiling such abuses, and a number of court cases ensuing, some, but regretfully not all of the false prophets of the 'not-so-new-age' gurus saw their fortunes plummet. Many of us breathed a sigh of relief when a famous false guru was expelled from the USA in handcuffs, leaving behind his hundred or so Rolls Royce cars and many broken hearts.

But there are other categories of practitioners who benefited from our drive to open new cognitive alleys. Many of us experienced relationship problems; many of us are divorce casualties in that we are either children of divorced parents or have gone through or are going through divorce ourselves. Divorce can reveal yet another dimension to the meaning of the word pain. This, of course, is good for the business of psychiatrists, psychotherapists and the like. I remember an aristocratic friend of mine, the last heir in a line of Counts. His wealthy divorced parents had delivered him, at a tender age, to a psychiatrist to sort out the mess he was in after their break-up. I was fond of him and he was sensitive, beautiful, but fragile. My friend saw such doctors for years. Later, we shared an apartment as students, and what had not changed at all was his fragility. I saw then that psychiatrists and their like aren't always able to provide the right answers.

A couple of years later, I spent time with a friend at the home of a young couple who lived in a spartan log cabin in the Blue Ridge Mountains of Virginia. They were living off the sale of farm products and hash cookies. I loved the bumper sticker on their pick-up truck: "Don't blame me, I voted for McGovern." We were in the midst of the Watergate affair and this was not Nixon country. But political affinities were not enough to maintain the household's harmony. Bob and Liz (the names are fictional but not the story) were having problems in their married life; both visited the same psychiatrist.

Needless to say, much of the proceeds from the sale of their farm products were flowing into his practice. The wife had developed a romantic infatuation with the good doctor and the therapy was concentrated on the husband who had to overcome his possessiveness and petty jealousy. Of course he was paying the bills, and I guess the therapy worked out in a way. Liz finally left Bob alone in his little house with the smell of grass in the kitchen and Bob Dylan music in the background. Liz later found out that the psychiatrist had voted for Nixon, but never mind. He was such a persuasive fellow.

I did mention hashish. Those who, like me, studied at postgraduate level at a US Ivy League university in the middle 1970s, probably discovered more there than the taste of grass. I never was heavily into drugs but being consistent in my curiosity, I did my homework. In the hills near Santa Cruz, California, I briefly visited a hippie commune. Every morning the princesses on the balcony waved goodbye to their men, who astride their motorcycles, like a modern version of medieval knights, zoomed off on some lost crusade. It did not evoke much of the Middle Ages however, for none of the women were wearing clothes. Drugs were the way to knowledge. One girl there offered me some and, in a sort of ritual, took some herself. I obliged and went for a walk in the nearby fields. First, I felt very powerfully my own unity with nature. The earth felt as if it was penetrating my bare feet in a deep, loving caress and the brilliance of the sun covered me in a warm embrace. The girl had followed me on the narrow path and was staying a few feet behind. I turned to welcome her at this point. She stared at me as if dazzled by a blinding vision and could hardly speak. I knew it was just the sun and I treated her as a gentle brother; she had a boyfriend and a child and I was not going to mess things up. A few moments later, the trip started to crash and I hid in a sleeping bag, feeling paranoid and with a big headache. This, along with other experiences, taught me that drugs may take us down some new cognitive lanes, where we visit new places indeed, but the trips are damaging to our brain cells. A car may force its way through a security fence, but it suffers damage such as burst tires and it cannot then speed away. In the same way, drugs can somehow break through the barriers of the conscious mind but they bring us nowhere, and wherever we go, the price we are called upon to pay is often high.

Half a year later, I received at my home in Kathmandu, Nepal, a letter from the Californian girl that included another 'offering'. "Take it, my love, and be next to me." This time I didn't feel obliged and the drug went into the trashcan.

KNOCKING ON HEAVEN'S DOOR

Qui vit sans folie n'est pas si sage qu'il croit.

Living without madness is not as wise as it seems.

— François VI, Duc de la Rochefoucauld

The picture of scattered seekers in the 1970s looked complex, and I was at the age where it is easy to look for meaning in another way: enjoyment. As the big picture looked pointless, I saw myself as a hedonist, trying to taste the fun of all the aesthetics and pleasures that could be grabbed. In one instance I really had my wishes granted with spectacular generosity, but it was just to let me find out by how far we can go too far.

In 1973, I spent my summer vacation in Greece. On the boat between Hydra and Athens I met Bia, a slender Danish girl who fulfilled my ideal of an Aegean dream. She had this utter blondness that marries so well with a golden tanned skin. I was encouraged to discover that her liquid blue eyes were looking at me with more than sympathy. We met and we fused. We ended up in Mykonos, the island of Utopia made real for the international summer pleasure crowd. The hotels were full and so we camped in the garden of the house of a hospitable native. It was every element of a teenage dream, every bit as tasty as a chunky Greek breakfast of yoghurt and honey. Satisfaction was suitably reciprocal and we made sure that the dream came true, that we relished the honey; and as we were lazing on a lonely beach under that immense blue sky, I was feeling, yes, this is what I desired and it has now been given to me. I was looking at the sky so as to scratch heaven's door and wishing that these heavenly moments would become eternity. After all, the Greek gods were quite human and perhaps they would deliver me a piece of their heaven if I knocked hard enough.

Yet, in the same way that the sand of the beach was flowing through my fingers, so was this time of perfect pleasure seeping away. I then knew, as the French poet Ronsard did when he was looking at the falling petals of a rose, that I could not retain the fleeting perfection of the moment. Knowing this slowly killed the perfection; time carries a sort of death, an emptiness that my enjoyment could not fill. I realized then that my desires were too short sighted and that I needed something that neither time, nor anything else under this impeccable heaven, could take away from me. Why not? It is for the young to dare.

I tried to recreate Greece in Morocco but it did not work out. I felt sick. As I spent the next years of postgraduate school life in Bologna, Italy and Baltimore, Maryland, I focused more intently on searching for 'I-don't-know-what' with a diffuse impression that I was running out of time.

This book is not meant to be an autobiographical account of my trials, tribulations and eventual amazing luck, but I believe that a tremendous amount of energy was spent by our generation in pushing open the doors of perception, as William Blake would have said. We tried to speed on the highways of alternative cognitive processes; we lived fully and we burned fast. Looking for reality, we have run further away from it and into magnified delusions. Yet, despite the fact that many of our adventures may have ended in ridicule or disaster, I feel it was not all in vain. After all, this is a bit like hide and seek, and curiosity is about searching. If we find a piece of the answer then the game is not over yet, and the play takes another turn.

And this is how I came to the most extraordinary moment of my life. At the end of my search, in the summer of 1975, I felt exhausted and distressed, having spent so much of my energy and purpose chasing the elusive meaning of life. While I was staying in Pacific Palisades near Los Angeles, I was given the address of a lady living near London. The information came from an Indian student in Berkeley, California named Rajesh. He had told me that Shri Mataji – this was a sort of spiritual title meaning revered Mother – was a wonderful person and an exceptional yogi, a great master who had the power to raise the Kundalini. Actually, Rajesh told me that she was an Avatar, that is, an Incarnation of the Divine Force. Indians believe that the Divine incarnates at different times in history to protect and guide mankind. However, for me, this was not the sort of thing you believe simply because you are told it.

Later, in Arizona, a few days after this conversation, which had taken place near the observatory of San Francisco, I witnessed strange but beautiful natural occurrences. I prayed for and obtained, within minutes, a beautiful rainbow over the Grand Canyon. It is hard to render such an experience in words. More or less at the moment it happened, Rajesh was in London telling Shri Mataji he had met a fairly burnt-out seeker, who had traveled through the deserts of Arizona and New Mexico and who needed some help. She told him: "Tell him to come to London and to see me."

Back in California, Rajesh passed me the message. I was intrigued because the possibility of awakening the Kundalini was rather challenging. The Kundalini is known to be a most mysterious energy, hidden within the sacrum bone, whose awakening triggers a breakthrough of consciousness. It is described in ancient texts but its awakening was described as extremely difficult and hazardous. I was solidly skeptical, I must admit, but Rajesh was otherwise a very bright and talented fellow and not someone prone to believing in nonsense. It seemed worth checking out.

I hitchhiked to Chicago, took a plane to Philadelphia and, from there, to London. I spent my first night there in the flat of Hector, an old and dear friend. He was an officer in the Life Guards of the Queen of England and stuttered deliciously. The mess in his flat, near Holland Park, reflected the mess of his life, invaded recently by some hotheaded South African lover. Hector used to be quite handsome but his face was slowly degrading, something which reminded me of Oscar Wilde's novel, *The Portrait of Dorian Gray*. Everything seemed so confused and, at times, desperate. I did not share his inclinations and knew that he was not happy, but did not know what to do to help him. Actually, helplessness was probably my prevalent mood at the time. It was from his flat that I called Shri Mataji for the first time.

Her voice seemed to come from far away and yet it sounded quite close. It was soft and enveloping. At times a voice can mean a lot. It emanated something that felt to me very refreshing and transported me from my less than heavenly surroundings to a feeling of excitement and joyful expectation. Can it be? Can a solution really exist? Can she really help me? She invited me to her home in Hurst Green, in Surrey, a short train ride away from London. I boarded the train at Victoria Station with some trepidation. It was a sunny day and my blue and yellow suburban train looked like a happy toy. Hurst Green is a sleepy suburban town where the English bourgeois look inquisitively at new faces from behind net curtains. I walked through quiet paths to the address where Shri Mataji resided. I saw a comfortable house with an inviting front yard and a back garden. I took a deep breath and knocked at the door.

PART TWO

THE SEARCH FOR MEANING

All human beings by nature have an urge to know.
> — Aristotle, Metaphysics 1,1

Look and you will find it - what is unsought will go undetected.
> — Sophocles

Thomas Mann, regarded by many as one of the major German novelists of the twentieth century, captured the essence of the human dilemma when he recognized that the immense value and beauty of human beings lies precisely in that they belong to the two kingdoms of nature and spirit. Overcoming the romantic and more Wagnerian impulses of his youth that focused on the pessimistic dimensions of this contradiction, he matured to seek, like Goethe, a human synthesis that would go beyond the tenets of the dualist Christian dogma of body and soul. In this he projects a Trinitarian vision of humanism that has some parallels with Joachim. He says in this respect: "I am convinced that of all our strivings, only those are good and worthwhile which contribute to the birth of this new human feeling, under whose shelter and sway, after the passing of our present forlorn and leaderless age, all humanity will live. I am convinced that my own strivings after analysis and synthesis have meaning and value only as they stand in groping, intuitive, tentative relation to this coming birth. In fact, I believe in the coming of a new, a third humanism, distinct, in complexion and fundamental temper, from its predecessors."[1]

At the core of this new humanism lies the unlocking of the oldest secret: how can we, living in the material body, unfold the potential of our dormant spirit in such a way that body and spirit live in happy concordance?

---

[1] Thomas Mann, *What I Believe*, (ed. Mark Booth), Firethorn Press, New York (1984), p. 44.

3. THE CHRONICLES OF AN OLD FALLACY

The faith that stands on authority is not faith. The reliance on authority measures the decline of religion, the decline of the soul.

– Ralph Waldo Emerson, The Essays of Ralph Waldo Emerson

I need now to take you, by a roundabout way, into the woods, the vestiges of bygone centuries and the tapestry woven by our common past and common mistakes. Only then will it make clear sense to tell you why knocking at this particular door related to knocking on heaven's door. Please forgive me for this; we will return to Hurst Green. But to grasp the nature of the pilgrimage the Westerner has embarked upon in his search for meaning, we need to retrace our steps to the moment of our origin or rather to a Book that symbolically relates our genesis.

THE ORIGINAL CONFUSION

To him who conquers, I will grant to eat of the Tree of Life, which is in the paradise of God.

– John, Revelation 2.7

The plucking of the apple in the Garden of Eden is a specific instance of karmic law at work, of a story that deeply influenced history. Let us look back to this tale to identify the initial trace of our search. It was a search for meaning, but as the story reached us, it identified woman with evil and seeking after spiritual truth – which was also considered dangerous by the establishment. In this, we may also uncover a fundamental fault line in the very fabric of Christianity.

Holy books such as *The Bible*, *The Koran* or *The Gita* must be special; after all, so many people already think so. These books must transmit precious messages about the spiritual inheritance of mankind, even if these messages are often blurred or even falsified as they pass down the corridors of history. It is men who write the books and with such influential writings, distortions or lost meanings of the original message are unavoidable. Of course, I do not expect the keepers of the books to agree with this; they would insist this insinuation to be anathema, for their authority rests on an unquestioning adherence to the written word.

A most interesting attempt at looking through our traditions with a sensitive yet scientific mind can be credited to the Swiss psychologist, Carl Gustav Jung. His analysis of symbols, legends and dreams reveals archetypes and meanings that are the keys to unlocking the secrets of consciousness. Jungian analysis helps to better grasp of the content of the human psyche. *The Book of Genesis* can be approached in this manner. After all, it recounts the famous 'original sin', a story that influenced the three great religions of the Middle East: Judaism, Christianity, and Islam.

In the garden of heaven (Eden) the woman, Eve, tempted the man, Adam, to taste the fruit of the tree of the knowledge of good and evil. She did so under the influence of a serpent coiled around its trunk. Biting this apple had consequences indeed, *homo sapiens* was thereafter born in sin and Adam paid dearly for his trust in his beloved. They were thrown out of paradise and their offspring, our whole race, was said to be cursed.

Let us revisit this scene in the Garden of Eden: the tree is in the midst of the garden of heaven, which was created by God for his children's enjoyment. This enigmatic tree is about the knowledge of good and evil, wisdom and discrimination. If the garden is good, how could the tree be evil and how could Satan gain entrance? Were there no gatekeepers at the entrance of this heavenly and most protected place, God's own garden? How could the Devil have sneaked in? Maybe someone got the script wrong?

The serpent was there for a purpose, and according to a Jungian analysis it is not satanic as depicted in the *Genesis* account, but rather a symbol of a positive energy. You can still see the symbol of the serpent on the door of most pharmacies. It is described in mankind's mythological memory as the Aagathodaimon, the healing power that is coiled on the caduceus of Hermes in ancient Greek mythology. It represents the residual power of Kundalini, a secret redeeming energy in Hindu mythology. The serpent represents a powerful, mysterious inner energy that invites Eve to look forward towards knowledge, growth, development and fulfillment. It symbolizes the force of evolution that moves things ahead. "*Eritis sicut Deus,*" said the serpent. "You will become similar to God." It is a promise of higher awareness. After all, as God embodies all the highest qualities, should not his children strive and aspire to reflect His perfect attributes? Is it not the attitude of loving children to try to emulate their parents? This being so, where is the sin?

"Womanhood leads us above," says Goethe in the second Faust. Actually, in the sensitivity of simple folk and in the countless manifestations of universal art, the woman, as mother, wife, sister or daughter, is the companion, sustainer and often the protector of men. The fact is that womanhood brings us upwards. Woman inspires man. Eve was to Adam as Beatrice was to Dante: she dares man to raise his gaze, to rise and fulfill a higher potential, to choose his destiny instead of his mediocrity. Rather than staying in the protected shelter of the garden of certitude, man began a long quest for his true Self. All the great instructors of mankind, such as Moses, Socrates, Lao Tzu, Buddha, Jesus or Mohammed guided, led and pointed the way. To progress on this path of equilibrium and balance, Adam needed Eve and vice versa, and their equal, complementary balance is key to the harmony of the cosmos. According to Taoist cosmology, the human psyche consists of two elements: Yin and Yang, the feminine and the masculine; understanding this bipolarity leads to a higher synthesis, whereas negating either of the poles leads to a dead end.

Yet in the great sacred books of the Middle East, the feminine dimension is associated with evil. The consequences of this distorted paradigm did not lead to a higher synthesis but instead to a deep trauma in the Western mind. I would say that it opened a gap between man and woman that accounts for much of the hidden assumptions that fashioned Western civilization. The first sin was not the bite of the apple but the implicit degradation of woman. Once the inferior status of women is assumed, the results, reached through many roundabout ways, are the psychological hardships we still face today. Of course I understand that women have also been exploited in other cultures, but I am more interested here in pointing out the ideological undertones and their consequences in ours.

The assumption made in the story of the original sin occults or degrades the feminine side of the psyche, that is, the right hemisphere of the brain that relates to the emotional side of the psyche. It is said that we are deceived by the feminine side: we cannot trust our emotions; we cannot follow our hearts. Thus the contemporary Judeo-Christian West relied heavily on the male side, that is, the mental dimension and the will to power. These trends ushered in dynamic centuries of conquests and discoveries, and certainly fostered human progress in many fields. The West developed the industrial and technological revolutions and benefited from the resulting economic growth, but something went awry. Adam without Eve is not a complete entity. The lack of access to emotional intelligence affected the coherence of our civilization. The male paradigm strived for action but all too often it neglected the needed input of the Yin feminine qualities, the capacity to sustain and love, and the compassion and attention to social welfare needs. The great confusion between woman and evil activated inequality between the sexes manifesting in the exploitation of women in Muslim countries and the war between the sexes in modern, at one time Christian countries, which led to sterile competition, to misogynistic oppression, related ethical shortcomings and familial breakdowns.

The reification of women as sex objects in our red light districts became ultimately possible because the spiritual nature of womanhood was not recognized. The roots of decay in modern post-industrial societies plunge deep into the crevice created by our present understanding of our original myths.

Millennia later, this account of our first wake-up in Eden proved a convenient theory for a church making its livelihood out of saving men from pre-ordained damnation. When the priest who taught me religion in my Catholic boarding school referred to this fateful apple in order to explain the existence of Evil, I discovered as a fourteen-year-old the spirit of rebellion. I did not want my life messed up because of Adam's fondness for Eve and her apple. It did not make sense to the boy I then was and much of the time spent by the adult thereafter was invested in a journey of enquiry in order to explain to myself why such a thing as evil existed in the world. How could a loving God have created such an evil serpent and allowed it to crawl where it would do the most damage? Why in this protected garden, could a little snack with an apple create cosmic havoc on such a scale?

Modern rationalists claim that the story of Genesis does not mean anything much. However, you could suspect them of being wrong and here I submit, to you the reader, a first hypothesis, wherein the *Book of Genesis* indicates two possible directions: running towards the exit of the Garden, or penetrating inside the mystery of the Garden as contained in the Tree of Life. Through its coded message, *Genesis* reveals something of our psyche and of its confusion; of man's fear of change; of the worrying power of desire and of our inability to integrate harmoniously thoughts (Adam) and feelings (Eve). As the humans moved out of the Garden of known certainties to travel on their own discovery channel, they were equipped with both freedom and ignorance. We lost our primeval connection with God and His reality and under such conditions we made mistakes. Mistakes beget evil and this is what the story of the first apple is really about. But the story of the first mistake heralds, too, the promise of our ultimate success.

INFILTRATION AND BETRAYAL

Truth is the only merit that gives dignity and worth to history.

– Lord Acton

There are some risks we cannot afford not to take. Adam, the driving force of the male principle, was a courageous man. He was right to follow the guidance of the feminine intuition and to initiate a trail of self-enquiry. This is early teamwork in action: Eve and Adam, Yin and Yang, embracing toward a higher synthesis. Adam, the first born, was already looking for the passage to the other side. This is just to remind us how old our curiosity is: biting the apple meant accepting an invitation to play the game. Despite the cozy comfort enjoyed in the Garden of blessed ignorance, men and women have since been on a quest, but the path was never going to be an easy one. The centuries unfolded a tapestry of light and song, blood and fire, screaming darkness and radiant dawns. During the Second Age, starting with the birth of Christ, we can discover how the plot thickened.

Is it not amazing that their immediate followers betrayed both Christ and later Mohammed? In Islam, the drive for power and the Caliphate led the companions of the Prophet to fight his own family, that is, his daughter Fatima, his son-in-law Ali and his grandchildren Hassan and Hussein. The family of the Prophet was murdered and the tragedy at the battlefield of Kerbala opened the great schism between Shiites and Sunni. Did Christianity fare any better?

The development of Christianity can accurately be described as tragic. The Gnostic writings give us a picture of what happened after the death of Christ, which is very different from the one we are officially taught. According to the *Apocrypha Gospel of Thomas*, who is said to have followed Christ to Kashmir after His Resurrection, Jesus had entrusted the leadership of the young Christian collectivity to James the Just but that dissent occurred through the entry of a newcomer.

Saul of Tarsus was an astute Roman citizen who persecuted the early Christians in Jerusalem and had Stephen stoned to death. On the way to Damascus, he hallucinated, a sort of psychedelic conversion, and returned to the Christians, this time to destroy them from inside. He was an intellectual, a bureaucrat and a busybody and he outsmarted the simple-hearted Disciples of Christ although it is reported that John, Thomas and James all opposed him. Peter and Judas were the weak links amongst the early followers. Saul, now known as Paul, falsified the early Gospels, developed his evangelical zeal to establish his power base in various cities of the empire and managed to use Peter as his front man. Peter looked less brainy and probably tried to do his best, but he sounded vain, rashly impulsive and jealous of Christ's affection for John. After the passing of the Shepherd and on the assumption of being the Vicar of Christ on earth, he waited for Paul to deliver him prestige, followers and prominence. Paul knew that he could not take the front role, as he did not belong to the small circle of Jesus' immediate followers, nor had he known Jesus personally. According to the *Apocrypha* writings, he was also wary of Mary, the Mother of Jesus, and tried to marginalize her.

The early followers of Jesus were simple-hearted people and predictably enough, the bureaucrat won the struggle for control of the new community. John went to Patmos, Thomas to India and James to Spain. Jesus himself, after His Resurrection, is said to have gone to Kashmir where there are many accounts of His presence there as Issa, as documented by recently compiled studies and research. Although the Gnostics would uphold the mystical inheritance of Christ for some centuries, they lost the ultimate battle with the followers of Paul, the clerics who went on to develop the institutional and political might of the new church. The way was thus free for an early betrayal of what Christ stood for, and today both Peter and Paul have their own basilica in Rome.

Paul, a Jewish turncoat and proud of his Roman citizenship, was also the first anti-Semite in the Christian world and because the true Apostles who had been close to Christ were Jews and unlikely to bow to his schemes, he turned the Church away from its original mystical heritage. When the Roman Emperor Titus destroyed Jerusalem, the Pauline doctrine within the young church took the upper hand. Paul, in his attempt to marginalize the early Jewish Christian community, also encouraged the fallacy that the Jews had condemned Christ and were therefore to blame for his execution. In fact, it was the Proconsul of the occupying power, Pilate, who orchestrated the trial of Christ. He was another bureaucrat who wanted to artfully 'pass the buck' to a Jewish crowd: he did not want to stain his hands with the death of the Just. Hence, it was the Romans who killed Christ, with the help of collaborators such as Erodes and Caiaphas.

This false charge against the Jews, defaming a whole people with a few sinister rulers such as Erodes or Caiaphas, had terrible and ongoing consequences. Millions died for it and the Catholic persecution of the Jews, from the Middle Ages onwards, was a despicable feature of the Pauline heritage.

The institutionalization of faith cast a long shadow over spiritual enquiry in the Second Age and some arguments to this effect are presented in the Addenda to this book. The calcification of western spirituality is related, at its roots, to a male dominated Semitic paradigm in which the established doctrine is the authority that considers all free enquiry as sinful. At every opportunity, the Catholic Church paralyzed any sort of intelligent enquiry from the Middle Ages through to the nineteenth century whenever its considerable might and influence allowed it to do so. The dogma handed down from above led to the repression of all dissenting opinions and the Church created a black hole: critical intelligence disappeared when it came to answering the fundamental quest for meaning. From schism to schizophrenia, dogmatism favored a split personality. For many centuries, the westerner was able to be agile in temporal affairs where his energy was freed for material pursuits, but he was obliged to remain servile and obedient in religious ones. Of course, Protestantism rejected the temporal power of the pope but it was unable to go back to the long lost mystical sources of Gnosticism. With the advent of rationalism, modern man rejected dogma and thence 'threw the baby out with the bath water.' Since the eighteenth century, when Europeans turned their backs on metaphysics, religion survived mostly as a devitalized cultural life style. Baptisms, marriages and burials need, after all, some ceremony and ritual.

Just as with the Pharisees that Jesus complained about, the clerics who pretended to follow Him blocked the gate through which He invited all of us to pass.

There was another Pauline temptation that relied on the story of the apple to turn itself into dogma: deal with your libido by denying or demonizing it. Sex was every bit as dangerous for Adam as it was for Eve, the temptress. Some of Paul's writings show clearly that he was misogynous and his Epistles, in the name of a Christ he never himself met, led ultimately to celibacy being imposed on the priesthood in the name of a higher calling. This created an artificial antinomy in western thought between spirituality and sex. Sex and Eve are given a lower status, one easily associated with guilt. The twisted relationship between sexuality and self-enquiry is a consequence of the fact that the Church repressed sexuality.

We need to dwell for a while on the subject of sex, a topic that absorbs much of our attention in today's world. If woman under the male God paradigm is given an inferior status both in mythology and society, the consequences for all of us are more than regrettable. As her redeeming mystical properties are negated, woman is present in man's consciousness in a mostly carnal sense. On the whole she is not encouraged to activate her own spiritual potential and much of her magnetism is turned instead to winning at the game of seduction. Repressed celibate priests, who understandably fear women, for they see sexuality as leading to their spiritual downfall, manage religion and spread misogynistic concepts. They perceive sexuality as the antithesis of spirituality and this trend, when perpetuated during centuries of asceticism, led to alternative cycles of sexual repression followed by explosions of licentiousness.

Sexuality has been, and continues to this day, to be a problem for the Catholic clergy. The obligatory celibacy has no anchorage whatsoever in the teachings of Christ, but represents instead a fabrication by the Church which will sadly associate spirituality with repressed sexuality, tortured lives and the continued perception of women as inferior beings, temptresses who are an obstacle to spiritual growth. The lives and writings of Paul and Augustine, authoritative leaders of the Church in matters of morality, betray their own difficult relationships with sexuality: "A thorn in my flesh," said Paul, and all Christians were subsequently to pay dearly for it.

With the sexual revolution of the 1960s and the dogmatic position of Pope Paul VI on contraception, the Church became increasingly estranged from modern reality. Its teaching on contraception runs against efforts by poor developing countries to endorse birth control.

Of course, repression created its contrary response and in true dialectic fashion, sex came back with a vengeance. But it came back without Eve, disconnected, so to say, from the finer emotional dimension of exclusivity, which makes it so precious and dear. The powerful swing of modern licentiousness destroys the harmony of couples and the consequent stability of families. After all, it was in the modern day 'Christian countries' that pornography was developed to the point where it is now a multi-billion dollar industry. Running away from Eve was not a good idea. The point I am trying to make is that when the archetype of the Adam-Eve pair works well, that is, when couples are emotionally, physically and sexually satisfied, relationships tend to be stable.

A new dogma of license was created after World War II and it is politically incorrect today to suggest that currently accepted behaviors of sexual promiscuity might not deliver the expected level of satisfaction and fulfillment. Even anti-AIDs programs are shy in extolling the virtues of fidelity for the couple.

By the seventeenth century, modernity was characterized by the peculiar conviction of being right. Modern people know best. It is easy to think so when one has lost one's memory, and the fallacy that grew, as a dark shadow over the Second Age, was to set man against woman and flesh against Spirit.

We can be visual about it. On the Muslim side of the Mediterranean, a fundamentalist woman hides behind the veil of the chador and her throat may be slit if she does not do so. At the same time, on beaches, just to the north, many French and Italian girls go about without clothes or shame, undressed in quasi-invisible G-strings. The divide between the two shores is culturally deep: Muslim traditionalists see the European girl as provocative and immoral; the Arab girl, in the eyes of her European sisters, is repressed and dominated by a male chauvinistic system. Both points of views are understandable, even legitimate. Between prostitution and clitorectomy, girls of the modern era must defend themselves and live with the consequences of a unisex Semitic mythology.

FROM SCHISM TO SCHIZOPHRENIA

The psychological aftermath and consequences of a misguided religious paradigm are not difficult to identify. They are buried deep within our subconscious. Catholic comes from the ancient Greek 'kata holos' which means 'universal.' In the original vision of the Gnostics, the Catholic religion was meant to be universal, all-inclusive and fostering the holistic spiritual dimension of man. Sadly, the Church turned into a sectarian and partisan institution, which does not believe in the free market of ideas and it tried ruthlessly to root out all semblance of anything that looked like competition. By 1204, Crusaders had ransacked Constantinople, a date of infamy in the annals of the eastern Orthodox world. The apologies of Pope John Paul II cannot change or atone for the fact that western Christianity fatally wounded the Byzantine Empire on the eastern edge of the Christian world. This intolerance, over the centuries, took countless forms and generated many schisms but, more seriously, the dogma of the Catholic Church left an imprint on the Western psyche itself, which is akin to inducing a split personality.

A Catholic is someone who aspires to be analytical, inquisitive and scientifically minded in the course of daily life or professional activity. But when it comes to spirituality, he must, as Kierkegaard observed, grab himself by the neck, put his intelligence in parenthesis, shut off all critical sense and turn into a servile follower of obscure or dumb clerical beliefs, as glorified in the pope's encyclical writings. This capacity of putting parenthesis in one's perception of life facilitates parallel behaviors and double standards. It encourages a dichotomy between what is said and what is done. This attitude of necessity breeds hypocrisy, and it explains why the Church literally got away with more than murder. Critical intelligence disappeared into a black hole, sucked away by two thousand years of crafty conditioning.

I sympathize with Catholics who became discouraged by the incapacity of the Church to reform itself. Sincere Christians have left the Church in droves over the past forty years. The process had started way back, with the advent of Protestantism and it carried on with the arrival of Marxism. When spirituality is reduced to the hopeless level to which Catholic dogmatism brought it, it is logical to look for a path elsewhere. The decline of the philosophical influence of the Church started in the eighteenth century and the decline of its political influence was confirmed in the nineteenth century.

However, in a dialectic manner the Church, by the twentieth century, managed to generate its opposite: a strong reaction against spiritual values, leading to contemporary atheism and materialism. This is perhaps the most severe impact of the dark fallacy that clouded Western thought. The gate was shut when it came to the relationship between man's intelligence and his spiritual potential.

Since the eighteenth century infatuation with rationalism and the nineteenth century claim that God is dead, Western thought turned away from the spiritual dimensions of man. But the totalitarian ideologies of the twentieth century, which were meant to replace religion, themselves faded away before the end of that century and today, on the world stage, religion is back as a dividing geo-strategic issue that generates conflict in many parts of the world. The paradox that, for so long, a God of love should be the pretext for so much hate remains puzzling. Something, somewhere seems to have gone wrong in the long corridors of the Second Age.

As we review this legacy, it may be fair to assume that the issue of religion will play a growing importance in the management of world affairs in the future, but a fresh understanding of the religious phenomenon is now required. In the Addenda, we shall elaborate on the subject of the Church. Why spend so much of the reader's time here on the fate of priests?

We shall explain later that priests represent the class of society in charge of clarifying meanings, that was meant to provide the appointed pathfinders for the trail to the beyond. They accordingly guarded the doors of the passage and they influenced societies' primordial beliefs. The extreme extent of this influence is still illustrated today by populist fundamentalism. On the other hand, paradoxically, dwindling numbers of attendees hang around our churches in petrified boredom, as attempts to add glitz, glamour and 'street credibility' cannot fail to resurrect a dying theology.

The first decade of the Third Age is a time that invites strategic reflection and introspection. Many thinkers now direct their attention to identifying a global perspective for the future of civilization.

4. THE FOOTSTEPS OF GOD

Going is not what one should desire to understand. One should know the Goer.

— 3.8 Kaushitaki Upanishad

The first hypothesis postulated in the previous chapter submits that The Book of Genesis indicates two possibilities: running towards the garden's exit or penetrating inside the mystery of the Garden contained in the Tree of Life. The second hypothesis is that, in this quest, we are not on our own. It is the Divine Power itself, which helps us along the path. This chapter is a cursory account of the history of seeking, but also an opportunity to present the notion of femininity hidden within the divine trinity. This is a prelude to the notion that we may all benefit from the awakening of the feminine spiritual power within ourselves.

THE PROVIDER OF MEANINGS

The Lord looks down from heaven upon the children of men, to see if there are any that act wisely, that seek after God.

— Psalm 14.2

In his well-researched book, *The Bible Enlightened*, Dan Costian, a Romanian scholar, makes the following observation. "The message that we should like to communicate does not concern the priority or superiority of one or other religion, but that the progress of human spirituality originating in diverse archetypes found in people from different geographical areas and historical periods, has a universal value."[2]

No one familiar with the history of ideas will be surprised that various forms of spirituality played a role in the organization of societies and in the rise and fall of civilizations. The pre-Colombian priests, Hopi medicine men, Burmese shamans and African marabous were the chief advisers to their respective communities, and they provided interpretations and meanings in order to guide the life of a village in the right direction. Their advice would be sought and respected by the elders of the tribe. This veneration suggests that they played a socially useful role. What was this function? Anthropology provides ample evidence that the chief business of religion was to provide meaning. Whatever the method, be it by reading the flight of eagles or the viscera of slain animals, the wizard or the sorcerer had to provide a sense of direction. Meaning made it possible to prioritize actions: should we go to war with nearby clans or go hunting instead? The priests were the strategic thinkers.

The search for direction covered both the material world as well as the other world and also dealt with how we should relate to both. The first steps of law, for instance, the *Jus Quiritium* of the early Romans, consisted of a set of measures to satisfy the souls of the departed ancestors. Their purpose was to protect the living from the dead and we find the same orientation in the earlier animist practices. The living were scared of the spirits of the dead and they wanted protection against attacks from the dead (white magic) or they wanted to control their souls. Know-how developed to manipulate ghosts in order to obtain material gains, harm rival concubines or business competitors

---

[2] Dan Costian, *Bible Enlightened: Hidden Teachings Revealed*, Bombay (1995), p. 8.

in the world of the living (black magic). We can still buy these kinds of services from white-collar sorcerers practicing witchcraft virtually everywhere. Ancient Egypt is the best example where the living sought satisfaction by preparing for the journey into the realm of the dead. The dead person was buried with the paraphernalia needed to keep the spirits pleased. On the whole, ancient beliefs recognized that dealing with the dead could be a tricky business. This is one area that has been obliterated by modernity's loss of memory.

Religions meanwhile evolved and in Ancient Greece and Rome, and in the Vedic Age in India, Deities corresponded to the forces of nature: the earth (Demeter and Bhoomi Devi); the water (Poseidon and Varuna), the sun (Surya, Aton and Apollo) or fire (Agni) worshipped by Zarathustra, the Roman vestals and the rest of the Aryan world. Interestingly, the ruler of all was the God who controlled the weather: Indra in India, Zeus in Greece or Jupiter in Rome, who was equipped with the thunderbolt. The ecological dimension of the antique pantheons was perhaps not fully realized, but the devastation recently caused by *El Niño*, the holes in the ozone layer and other forms of climate change may suggest today that our ancestors had good reasons to respect nature and to keep its powers pleased and at bay. For centuries man worshipped the forces of nature through his Gods in order to maintain his sense of unity with the universe. It is only in Hollywood's optimistic catastrophe fictions that we triumph over nature and can watch on the screen how man destroys twister tornadoes and nukes incoming asteroids. In the real world, natural catastrophes are a deadly business and their frequency is increasing.

History moves on and so does man's understanding of the cosmos. A further and well-known step in the history of religion is the appearance of monotheism in the Middle East with Jews, Christians and Muslims proclaiming the one and only God. This is, of course, still their ruling belief today and with typical ethnocentrism, Westerners overlooked the fact that the image of the Father had already been evoked millennia before Christ in the person of the Hindu Gods, Lords Rama and Krishna. In other words the First Age of Joachim started between 8000 and 6000 B.C. and probably opened with the battle of Kurukshetra, as described in the epic, the *Mahabharata*.

The advent of Lord Krishna marks the end of the prehistory of religion. One important aspect of His incarnation was to show that the Father is not a severe, remote figure disconnected from His children. On the contrary, He helps us on the way forward to the Gate of Passage with affectionate and playful coaching. The notion of play is such an important insight for modern man who is increasingly stressed out by the pressures of modern living. Through His eventful life and comprehensive teachings, the great Lord Krishna brought a quantum jump in our grasp of spirituality. Of the three great Books, the *Gita*, the *Bible* and the *Koran*, the *Bhagavad Gita* is the oldest and the most precise in terms of the psychological guidance and direction provided. In the *Gita*, Krishna spoke about the trunk of the Tree of Life as a channel, the *Sushumna nadi* that leads to a higher state for man. He also described other aspects of this secret landscape and warned against lust and anger, the pitfalls of desire and action, which may turn into the gates of hell. Purification of desire leads to righteous action, which in turns activates our potential to evolve. We may venture here a third critical hypothesis: it is the Divine Power itself that takes interest in gradually bringing us to the threshold of the Gate of Passage. But the trials and tribulations of the First and the Second Age express the difficulties we faced in trying to meet the lofty standards of introspection and self-mastery set by Shri Krishna.

RELIGION AND MODERN SOCIETY

Most of us spend too much time on the last twenty-four hours and too little on the last six thousand years.

– Will Durant

The arrival on the scene of Hebraic concepts caused a crisis in the philosophy of the ancient world. In ancient mystical traditions, the seeker of higher levels of consciousness could eventually unite with a God who was seen as an all-encompassing energy. But the Jewish God was a providential and personal God, Father of his chosen people, yet also out of reach. Intellectually speaking, He corresponded to the early Greek conception of Zeus. By definition, a 'persona' has a form and one form excludes another. The union with an impersonal energy becomes impossible in an anthropomorphic conception of divinity. Hence again, on a practical level, man's path towards godlike perfection was drastically cut off. Such an attempt would have been in fact a response to the instigation of the snake in Eden: *"Eritis sicut Deus."* (You will become similar to God)

On the speculative level, logically, if man cannot progress towards God, it means that by himself he cannot know anything about Him: knowledge is only therefore to be found in the sacred books, given by God to Moses or to Mohammed, which are then the sole and complete source of revelation. The narrow limitations of *Biblical* or *Koranic* space were to act as a permanent restraint on Christian and Muslim speculations. Belief and not experimentation is the right attitude. Of course the Protestants, who claimed back a right to enquiry, challenged the Catholic orthodoxy and in Islam, the Shiite branch challenged Sunni orthodoxy in order to go back to the true traditions of the Prophet, but the imprint of centuries of religious conformism on the minds of the followers discredited the search for inner meaning.

Religions influenced economics and society but they also developed intimate relationships with politics, that is, the exercise of power. Indeed, rulers the world over used religious prescriptions on a grand scale to maintain their grip on the minds of their subjects. This proved true for the Maurya Buddhist dynasty in India, the role of the Japanese Emperor in the Shinto cult, the period of Muslim Arab expansion and in more recent forms of Christian colonial evangelization. The Chinese Emperor was the Son of Heaven; Europe at the time of Dante was split between the secular might of the Emperor of the Holy Roman Empire of German Nations and the spiritual position of the pope in Rome, both claiming to represent God on earth; the French and English kings and queens claimed to rule by divine right. Such claims for superhuman legitimacy lasted into the nineteenth century. Only a Napoleon dared to take the crown from the hands of a scared pope and to have it put on his own head during his coronation ceremony. Yet later, Charles X, the last Bourbon king in France, was kneeling in the cathedral of Reims to be anointed again by divine right.

As Middle Eastern religions did not favor the free enquiry of spiritual phenomena, Western metaphysics entered the terminal phase of its long illness.

A withdrawn, yet elegant professor, Immanuel Kant (1724-1804) never set forth outside his native Prussia. However his mind traveled far and wide and the clarifying precision of his thought cut through the implausible paths and artificial constructs of western thought. Kant argued that our perceptions are clothed in thoughts and that thoughts are limited. Thus the essential object of knowledge, the thing-in-itself, *"das Ding an Sich,"* is beyond the reach of our cognitive resources. So is, I may add, the other side of the screen of our existential movie in that the entire structure of theology seemed to totter under the rigor of Kantian analysis. *The Critique of Pure Reason* ranks among the most important works of philosophy for it clearly demonstrates that the tunnels towards the other side dug by metaphysicians and theologians were leading nowhere.

Earlier, religions gave some respite to politics, or so it seemed, but with the advent of rational man and critical enquiry in the eighteenth century, religion lost center stage, for in the West, it clearly did not 'deliver the goods' anymore. Following the implausible social contract of Jean Jacques Rousseau, democracy drew its legitimization from the will of the people. Today religion survives in advanced cultures as a post-life insurance scheme to alleviate that old fear stirred by the journey into the world of the dead, but it no longer plays a role in regulating our lives or the market place. By and large, it is no longer a factor in the decision-making process or behavior of the 'material' boys and girls who came of age at the end of the twentieth century.

On the shores of our disorderly pursuits, the footsteps of God were almost washed away. The best brains of those societies turned away from spiritual thoughts and invested their energies more decisively in the material world. The impact of Christianity on Western societies took new forms. Max Weber saw the spirit of modern capitalism as having been born from the spirit of Christian asceticism.

Modernity and its ghosts, described by William Blake, emerged from humming furnaces and 'dark satanic mills.' The industrial and technological revolutions changed the face of the earth. We produced more of everything but unfortunately this did not translate into greater happiness or enjoyment.

'To have' and 'to be' are not automatically correlated concepts, yet 'to be' or 'not to be 'is not the question; rather it is the answer. Spirit is not Matter. The difference matters but can we bridge the gap? Joining the effulgent Being of the Spirit, described by Lord Krishna at the dawn of the First Age, already depends on consciousness, not ownership, and seeking satisfaction in matter only leaves us with a post-party hangover. Following the imprint of the footsteps of God throughout history, can we sense another direction to take us inwards? The footprints suggest that He walks toward us, toward our most intimate Self, but how do we come to terms with spirituality in the twenty first century, and can the spirit within us play a role in the way ordinary people, as well as those who govern us, run their lives and their businesses?

CONFUSED SPIRITUAL PURSUITS

Some proclaim themselves Teachers
And collect a crowd of followers.
These are not men but dogs,
Though they have neither a tail nor four legs,
Adulterous and drunken brutes,
They fatten their bodies.
Tuka says: they are fully equipped
To go down the Pit.

— Saint Tukaram

Es ist doch lange hergebracht
Dass in der grossen Welt man kleine Welten macht.

It is a well-known fact that man creates his little worlds within the big one.

— Goethe, Mephisto in Faust

In the West, Zeus was the external God while in the East, Zen was the inside path. A significant revival of interest in alternative spiritual methods took place in the 1970s in the more affluent countries. This would validate the argument that material affluence and security facilitates spiritual research. The poor may be spared the temptations of the rich, but on the whole, seeking the beyond is a luxury they can ill afford as they seek today's bread instead. On the other hand, for the rich, when the sirens' song of the material world becomes too enticing, the spiritual urge fades away. There are so many 'material girls' in the candy store, so many cars in the showroom, too much buttered popcorn in the movie hall and, for serious people downtown, for a time, too many good prospects for juicy corporate takeovers. Why bother? Matter, not spirit is for them the source of satisfaction because Spirit, whatever it is, cannot be owned. Too many smells, flavors and temptations cover the scent of the great quest of mankind for deeper meanings. The purpose of life is not high on the agenda: the mainstream of contemporary thought in our democracies has silenced the discussion of fundamental questions or reduced it to ridicule. Apathy of intelligence became the order of the day, as described later in Chapter 7. In this book, we will concentrate on surveying the Clinton decade, the last one of the Second Age. Granted, it is already behind us but it is still rich in lessons.

I described in Chapter 2 some aspects of the landscape of seeking in the 1970s. As trends went in the 1990s, within the established circles of society, conversations were mundane or businesslike, rarely spiritual. Interest in spiritual questions tended to come across as trivial, naïve or inconsequential. Spiritual activities were broadly tolerated but seen by the mainstream as largely irrelevant. I am tempted to say, rightly so. Witness the array of commodities on offer in the New Age discount shop: stones, cards, crystals, herbs, mushrooms, mantras, chakras and tantras, magnetism and yoga, witchcraft and parapsychology, planets and stars. New movements and sects proliferated: some were harmless and provided emotional support for their members. Some were outright frauds, totally unable to deliver what they promised; they robbed followers of their critical judgment and, needless to say, of the contents of their wallets. All the while, the larger monopolistic sects devoted themselves to the pursuit of power by other means. The depleted ranks of Catholic and Masonic groups were hunting and seeking to persecute some new sects in the name of honorable values such as 'defending the family.' At the same time they joined hands in the secret Masonic lodge of the P2, bent on an Italian opera of extortion, racketeering and murder. In France and Belgium, they chased alternative belief systems with the familiar zeal of the Inquisition extirpating the heretics.

The media, of course, was always on the lookout for a good headline. The French press was delighted: the cosmic guru of the Mandaron sect in Castellane, who bashfully claimed to have been Jesus Christ, Napoleon and Genghis Khan, was arrested on a rape charge. In Japan and Switzerland, murderous versions of the clubs of avenging angels of the last days, dropped Sarin gas in the underground or committed suicide bucolically in holiday chalets. They too made front-page stories and sect members saw themselves as the 'Chosen' and as the engineers of purifying doom. Apocalyptic prophets used to be figures of fun because Armageddon failed to arrive when they predicted it would. To be on the safe side, the apostles of doomsday now make plans to make sure their predictions come true. The leader of the Aum Shinkyrio cult in Japan enrolled people with PhDs and mobilized more than $1 billion US dollars for developing poison gas and biological weapons - including the Ebola virus - and all this in a country of highly educated citizens. How did he do it? This shortcut from fantasy cults to real nightmare shows the extent of spiritual alienation in an advanced society.

Let us turn to the established religions. When religion shows its face today we are sometimes in for a Rocky Horror Picture Show. It appears in the hairy face of a fanatical mullah covering the walls of Teheran or in the hypocritical mildness of a child-abusing Roman Catholic priest. Traditional aspects of religion have turned bizarre. On the walls of Jerusalem's strictly orthodox neighborhoods, posters proclaim, "When the Messiah will come, the first thing He will do is eliminate the wig." Evidently, hairdressing fashion has always been at the core of theological feuds: the Sikhs grow their hair while Buddhists shave theirs. Pious Muslim males grow their beards and good Muslim girls hide their hair.

These conditionings all start in childhood. I remember my visit to the dzong (monastery) of Tsonga in Bhutan. In beautiful ochre and purple cassocks, hundreds of shaven-headed child monks were mindlessly cheeping the Holy Scriptures for hours at a time. I had myself sung Gregorian psalms at 5 a.m. under the gothic vaults of an ancient basilica during my college years. This type of education strikes me as a strong narcotic against the use of critical intelligence. In their emptiness, songs and chants were at least harmless. I could not say the same of the fiery homily of the imam I heard in the Gaza strip, a pupil of the prestigious Al Azra University in Cairo. He was quoting God and Hitler to Palestinian teenagers on how to handle the Jews. "Hamas future martyrs, unite!"

He was also saying that the West is decadent and while we may prefer our decadence to his militancy, we must grant him the point: Western morality is crumbling, the European churches deserted. Where did our religions go wrong? Were they always meant to end up in factional violence or outright boredom? Yet, from a logical point of view, religious beliefs are such a constant element of human life that there must be some rationale behind them. Is it possible to find a contemporary answer to the question: what were these religions about in the first place?

BETWEEEN ZEN AND NIKE

L'on souhaiterait une theorie générale de la vision qui n'entrat pas en contradiction flagrante avec les faits d'observation quotidienne.

One would wish for a general theory of vision that would not blatantly contradict the facts we observe on a daily basis.

    — Magritte

Many kids in the 1970s became involved in Tao and Zen whereas kids in the 1990s aspired to Reebok and Nike. Each generation, of course, finds the interest of another frivolous but they have one thing in common. They all seek satisfaction. Trying to get satisfaction is the theme of one of the best song of the Rolling Stones and it is also the fundamental law of economics. After all, goods and services are supplied to satisfy demand. Producers will be successful only if they meet their customers' satisfaction thresholds. They need not think much further but these thresholds may change despite the all-pervasive manipulations of the advertisement industry. Its job is to make the customers believe that they need a certain product by stimulating desire for it. The assumption, mostly proved correct by sales, is that I am satisfied if my ego is satisfied. The trick usually consists in associating brand recognition with the purchaser's ego gratification. How long can such tricks last?

Let us return to the temptations of religions. In the past, two tendencies had emerged to meet the challenge of providing satisfaction to believers. The first one, very simply, cashed in and took the money. How? The traditional fashion was to call for unquestioned faith in the dogma and to present a specific clerical hierarchy as the guardian of that dogma. From this monopolistic position, the hierarchy would commercialize spiritual proposals: the supplier of religious orthodoxy would draw from his trade, status, wealth and power. The Catholic Church in the Middle Ages, the Caliphs of Baghdad, the Dalai Lama in Lhasa, as well as many astute self-appointed gurus of the New Age, embarked on this road: they accumulated wealth as carriers of various gospels; they built themselves palaces in Rome or Malibu. Looking at the long term, this approach corresponded invariably - if not immediately - to a degradation of the product, customers' lack of satisfaction, diminishing returns and loss of market share.

Most New Age sects burn out fast at a quicker pace than before, as followers get disillusioned. This is largely because demand has become more sophisticated. Scientology is attacked in the courts and despite sophisticated theories, seekers are no longer impressed by the Transcendental Meditation flying squadrons, hopping on mattresses as they attempt to levitate. The neo-Freudian jargon of Rajneesh no longer meets the new quality standards.

The other tendency, intellectually more demanding, has been to understand that spirituality does not lend itself to commercialization. By its very nature, it must be acquired or communicated freely. For spirituality to be meaningful, it must be based on direct personal experience, which is the only basis for having faith in the Spirit. The problem is how to achieve the right sort of experiences? What is it in the message of spirituality that can deliver solid satisfaction? How can spirituality reach out to the men and women seeking it? Can it deliver the 'genuine article' in such a manner that it does not degrade it? Parmenides, Spinoza and other seekers were interested in the 'Real Thing' well before the advent of Coca-Cola. This search is not new and we can see that trust in the concept of the perfectibility of man has been a constant trend in all the major world cultures.

However, we have yet to show that concrete results can be achieved in this pursuit. It should be possible to show that such achievements are verifiable in a manner that satisfies the requirements of Hume's skeptical empiricism. In presenting our fourth and most critical hypothesis, the possibility of experiencing Self-realization, we are treading on this path and must ask the reader to take a broad look at the relationship between achieving spirituality and achieving satisfaction.

The 'I' investigated by Gurdjieff may be more than ego, and it may well have its own needs. There is a line of enquiry and research which has suggested that spirituality could make an eminently practical contribution to a more holistic quest for satisfaction. The older scripts were telling us that Spirit in man is the big 'I,' the divinity within man. We may thus formulate our fifth hypothesis: Spirituality caters to the needs of the 'I' and when the 'I' takes itself as the object, it is called the Self.

WHAT WE DESIRE MAKES A DIFFERENCE

It is preoccupation with possessions, more than anything else that prevents man from living freely and nobly.

— Bertrand Russell

But we run in the opposite dimension, sucked by the gravitational pull of matter. Adam raced away from Eve, the Tree of Life and the Snake of Mystery. Where does this leave us? He ran fast, down the corridors of time, and achieved much indeed. His course took him inexorably towards his apparent mastery over matter.

Both Pharaoh Seti I and Napoleon had a perception of time and space conditioned by the pace of the horse. Millennia separate them but between Napoleon and my grandfather, who shared the same century, man's environment started to change at an ever-increasing pace. Yet their worlds were still related in some ways through comparable conditions. My grandfather, at the age of seventy, climbed Mont Rose, the highest mountain in Switzerland. He never owned a car or played the stock markets and his life was not that different from the lives of his ancestors. I can hardly climb a couple of stairs without losing my breath but I live in planes, fish for barracuda in Djibouti, buy emeralds in Bogotá and chat on the Internet. My life is very different.

Even a cursory glance at the phenomenal acceleration of history over the very short period of the last one or two centuries shows signs that the engine that powers us is overheating. The Adam-led, one hemisphere brain type of growth has pushed through by means of willpower, creativity and action. Throughout the industrial revolution and the ensuing breathtaking scientific and technological advances, the pace of faster change favored and enhanced continuing material affluence for some: Descartes' paradigm, "I think therefore I am" is replaced by "I have therefore I am." This shift largely happened, though not exclusively, in the so-called democratic countries.

"Who am I?"

"Ask your bank account."

In the USA, they ask: "How much is he worth?" not "How much does he make?"

Owning, owing! This has become the real engine of life. Driving down to Manhattan, I once read on the bumper sticker of a BMW: "I owe I owe and off to work I go." Owing keeps you busy not free.

A pretense of politicians in the western democracies is that they provide at the material level the greatest happiness for the greatest number; it is the principal vote winner. They sing the same tune, "I shall lower taxes, I shall create jobs." Ownership explains the success of capitalist democracy.

Let us now step back to a time when philosophy was more than just obscure linguistics. To be bold, let us intertwine two nineteenth century arguments, the first borrowed from Hegel, the second from de Tocqueville. The first was a man of vision, the second, a man with keen sight. Hegel saw history as the actualization of consciousness. The view of de Tocqueville was more down to earth and closer to our turf. In his study of democracy in America, he saw that the main foundation of democracy's stability and prosperity is its capacity to open a wide access to private property. When business is in power, it would logically strive to achieve this. Market economy democracy is the successful norm for the world community as it ensures access to ownership. At least we have established that the desire to own is powerful indeed. Placing de Tocqueville on Hegel's evolutionary ladder, we could say that market economy democracies represent, in the scheme of history, the necessary step where the collective desire of mankind to successfully use and exploit matter is fulfilled, at least for many in the richer countries. At this stage, material affluence provides consciousness with security. Within modern democracies, people's age-old desires and aspirations for private property and material affluence seem indeed more largely satisfied than ever before.

The perceptions of de Tocqueville and Hegel need not be contradictory. Perhaps, and this is our sixth hypothesis, we needed first to secure our grip over matter before soaring towards the spirit. On its way towards the Spirit, following Hegel's spiraling scheme, human consciousness first invests its creativity into matter. The human consciousness achieves security at the material level before it ventures ahead on the spiritual journey. The sky of the spirit may seem the destination of the few, the ground of materialism the limit of the many. However, we walk on the ground while looking at the sky and some wonder: Can we fly? If our awareness does not grow upwards, will we regress downwards? At the end of the second millennium, on which step of the ladder are we standing?

Let us accept, for the sake of argument, that in the Hegelian scheme, evolution pushes forward with a purpose. If that primordial desire which guides history is for the actualization of spirit and not merely for the mastery over matter, it implies that the step on which capitalism is currently standing is not the final destination. Seen as such, material progress has been helpful, provided we now discover how to go on to the next step. This discovery is the essence of the Third Age of history that Joachim attributed to the Holy Spirit, when he wrote the *Expositio ad Apocalypsim* in 1183. But in his mind the monks would find the solution. Our old philosophers pretended all along that neither our desires nor evolution would stop at matter. Are we climbing the ladder or are we glued to one step? Maybe the ladder to climb is within the once famous yet now mostly forgotten Tree of Life?

DESTRUCTION AND REDEMPTION: THE RETURN OF THE FEMININE TRINITY

The Divine Humanity: A Three-fold Wonder, feminine, most beautiful, Three-fold, Each within the other.

— William Blake, Jerusalem, Chapter 3, Plate70

Next appeared a great portent in heaven: a woman robed with the sun, beneath her feet the moon, and on her head a crown of twelve stars; she was with child and she cried out in her pangs of birth, in anguish for delivery. And another portent appeared in heaven: behold a great red dragon, with seven heads and ten horns, and seven diadems upon his heads... and the dragon stood before the woman who was to bear a child, that he might devour her child when she brought it forth; she brought forth a male child, one who is to rule all the nations with a rod of iron.

— Saint John, The Book of Revelation, The Apocalypse, Ch.12

Joachim was not, of course, the only prophet of the coming age. There are scores of prophetic texts suggesting that our new millennium opens with tremendous ordeals followed ultimately by redemption. After the twin towers of the World Trade Center in New York crashed on the 11th September 2001, many revisited such texts. A coming of a phase of destruction would be in conformity with the predictions of the Apocalypse and of the *Kalki Purana*, which predicts the destruction of things that are corrupt at the end of the Second Age. In the Hindu faith, Kalki, the tenth Incarnation of Lord Vishnu, corresponds to the return of the Christ King, as described in a mighty vision in *The Book of Revelation* of Saint John. (19.11) Kalki, it is said, will appear at the end of the age of darkness when virtue will have vanished; there will be famine, wars and criminal rulers. Women will bear too many children, Brahmins will have lost the knowledge, substance and real worth will depart from everything. The sacred rites will be finished and the earth will be worshipped for its minerals only. Men and women will live together without being married, bound by sensuality only. Women will be like men and men like women.

In the days following the catastrophe in New York City, I received this bit of numerology in my email:

The date of the attack: 9/11; 9+1+1 = 11

September 11th is the 254th day of the year: 2+5+4 =11

After September 11 there are 111 days left to the end of the year.

119 is the area code of Iran and Iraq: 1+1+9 = 11

Twin Towers - standing side by side, looking like the number 11

The first plane to hit the towers was flight 11

Flight 11had 92 on board. 9+2 = 11

Flight 77 had 65 on board. 6+5 = 11

Afghanistan = 11 letters

The Pentagon = 11 letters

New York City = 11 letters

The State of New York: the 11th state to be added to the Union

I did not check these numbers but when I read the lines, I recalled having been told a long time ago about the esoteric symbolism contained in the number 11. Kalki is identified with the *Ekadesha Rudra* principle, that is, the eleven destructive powers of Shiva or of the returning Christ King. As we shall see in the Appendix, a similar expectation is found in the Shia branch of Islam, in the return of the Mahdi, the twelfth imam. We will state elsewhere that such archetypes in our unconscious influenced history very directly. If we accept for a moment the possibility of the symbolic content of such traditions, we could infer three things: a) there is a period of destruction unfolding now; b) this period was prophesized in various religious writings; and c) this period may lead to the purification of man and a new age of spiritual renewal for mankind. And all this has something to do with womanhood. The knight John of Jerusalem, in the eleventh century, wrote in his Book of Prophecies: "Because a woman will arrive to reign supreme. She will be a great master of the future time…She will be the Mother of the Millennium that comes after the Millennium. After the days of the devil She will make the softness of the Mother flow. She will, after the days of barbarity, embody beauty The millennium that follows the millennium will metamorphose in an age of lightness: men will love each other, share everything, they will dream and their dreams will turn into reality … So an end will be proclaimed to barbarity. It will be the era of a new strength of belief. The dark days at the beginning of the millennium that follows the millennium will be followed by days of jubilation: man will once more find the righteous path of humanity and Earth will find harmony once more."[3]

As indicated in the texts above, the shape of destruction is balanced by the protecting appearance of a feminine figure. What is the role of the feminine paradigm in this coming revolution? Is it to bring spirituality down to earth?

---

[3] The Knight John of Jerusalem, *Prophecies on the Adi Shakti*, Cabella (2002), p. 13.

At the dawn of the Third Age, we see the re-emergence of the experimental approach to spiritual reality. Centuries of monopolistic dogmas and the naïve pretensions of the rationalists had erased it from western consciousness. Self-realization was depicted in the past as a metaphysical illumination that no one could explain. The thesis presented in the next chapter suggests instead that it can be felt through specific neuro-physiological sensations and expanded states of consciousness.

A power leads us gently on this path. In the *Gospel of the Essenes*, the earthly Mother is She who will restore the world. Like the Virgin Mary at the end of Goethe's second Faust, She is the helping guide who brings man to the level of higher awareness where he can reach the Heavenly Father.

During the last supper, Christ told his disciples, "These things I have spoken to you while I am still with you. But the Counselor, the Holy Spirit, whom the Father will send in my name, will teach you all things." John 14.25.

The Aquarian Gospel of Jesus the Christ is an apocrypha with more specifics: "And now, I go my way, but I will pray to my Father God and he will send another Comforter to you, who will abide with you. Behold, the Comforter of God, the Holy Breath, is one with God, but She is the One the world cannot receive because it sees Her not; it knows Her not. But you know Her because She will abide within your soul." [4]

Again, the Feminine Power is identified with the Holy Spirit and the Grace of the Holy Breath. Verily, the vision of Joachim is not a solitary occurrence. It does look like, in the Second Age, that the Good Shepherd, the Son, brought the seeking man to the point where he can receive the teachings of the Master of the Third Age. In the fragments of the lost *Gospels of the Hebrew* commented on by Origene (in *John 2,6*) Christ is reported to have said: "My mother who is the Holy Spirit just took me by one of my hairs and carried me on the top of Mount Tabor." And in commentary 4 on Isaiah we read: "As the Lord returned from the water, it so happened that the entire source of the Holy Ghost came down and rested on Him and She spoke to Him: 'My Son, among all the prophets, I was waiting for Your coming, that I may rest in You. For You are My rest, You are My first born Son, who rules in eternity.'"

One of the overlooked features of Middle East monotheism is that God is a male figure only. This contrasts with the countless manifestations of a feminine Divine principle in ancient times. The divinity of the feminine element had been the rule in Europe during the Neolithic period. Hathor of Egypt and Surabi in India represented the universal mother as a milk-giving cow. Kuan Yin in China, Ana for the Celts, Isis in Egypt, Isthar in Mesopotamia, Astarte in Phoenicia, Artemis and Athena in Greece, Cybele in the Phrygian and Hellenic world are only a few of these countless forms. In Tibet She is the *Boddhisattva Tara*, the "Savioress." Very often, the Great Goddess is represented accompanied by a feline (lion, tiger, panther) and, again, a serpent, seen on the scud of Athena. Fertility cults and Mother worship were gradually swept away by waves of nomadic invasions from central Asia. In Assyrian mythology, the son Marduk kills the mother Tiamat

---

[4] *The Aquarian Gospel of Jesus the Christ.* Ch. 161 v. 35.

and this marks the brutal assertion of the male principle that was to influence the modern era. But even in Mediterranean Antiquity the sanctuaries of the Goddess were of paramount importance: Isis in Egypt and Artemis in Ephesus. The Hindu religion contends that God is both male and female and figures of the Goddess are objects of intense devotion. In the Christian world the Marial cult runs strong and deep, though the Church never gave Mary the status of a Goddess. Typically She is seen as '*Advocata nostra*,' the One who pleads for us before the divine tribunal of judgment and who extends help and protection to those who struggle in the valleys of tribulations of this world. Let us listen to her praise by an anonymous poet of the tenth century:

Salve domina coelorum,	Hail Sovereign of the heavens
Imperatrix angelorum	Empress of the angels
Dignans tamens miseros.	You however accept the down trodden.
Salve mitis, salve digna,	Hail, you are tender and dignified
Salve dulcis and benigna	Hail to the sweet and benign One
Trahe nos ad superos!	Carry us above!

In the Indian tradition, the primordial power of God is venerated as the feminine aspect of God, the Adi Shakti, and Mother of creation, the universal Goddess that divides Herself into three main aspects: Mahakali who steers our inner power of pure desire; Mahasaraswati who governs our power to create and act and Mahalakshmi who leads the path of evolution and the spiritual ascent of the seeker. The advent of this triple power is announced in Buddhism, which expects the coming of Maitreya. Mai-treya, the mother with three aspects is the savior and future Buddha. This advent is also predicted in the Gnostic vision of the *Trimorphic Protonoia*. A representation of the triple power of the Goddess is enshrined in the beautiful medieval "*Wiener Neustadt* Altar" in Saint Stephen's Dome in Vienna. The same power is extolled in the praises of the sacred wisdom, (*Hagya Sophia*) and the hymns of King Solomon.

However, statues, poems, tales and paintings use a metaphoric expression to describe or announce a subtler liturgy. We must understand such liturgies in relationship to a state of being. This state is referred to in the Hebrew concept of Shekhinah, which is the blissful perception of the Divine presence or manifestation of God in the consciousness of collectivity. Henceforth, the steps of God seem to lead towards the inner secret of our sacred being, for Jesus is also reported to have said: "Your Mother is within you, and you are within Her. It is She who has given you birth and given you life."[5]

Can an inner, spiritual transformation exert any impact on the world as we know it? This book attempts to explore this question but others have answered it before. In the above-mentioned text of the knight John of Jerusalem, a manuscript discovered in Moscow in the archives of the KGB, we also read that, after the days of destruction, a glorious dawn will shine. An end will be put to turmoil, the Golden Age will start: "Thus man will have his second birth. Spirit will possess the mass of men who will be united in brotherhood." But looking around, I shrug. Before we see the light, we should be prepared to face the darkness. Anyone who reads *The Bible* or *The Koran*, and takes these texts seriously, will be scared by the prophecies of destruction that they contain. In so many ways, this destruction is already

---

[5] E Bordeaux-Szeleki, *l'Evangile Essenien*, Geneva, p. 257.

upon us, even though we do not always see it. I hope the reader will not mind as I am about to take him through chapters burdened with the very real problems we face.

Modern man has identified his sense of security with material affluence. He has not built his identity inside, on the inner worth of spiritual accomplishment, but instead has constructed his identity through outside devices such as the accumulation of appearances and possessions. He has shielded himself from the unknown with insurance policies. Thus we seem to bask in a false sense of security and may not be aware of the many paths taken in the process of self-destruction of our civilization. Let us follow the trail in the last decade of the second millennium. This period sadly illustrates what sort of load we are passing on to the generations of the third millennium. Interestingly, the dysfunction of our society relates directly to that of the modern psyche.

The modern era is about speed. It is ushering man to a new condition: having conquered matter, man could theoretically now use time to enjoy the freedom from wants and to explore the frontiers of the spirit. But it is not so and just like an athlete who gets punished for having pushed the physical limits too far, man has to pay a price for gathering so much speed throughout the industrial, technological and information revolutions. We have overstrained ourselves and must now register the damage done to our psyches: the numbing of the brain, the scorching of the liver and the freezing of the heart. These were the three organs through which we were meant to play the 'game of the *gunas*.' We will now explain.

PART THREE

TRAPPED WITHIN THE GUNAS

This book investigates connections between the cosmos and the human microcosm. What is it in the structure of the cosmos that affects our daily lives and society alike? In *The Bhagavad Gita*, we find an explanation of the workings of the world and of our race. The *gunas* are moods or types of influences that drive nature and men and the interaction of these influences generates man's world of contradictions. This mode of analysis of patterns in history is the underlying method of Hegelian and Marxist dialectics and of that used by Oswald Spengler in his book, *The Decline of the West*. But the link with psychology was still missing. In Part Four, I shall explain how three main channels of energy at the cosmic level – the moon channel on the left side, the sun channel on the right side and the central channel of equilibrium – are reflected in our own psychosomatic structure. A more detailed description of this mode of interpretation of both psychology and history is contained in Chapters 15 and 16.

The failure of these channels of energy to function harmoniously in our body generates behavior leading to the problems described in Chapters 5 to 7. An obstruction on the moon channel diverts desires, on the sun channel misguides action, and on the central channel, hampers knowledge.

A few of these chapters were written in the 1990s and since many of these observations subsequently came to pass: the resurgence of fundamentalism, the collapse of the stock markets, the problems of globalization, criminal CEOs, acceleration of climate change and natural catastrophes. I did not want to update the illustrations of the problems of the world society with events in the opening of the third millennium because the purpose here is to illustrate trends. Sadly, these trends were only confirmed over recent years. What sounded prophetic then has unfortunately become common knowledge now.

READING INTO BALLISTICS

Like most little boys, I used to throw pebbles across the surface of a pond and to try to count the ricochets. When, later, I became an artillery officer, I learned how the trajectory of a shell is determined by a set of parameters that are calculated in order to hit a specific target. The point of impact depends on the curve of the trajectory. If you imagine that the shell is an allegory for the present, it follows that the future depends largely on conditions laid out in the past, a theory of history that seems somewhat deterministic. This is the point of view defended by the karma theory of eastern religions. They tell us that we will be visited by the consequences of our past actions, good or bad. If we generalize this approach, we can be lured into seeking clues about the location of the target. Can we anticipate the future by studying the trajectory?

Let us visualize our society on some point of a ballistic curve that may yield information on the point of impact. I am not deterministic by temperament and I would hope we might improve this allegory. The shell would then turn out to be a smart missile perhaps, with some cybernetic guiding system, which allows for modifying its course during flight. But even so, some questions remain: what data should be entered into the targeting system? What can we learn from the ongoing path of the missile? In which direction is it heading?

As a student of political sciences, I became interested in the tracking system for the missile. I studied political philosophy to find out what our well-meaning forefathers deemed to be a proper stewardship for the course of human society. I found a global wisdom across world cultures which prescribed some 'do's and don'ts' to avoid misfiring or missing the target altogether. A broad consensus emerged through various teachings identifying the kind of behavior that is best conducive to the survival of the species. Moses, Confucius, Lao Tzu, Socrates, Mohammed, Guru Nanak, to name a few, are quite consistent in their teachings.

I have been puzzled as to why modern man felt able to do away with this body of ancient wisdom and how confidently he threw away the radar system. The result is that never has society zoomed so fast into an unknown future, in circumstances where a good radar system is needed. Today, critical intelligence is allowed to function mostly under the narrow constraints and hidden assumptions of the ruling one-dimensional thought of materialist modernity. Perhaps we should unveil and question some of these assumptions.

The contrast presented by world society is straightforward. The developing world is facing overpopulation; the developed world is running out of babies and young productive workers. The rich have never been richer, while at the same time billions of people in the Third World are living under the threshold of poverty in a fast degrading environment. These imbalances present a huge challenge. When facing this mess, we, the citizens of the Western democracies, may feel vindicated that we have spared ourselves such a plight and that we are still on course. We may feel that our relationship with the rest of the world is under control. Yet those of us with a better memory would fear that we put too much faith in technology and not enough in caring about relationships. The ghost of our deeds may yet visit us; we may see in our nightmares Chief Seattle, the slave traders or the emptying cargoes of sunken oil tankers. Are we aware in what ways our actions affect us? In fact, do we pay enough attention to more subtle forms of destruction that are at work through our modern economics and lifestyle? Our society is racing through time and space, toward some catharsis or impact point as predicted by the Christian scriptures, carried by the compounded result of the sum of its past misdeeds and achievements.

When Daniel Cohn Bendit, Danny the Red, almost brought down the government of General Charles de Gaulle in the streets of Paris in May 1968, many of us thought the world was changing. Change did come, but in what sense? I started reflecting on the evolving nature of our western democracy some thirty years ago but it is really at the end of the 1980s that trends started crystallizing to shape the present day pattern of modernity. This is why I have chosen to focus on the end of the Second Age, the last decade of the twentieth century. Many sociologists agree with me that the last twenty years present significant trends that provide glimpses at some possible shapes of the future.

5. THE FREEZING OF THE HEART

This chapter submits that our capacity to love is largely frozen and is no longer operating in a collective manner. Thus, we need to get back to a condition where we can know again how to express our love and respect, to our kith and kin, to the entire world community and to nature itself. The family, the nation, the nature around us, that is, the functioning of social ecosystems are like the concentric circles of what encompasses us. But each of these circles is disturbed because we are not sufficiently channeling the energy of love to each of them.

WHICH WAY TO FEELING, PLEASE?

Le petit Prince dit: "On est un peu seul dans le desert..." "On est seul aussi chez les hommes," dit le serpent.

The little prince said: "One feels a bit lonely in the desert..." "One feels lonely also in the midst of people," said the serpent.

— Antoine de Saint Exupery, The Little Prince

I am enjoying a pleasantly cool evening on a Nile boat cruise in Cairo. The sky offers its deep blue immensity. Luxury hotel towers on the banks of the river rise in Pharaonic and panoramic splendor. I relax after a long working day. The food is rich, the audience on board, excited and friendly. Loud music brings us to the climax of the evening's entertainment - here comes the shapely belly dancer, her eyes smoldering, her smile flashing and her flesh trembling in expert fashion. She is sure of her command over her largely male audience. While dancing, she picks up guys in the audience to dance with her in the crude stage light. I remember; it had happened to me once before in Morocco. I try to hide, but here she comes, there is no escape. I hop on the stage, circling her like an Iroquois around his totem, avoiding looking at her charms from too close a vantage point. My penance ends and I withdraw under an umbrella of ovation. The dinner goes on. Later, I climb on to the top deck of the ship to get a moment of blessed solitude and tranquility. The belly dancer is there too, smoking a cigarette. She is sitting on a chair, sad and alone. At first I do not recognize her, all her glamour vanished, all vitality extinct, nobody behind her eyes. I want to tell her that she danced well, that she doesn't need to be sad; I want to say something nice but I can't. We had never really met. I am just one of those she entertained.

I am using here the word 'entertainment' in the same way as the seventeenth century French philosopher, Blaise Pascal: to him, '*divertissement*' meant to turn away from real life. The yearning for entertainment, it has been argued, is called upon by the very stressful and rather dry lifestyle of modern cities. Entertainment takes us out of our lives as if we can find something better out there. What about a form of entertainment that would truly enrich our lives?

Entertainment, as we shall see later, has, on the whole, the important job of keeping us out of reality, the assumption being that reality is boring. But we may be better entertained if we could go beyond escapism. Entertainment should not divert our attention but, on the contrary, focus it on the real wellspring of fun, happiness and joy. This is why the great play of Self-discovery is so gratifying. Reconnecting with the heart in a deeper sense will open for us forms of entertainment that rest on simple but intense feelings of satisfaction and joy. Feelings, as realized souls experience, can bring us closer to each other and introduce us to collective enjoyment. Genuine emotional gratification through affection, friendship, caring or love is only too often denied, and yet aren't such feelings the seeds of life's joy? The best therapy to restore awareness would seem to be, somehow, to restore the connection of the heart to the brain.

LOVE AS A COLLECTIVE ENERGY

The supreme happiness of life is the conviction that we are loved.

     – Victor Hugo

The organ that can connect with direct certainty to the present is the heart. The heart gives balance to the brain through its intuitive sensitivity, and this epistemological added value to our cognitive process has been recognized in a number of books which contrasted the emotional coefficient to the more widely acclaimed intellectual coefficient. Without a subtle linkage to the heart as an organ of knowledge, the brain loses its navigational sense; it becomes disconnected from the truth and it searches for satisfaction in pursuits that cannot deliver satisfaction. It no longer trusts traditional benchmarks of ethical behavior and indicators of right conduct. It no longer finds itself choosing between good and evil but between hamburger and pizza, between vacuous pop culture and plastic. Without the inner capacity for enjoyment linked to an open heart, the brain seeks outside manifestations of its own phantasms. Actually the heart connects us to reality because it is itself connected to it through the energy of love.

Sages of the past allowed us to guess that Self-realization is uniquely connected to a higher world of enjoyment, for it establishes a direct capacity to love oneself. Usually we are not very good at it. We lack self-esteem and self-confidence, and to make matters worse, we too often feel guilty.

The heart is the seat of desire and, ultimately, desire leads to action. Let us search in our intimate memory. Have we not known moments of deep wellbeing, of serene joy and contentment, when we can say that we experienced fulfilment, where life was worth being lived and everything was as it should be? Love belongs to these moments. Love for the majesty of the sea; the silence on a mountain peak; for friends; for a woman, a man or a child. Moreover, in traditions all over the world, the organ that feels, that gives and receives love, is the heart. Love is a huge, collective energy but in the aftermath of decades of personalist psychology, love is perceived only as an inter-personal emotion, not as a collective force. Even worse, the Freudian fraud has promoted an absurd impoverishment of love. Love is sex. The influence of Freud on the West has brought us to a stage of infantile understanding of our potential. It has created a regressive, under-developed emotional culture. As such, the heart of our collective body is frozen.

Electricity is an energy that is enormously useful and it can be put to so many uses, but if a child puts its fingers in an electric socket, it will discover the unpleasant side of electricity. Love is one of the absolute values recognized in all civilizations but its use can also be misguided and misdirected. Language is often troubling, as can be seen in the literal meaning of common phrases: love is something you fall into, the tender trap; it is also something you make. In the West, love is sometimes described as a sort of flu of the heart, but a flu that killed Tristan and Iseuld as well as Romeo and Juliet. Like flu, it is contagious. Teenagers, lovers, couples playing with each other's hearts can all experience the pain, just as with kids putting their fingers in the electric socket. An extreme form of absurdity is to adopt the reductionist view that love is sex. The fact is that human love has many forms: affection, sex, tolerance, protection, companionship, fraternity, sisterhood, respect, compassion, admiration, dedication and worship. All of these attitudes generate positive interactions and are potentially huge sources of satisfaction. Many of them are crucial to maintaining cohesive groups and productive working environments.

Lasting satisfaction in interpersonal relationships is not to be confused with ephemeral gratification; it is a function of the degree of love invested in them. Our inability to give or receive love hampers the quality of these interactions and the collectivity suffers from the sum of these accumulated failures. Consequent behavioral responses to this inability may be registered as aloofness, mistrust, frustration, sarcasm or outright hostility. None of them are helpful or positive.

But how to love? It seems an odd question and the answer isn't something you can learn in a management course. If the emotion is construed or faked, it is no longer love. The energy is spontaneous, flowing from the heart, and no one knows where it comes from or why it is there. It is a great blessing to have loving parents and a loving family because the opening of the heart ideally takes place in early childhood.

At the end of the Second Age, we need a fundamental adjustment of desire, thought and action. How did we fail to open a path to a more humanistic and spiritual way of life?

The fight for survival of an individual may express itself in any form of competition or even in violence. In contrast, sensitivity for our fellow human beings, a sense of compassion, generosity and caring are needed for the collective survival of a community. These attitudes are expressions of the instinct for survival of a community as a whole. In the history of mankind, man is gradually learning to evolve and survive collectively, as a part of the whole. In a Darwinian sense, the fittest communities are those in which the heart, which cares for the whole, is alive to inspire the brain. This, by the way, was the authentic message of the great religious teachers. "Love thy neighbor as thyself." This is an eminently social message. The qualities of the heart keep the family, the tribe or the clan together more effectively and deeply than force or fear. Societies which could activate the primordial force of love are those that structure themselves to genuinely seek the greatest happiness for the greatest number.

Cultures that are destructive of good family conditions may well precipitate their societies on the road to decay. On the other hand, those that nurture love maintain the cohesion of human groups. This is equally true of corporate cultures in the business world. In any environment, a culture that promotes self-improvement will activate a deeper sense of togetherness.

SPLIT FAMILIES

It is time in the West to defend not so much human rights but human obligations.

— Alexander Solzhenitsyn

The family is the basic cell of our society but it is under pressure because of a number of factors including work pressures within the rich countries and poverty within the poor. Children suffer. Life starts with childhood and childhood used to be cherished. In the highlands of Maharashtra in India, there are eight sacred statues or swayambhus of Shri Ganesha, the God representing the eternal innocence of childhood, who is the object of tremendous popular devotion. He has an elephant head, symbolizing the strength and wisdom of the mightiest animal, devoid of human ego. He is the archetype for the primordial vibration of child-like purity, the first-born, and He is worshipped in India before each official ceremony or collective function for his auspiciousness brings good luck. In this millennial tradition, it is widely believed that the protection of values associated with childhood, such as innocence or spontaneity, are essential for the harmonious working of the community. This mythology made breaking news in the fall of 1995, when Ganesha's statues enjoyed a new prominence before thousands of bewildered and enthusiastic worshippers. Newspapers reported that in Toronto, New York, Vancouver, London and temples all over India, statues of the elephant-headed God were accepting offerings of milk in that the bowls were emptying by themselves. Maybe this was to tell us that innocence is reclaiming its place?

In the beginning was the child, and Christian art gave us countless portraits of the Mother and Child, which celebrate the charm of the divine infant, so well captured, for example, by the Spanish artist Murillo. Yet, modern times have, in many new ways, insulted the innocence for which Lord Ganesha or the Child Jesus stand for. Firstly, this occurred when Hitler captured the age-old Aryan symbol for Ganesha, the swastika, on the advice of occult Tibetan advisers and put it on the banners of the Third Reich's doomed legions. Another illustration of the highjack of a symbol for this same principle of innocence relates to the Aum or the Amen. "In the beginning was the Word, and the Word was with God and the Word was God." The Amen Word of *John's Gospel* has been annexed by silly false prophets, fake gurus and murderous sects.

Moving from symbol to reality is an even sadder affair. A child's smile warms up the heart, doesn't it? Somehow, in every society, primitive or so-called advanced, what happens to our children is considered a good indication of how well or badly the society as a whole is functioning. However, not every child is smiling these days. Paedophile networks on the Internet have multiplied sickening forms of child abuse and pornography, and it is on the Net that the demonic lure of money spreads the most blatantly. The highest selling films are those featuring coerced sex, rapes or torture. In the Middle East and Eastern Europe, thousands of over-painted young women receive easy visa clearance to cross otherwise closed borders under the category of 'artists'. Poverty breeds violence in men and degradation for women and it is now generating new forms of human slavery. An estimated 300,000 women have been shipped out of the former communist countries of Eastern Europe and the old Soviet Union by criminal networks. Trafficking in women is a form of sex slavery that is characterized by deception and coercion, and violence against these women is at its core. Each abused child and degraded woman is at the same time a testimony and a judge in the trial of a sick society.

Divorce rates are one of the main indices of the fundamental problems of modern societies for the destruction of families invariably affects children the most. Divorce rates have soared since 1970 in almost every developed country and the percentage of children born to unmarried mothers has grown steadily.[6] More than 50% of American mothers have jobs outside the home, meaning less nurturing for the children. In hospitals across the former Soviet Union, newborn children abandoned by their mothers fill maternity wards, and well-dressed children in school uniforms commit suicide in Tokyo. Poor farmers sell their twelve-year-old daughters for prostitution in Bangkok. 200,000 Brazilian kids are living on the street. In France hate starts at 12: the children are more violent at an earlier age than ever before.[7] In the Bronx, educators debated whether compulsory prayer in school is supposed to reduce teenage pregnancy; and metal detectors at the doors are employed to prevent the presence of guns in many New York schools.

In the meantime, we teach our children that being gay is like being Buddhist or black, that is, being American with a difference. The child is split: child or adult? Man or woman? Children with Kalashnikovs have been killing for a song in Mozambique, Sierra Leone and Cambodia. The child is split: killer or killed?

Ultimately the attacks on the family translate into a declining birth rate, that emerges as one of the main challenges industrial societies will have to face: how can economic growth and pension levels be sustained in the context of aging populations and fewer young people than before to swell the work force?

DISUNITED NATIONS

The United Nations was created after World War II to spare mankind the horrors of renewed conflicts. Is the broader family of nations faring any better than the nuclear family? The Charter of the United Nations starts with the words, "We, the people of the Earth..." but the intermediaries soon took over. The bureaucrats tried their best, they did what they could but the United Nations Organization, as it celebrates its 50th birthday, is under assault: governments cannot agree on reforms and this paralyzes the institution. The truth of the matter is that UN employees are probably neither better nor worse than their colleagues in the respective national administrations. Some countries have a proud tradition of public service and some do not. Nevertheless, on average, the attacks on the UN become self-fulfilling prophecy as the sabotage of multilateral institutions effectively lead to their growing paralysis. The UN is being denied the means to act and then blamed for not achieving results.

---

[6] The Population Council Families, *Focus*, New York (1995).

[7] *Le Nouvel Observateur*, (15 June 1995).

Some western governments dismantled the multilateral system of security that their fathers had put into place after World War II to avoid the resurgence of global conflict. This is because the large business interests of the West, no longer scared by the Soviet Union and the erstwhile communist camp, do not see the need for development aid any longer. The tobacco industry resents the campaign of the WHO to stop it promoting smoking in the poorer countries. The pharmaceutical, food and tobacco industries resent most types of regulation protecting consumers from some of their unhealthy products.

The international - and rather weak - regulatory framework of the UN must today be put aside as it could become the last hindrance to the economic monopoly of the masters of world business who have already marginalized the State. Typically, the United Nations Conference on Development and Trade, which used to present alternative economic analysis, risks being dissolved unless it reincarnates and sings the glory of the private sector. Its Center for Trans-national Corporations has been neutralized, and leading the charge against it are those Western countries most controlled by business interests.

Public opinion in the West forgets that the UN on the whole did far more good than harm. Decolonization, assistance to refugees, peacekeeping, human rights, environment protection, nuclear non-proliferation and fighting poverty are goals that were meant to protect the entire human race. They were worth pursuing around the world. In fact, the US Senate does not focus on addressing such matters and the European Union meekly follows, despite demagogic protests to the contrary. They want to be seen as doing something but do not want or feel able to act.

The United Nations' advocacy for more humane world development, socially acceptable and ecologically sustainable, is worthy of support and so are its efforts to reduce poverty. But the economic elite tolerates the UN's role in development only as long as it is nothing more than a slogan. Even impressive international conferences with Heads of State in attendance, such as the Rio Earth Summit, the Cairo Population Summit and the Copenhagen Social Summit, are carefully kept in the virtual reality of political talk. Countries take hardly any meaningful action as a result of these conferences and diplomats are asked not to notice. The U.N. became the surreal guardian of this irrelevance, wherein any initiative will die in an explosion of speeches, studies and action plans to ensure it never reaches the real world.

In the meantime, growing poverty in developing countries breeds more and more corruption. Taxpayers in developed countries are wary of supporting aid programs, if the money is unlikely to reach the intended beneficiaries and ends up instead in private pockets. The vicious circle goes on and the political will to break it is missing. The World Bank pretends to know better but bankers are not philanthropists, and as debt piles up, the divide between 'haves' and 'have-nots' is widening in the international community, just as it is within individual countries. About 1.5 billion people live under the threshold of absolute poverty. The conditions of life for twice that number are shockingly bad. With 10% of the world population, the 47 poorest countries have 0.1% of the world's income. The inequality gap between the richest and poorest, who make up 20% of the world's population, has doubled, from 30 fold to 60 fold.

The ruling ideology counts on the resourcefulness of entrepreneurs to save the world, but entrepreneurs are supposed to make money, not to keep society together. The private sector can play a positive role but alone, it will not do the trick: 75% of direct foreign investment in the developing world goes to less than a dozen countries and a small fraction of the $800 billion devoted yearly to military expenditure would go a long way to eradicate world hunger.

The Cold War, which at one time maintained a status quo from the menace of thermonuclear doomsday, is replaced now by a nervous hot peace. The challenges put on the states and the supranational institutions they generated (United Nations, European Union, NATO, ASEAN, World Bank and IMF) take many disruptive forms. Examples of volatile and murderous conflicts are many: the open war against the drug gangs in Rio, the blowing up of the Federal building in Oklahoma City, the conflict with the Tuareg in the Sahara, civil strife in Peru and Angola, the Kurdish and Chechen insurrections or the containment of Saddam Hussein. Geopolitical analysts have plenty of scenarios on how things could go badly wrong. We can mention: economic implosion in Latin America; instability in parts of Russia where the Kremlin could lose control over some of its 50,000 nuclear warheads; collapse of the central communist power in China and the emergence of provincial warlords; the overthrow of the House of Saud and Muslim radicals in control of oil supplies.

At the same time, the existing military capacity to face potential challenges is put into question. In just the same way that imperial Spain or Britain insisted on having larger armed forces than their contemporaries in order to maintain their status of pre-eminence, the United States, as the last remaining superpower is facing a severe dilemma. Previous 'Number One' countries found that the critical relationship between power politics and financial strength is hard to maintain when the over-stretched military capacities of the superpower place too heavy a burden on the diminishing wealth of the nation. Spending billions on space-based anti-ballistic systems is a pointed illustration of colossal waste through unnecessary military spending. Despite all the Rambo-like glory, the American forces who served in the 1991 Gulf War, were much like mercenaries, sending all the bills to the Saudi paymaster. They were the best soldiers money could buy, but they did not come cheap. Who else will pay? The capacity of the US to patrol a world fraught with uncertainties is not without limitations.

Disunited nations are ill equipped to face modern security threats, which, again, bypass the cash-starved nation state. The downsizing of national armed forces comes at a time when the forms of national insecurity multiply. To make matters worse, in the first half of the 1990s, it was estimated that 22 wars out of the 51 which were at that time were raging around the world, were partly environmentally induced. Scholars agree that ecological degradation and the shrinking of natural resources, both renewable and non-renewable, combined with uneven distribution of regional reserves are likely to trigger further social tensions, political strife or armed conflicts.

THE ECO WRECKAGE

We all belong to planet earth and Man belongs to concentric circles of systems that surround him. These circles maintain the conditions of our material and psychological wellbeing. When we break them we damage ourselves. We have shaken the stability of our families and a deepening income divide now splits our nations. The international community is made fragile by the weakness of its institutions. Beyond the family, the society, and the nation, man is sustained by the surrounding eco systems. In the film *The Matrix*, the nasty android Agent tells Nemo that he studied the behavior of the human race, which prospers and multiplies by destroying its own environment. The only other living organism that does this is a virus. He was not a pleasant character but was he wrong?

Our planet has often been perceived as a living organic entity. Our ancestors worshipped her, calling it our mother, Coatlicue in Aztec Mexico, Demeter in Rome, Gaia in Greece, Uma or Bhoomi Devi in India and many other names. The cycle of nature and the rhythms of the eco systems expressed the intelligence of this being. In our exploitation of nature we have gone too far, unable to understand the interdependence of the eco-cycles on which our race depends for its survival. We have broken the pattern of their consistency and have started to pay dearly for it.

We have yet to ward off the storm of the no-return ecological breakdown with incalculable consequences: gaping ozone holes, polluted air and water, slashed forests, chemical pollution and contamination of the food chain linked to the abominable way in which we mass produce meat. International experts are still guessing at the true impact of climate change.

They have found widespread evidence ranging from the thawing of the permafrost, longer growing seasons in certain latitudes, decline in plant and animal species, earlier flowering of trees and in the egg-laying of birds. In the twentyth century the planet heated up by about 0.6 degrees C. In the first century of the third millennium, the prediction is that it will hear up by up to 5.8 degrees C, the fastest rate of change for 10,000 years. This trend is attributable largely to human activities and the releasing of greenhouse gases into the atmosphere. We seem to have reached the stage where man is a causal factor of climate change and related natural catastrophes. The most silent catastrophe of all is the prolonged drought that affects hundreds of millions of lives and as usual the poor suffer the most. The press reports that increase of floods, hurricanes and drought over the last thirty years has cost from 10 to 30 billion dollars a year. For the 1990s the cost shot up to 43 billion dollars a year.

Yet the cost of non-action will have wider implications for everyone as scientists foresee the possibility of large scale and irreversible impacts. Experts predict enlarging deserts and declines in agricultural production in Africa and the Middle East, while in Southern Europe more droughts could reduce agricultural productivity. Europe will suffer widespread flooding and a decline in many traditional holiday resorts because of heat waves and unreliable snow conditions. Alpine slopes will be destabilized and landslides will threaten human habitats. Floods and droughts will affect Latin America and water shortages will be commonplace in Australia, New Zealand and in the southern states of the USA. Warming water temperatures destroy coral reefs. Much of Asia will suffer a decline in agricultural productivity. The disintegration of the ice sheets could raise global sea levels by up to 60 centimetres in the new century or up to 6 meters over the next 1000 years. Predictions include storm surges and coastal erosion on the eastern seaboard of the US. An increase in the intensity of tropical cyclones could displace tens of millions of people in low-lying coastal areas in Bangladesh, Indonesia and Thailand. The small island states may simply be washed away. These countries cannot protect themselves from the sea through extensive damming infrastructures, as the Dutch will undoubtedly do.

The inability of states to agree on reducing the use of fossil fuels, especially in energy hungry countries such as the US, is amazing. It reflects the fact that the cost of taking action to curb global warming exceeds the electoral gains for politicians. When the heart does not lead, the brain is lost.

The developing countries least responsible for global warming will have to pay the highest price. People will have to move on an unprecedented scale. The situation will be critical in countries affected by drought and desertification. Environmentally induced migrations can then contribute to crazy rates of urbanization in already crowded urban areas. For instance, the population of the cities of the West African coastline will triple over the next decade and are ill prepared to absorb millions of migrants from the Sahara region. The consequent demands in terms of infrastructures, waste disposal and drinking water will far exceed the supply: urban collapse is at hand. In the meantime transcontinental immigration will assault the borders of richer countries in the north such as the European Union and the USA. It can be feared that further youth unemployment in the Arab countries will strengthen the appeal of religious fundamentalists. The CIA already recognizes the implications of these trends on public security issues. Massive immigration may send xenophobic right-wing parties soaring in municipal elections to compound further social tensions and conflicts.

The World Health Organisation says that one billion people have no access to clean water and that 3.4 million people die every year from diseases that could be easily remedied by better supply and sanitation. Water consumption increased six-fold between 1990 and 1995, more than twice the rate of population growth. Two out of three people in the world will face water shortages by 2025. New Delhi, in India, is predicted to run out of groundwater by 2015. Lake Chad in Africa has shrunk 95% in the past 38 years while providing for 20 million people in 6 separate countries. Will the sacred egoism of the new American right encourage the needed investment in water supply and sanitation? Can we expect the necessary effort to reduce greenhouse gas emissions by 5 percent by 2012?

Pervasive factors of human insecurity such as poverty, social disintegration and environmental degradation end up in a humanitarian crisis of forced migratory movements that are far more expensive for society than the cost of preventive action. If we could bring some compassion to the solutions we propose to the contemporary global challenges we would be so much more efficient at managing them.

To be sure, we see progress. The emergence of 'green' industry such as appropriate technology, clean-up services and waste management is growing strong and the Organization for Economic Co-operation and Development estimates it was worth about $300 billion annually by the end of the 1990s. Big retailers and branded-goods companies are now defending human rights issues: Ikea, the Swedish furniture store will not sell carpets unless they are certified as having been made without the involvement of child labor. Levi-Strauss, the jeans manufacturer, introduced terms of engagement for sub-contracting partners, which exclude suppliers who force employees to work unacceptable hours. America's Department of Labor investigated 19 countries where 46 million children work making goods for American firms, often under appalling conditions.

But Third World countries are not a bit impressed by our moralistic leanings. They attribute the new interest in ecology and labor rights to First World protectionism. They do not credit the West with much credibility in matters of morality. They see in our countries pornography on the Net and in hotel bedrooms, sexual permissiveness evolving into sado-masochist pathology, broken families, and economic predators on the rampage. They do not accept Western civilization as a credible moral mentor and they reply to our virtuous exhortations: "Money may not bring happiness but let us discover this for ourselves. We will not remain virtuous chiefly for the purpose of maintaining your wealth at our cost." Can we blame them? They face survival issues.

6. THE STRESS ON THE LIVER

Must we not expect a general nervous breakdown? ... For we have been trained too long to strive and not to enjoy.

— Lord Keynes

This chapter is basically about our will to exert, which is activated by the cosmic energy of the sun channel, the *Pingala nadi*, as will be explained in Part Four. It fuels our drive for action and for accumulating wealth, which in turn, is enhanced by capitalism and technology. But gathering too much speed can endanger our course and spoil the journey. People run, run and run ever faster in the rat race but cover less and less ground. They are obliged to work more than ever before but end up with less. In the 1990s, rich people became very rich but most of the rest were left behind and the result, at the end of the year 2000, was a split society. If the wealth is not more evenly distributed, the rise of hopeless poverty encourages criminality, or worse still, the nurturing of terrorism in countries where there are no economic alternatives. How did we get so out of control; how did our leaders get it so wrong; what dictates the pace of our lives and of our institutions?

The speed of modern life has accelerated to the point where the engine that drives it is overheated and without lubricant. We may refer here to ancient Ayurvedic medicine: in which the liver, linked to heat in the body, is the organ that caters to the active and mental side of our being. If the brain is the organ for knowledge, and the heart the organ for desire, then the liver can be said to be the organ that supplies energy for action. Modern man has a need to balance these energies and to harmonize the working of the various organs.

As we will see in Part Four, stress expresses the gap between pressures from over-activity and the inadequate coping capacity of our psychosomatic system. We will show later how a spontaneous form of yoga can regenerate our energy through the action of the parasympathetic nervous system. But why do we need to do so?

There are not many countries in the world that I have not visited. I have erected my tent on a solitary ridge facing the Annapurna Mountain. I've watched the burial of a Tibetan abbot in the dusty loneliness of a remote Himalayan valley and I drank the holy water flowing from the spring of the Muktinath sanctuary. I have gone to faraway places: I deciphered the fight between gods and titans (*asuras*) on the walls of Angkor Vat, visited the tomb of Tamerlane in Samarkand and sat with elders in the Fouta Djallon mountain of Guinea. I drank mare's milk in the yurts of Mongolian nomads and I have attended numerous conferences from Los Angeles to Saint Petersburg. I cannot claim to know the world but I have seen much of it. I would hope too that this traveling helped me to lose most of my native arrogance. To me it is clear: every race on this planet has something beautiful to offer. Europeans should be able to see that what indigenous peoples have to offer is mostly what the modern polis is missing: dignity, respect, poise, wisdom, patience, exuberance, spontaneity, rhythms, music and, yes, feelings. We need freedom from the slavery of the clock.

In Auckland Airport I stopped in a shop to ask about a lamp, which bore the exact design of the three and a half coils that is the Hindu symbol for the Kundalini, the mysterious hidden power. The shopkeeper told me this is the *"Koru,"* the name given by the Maoris of New Zealand to the newborn fern frond which, when unfurled, symbolizes the beginning of new life, growth, peace and tranquility. Maybe one day we will finally be developed enough to learn something from such people.

THE DILEMMA OF THE WEST

The dogmas of the quiet past are inadequate to the stormy present. The occasion is piled high with difficulty and we must rise with the occasion. As our case is new, so we must think anew and act anew. We must disenthrall ourselves, and then we shall save our country.

— Abraham Lincoln

Since Marco Polo, Vasco de Gama, and the other Mediterranean navigators sailed to discover the New World in the fifteenth century, Western civilization has identified itself with the dynamics of change. Change spans the wheel of history, ever faster, bowling over in its path indigenous lifestyles, cultures and traditions. The Portuguese sailor, the Florentine condottiere, the railway baron or the global financial speculator, all moved by the will to conquer, have led this process. The world finally caught up and globalism no longer needs to serve the expansion of Western economic power only. But the question remains: does the change brought about by the shifting patterns of modernity take us where we want to go?

Paradoxically, the Third Age of material plenty may well already be on its way out but people in Europe and North America will be those most exposed to the social downside of the coming global liberalization. The Western middle classes, said to be the backbone of democracy, and living, as it were, on the ground floor, stand to lose the most from schemes devised by the trading predators in the remote aloofness of their 40th floor boardrooms. Strikers on the streets of Europe are getting the message faster than American workers. The production, trading and investment mega-networks can easily bypass the national trade unions and the unit cost of labor that in the West pays for a certain lifestyle; it includes social security, health insurance and some measure of environmental protection. Not so in developing countries where social security and environmental protection lag far behind. The capitalist is delocalizing production to Mexico or Vietnam and wage earners in the West are at risk from the combined effect of automation and the opening of the global labor market.

In the mid 1990s, the First World still had a dominant position with more than 90% of the 37,000 transnational corporations and their 200,000 or so foreign affiliates coming from the North (including Japan). But projections show a steady shift in favor of Asia for Gross Domestic Product in purchase parity terms, stock market capitalization and, more slowly, world trade. The public indebtedness of the rich countries is reaching dizzying heights, never seen before in peacetime: some US$17 trillion.

The Godfathers of the ultra-liberal revolution assume that they are the *Tyrannosaurus Rex* in Jurassic Park, and that the law of the jungle will forever go their way. Ironically, the liberal gospel of deregulation and privatization, which has been pushed down the throat of developing countries by the World Bank, will not, in the long term, benefit its Western advocates. It will empower emerging markets, a positive trend that illustrates how the dialectic of change finds its own momentum. Private investors, gradually turning their backs on the West, seek higher income in the emerging markets, which need about $200 billion a year for infrastructure development. In this sense, the dynamics of the market are working and will bring about a healthy transfer of wealth. The trend cannot be stopped and it will gradually destroy the economic podium of the Western predators. But what is the use, for society as a whole, of replacing one breed of predator with another one? Competition is as necessary as change itself, but it need not be brutish and blind, mindlessly trampling the lives of hundred of millions of people and devastating cultural identities and social achievements.

The force that drives history is playfully using the spiral movement of dialectics, the yin-yang oscillation and when there is no balance, every extreme ends up in its own contrary. At the beginning of the 20th century, Europe dominated the world; two European civil wars later, an end had been put to this hegemony. Now the Western economic pre-eminence and related social wellbeing is faltering. It is not threatened by external foes but by the smartest and most powerful Western economic operators; the human ego undoes its own doings.

Greed is an old sin, well known by the Middle Age scholastic fathers. "*Cupiditas radix omnium malorum est*": "Greed is the source of all evils." It breeds the uglier side of competition: ego, infighting and jealousy, and under its impetus globalization is not turning the world into the happy global village that was supposed to express our aspirations for communal togetherness. Instead it brings about Jurassic Park on the open prairie. Might makes right.

People in the Western countries are at a crossroads. They are betrayed and fooled by their economic elite, lullabied by their media, sick and tired of their politicians and weary of their bureaucrats. The system is betraying the people. Of course the manipulation of language and entertainment sketched in the next chapter is meant to hide this.

RUNNING FASTER TO STAND STILL ... OR LOSE GROUND

The economics that disregard moral and emotional considerations are like waxworks that, being life-like, still lack the life of the living flesh. At every crucial moment, these newfangled economic laws have broken down in practice. And nations or individuals who accept them as guiding maxims must perish.

— Mahatma Gandhi, The words of Gandhi selected by Lord Richard Attenborough

I need to take this point closer to our daily surroundings, again taking the 1990s as a test case. Like it or not, the ruthless competitive imperatives of that decade meant that considerations of personal quality of life were increasingly at odds with the objective of corporate productivity. The corporate tactics of cost-cutting and productivity enhancement rely on a combination of new technology tools such as robotics and computer automated design in manufacturing. The same is true in service industries, where increasingly powerful computing devices expand opportunities for managerial efficiency improvements. Super-fast global telecommunication networks and real-time transaction tracking systems cut out the intermediaries, and back-office consolidation serves as a quick fix for many transaction-intensive organizations, such as banks and insurance companies.

All these recipes for ferocious productivity enhancement have one thing in common: the pruning of excess workers. Life becomes increasingly tough for the hard-pressed survivors. While 615,000 workers were laid off in America in 1993 there have been dramatic increases in time spent on the job on the meaner and leaner assembly lines. Meanwhile, hefty pay increases, bonuses and stock options for the bosses were the order of the day. Blue and white collar workers, told to roll up their sleeves and give more at the work place, have not offered much resistance in the light of the ever present fears of job insecurity. Never mind a study by the Wharton Business School, which found that people who place high value on good family life and shorter hours at work are more creative and end up earning more money than those actually willing to sacrifice home life for a career.

Pressure, stress and psychosomatic disease, as evidenced by statistics, take their toll on the family life of workers who are relentlessly draining the energy of their liver, corresponding to their right-side, their sun channel. An over-stretched work force appears to deliver more in the short term and corporations are truly getting more out of their squeezed employees. This translates into increased efficiency and profit but workers do not get the rewards of their increased productivity. Efficiency gains merely get emptied into corporate coffers from where CEOs and other directors help themselves. The politicians pledge to put people first and their resolve to declare war on unemployment seems at odds with these mighty trends that accelerate corporate profitability.

The need to spread the benefits of economic efficiency more widely and equitably in society was one of the major challenges of the 1990s. Income inequalities in America, Britain and Switzerland, the true believers in deregulated market economy, are greater than at anytime in the past 50 years. About 14 million Britons, a quarter of the total population, now live below the threshold of poverty. During the last decade, income disparity in the UK grew twice as fast as in other comparable industrialized countries, according to a study of the Rowntree Foundation.[8] Sixty-four percent of British workers have no professional qualifications compared to only 26% in Germany. Societies with wide income inequalities have more instances of ill health, social stress and crime. Monetarist policies and deregulation seem to be missing something. Let's not forget too, the growing numbers of people in the 'rich' countries undergoing precarious working conditions, without contracts, insurance or pensions. Many worry about the longer-term consequences of such trends for democracy; for ultimately, what is the economic rationale for increased production efficiency if an increasing proportion of consumers lose their purchasing power? Admittedly, the question will be more acute in Europe andNorth America, threatened as they are by the Asian or Latin offspring of the raw capitalism the West itself has promoted.

[8] Inquiry into Income and Wealth, (1994).

The first world study on employment of the International Labor organization, released in February 1995, revealed that one-third of the world's active population is jobless: 870 million people, without counting under-employed workers from the threatened lower middle classes in Western countries who are sliding into poverty.

This scenario, at that time, did not cast any clouds in the blue skies of the wealthy. The number of rich people continues to increase: Chase Manhattan estimates that rich people in Europe and the Middle East own $1.5 trillion in cash or liquid assets. The growing entrepreneurial class of the emerging economies adds another $1 trillion. Salaries in the banking district of the City of London have shot up by between 50 to 100% since 1993. A CEO of British Gas gave himself a 75% pay increase, while at the same time announcing a lay-off plan for workers. Chief Executive Officers enjoyed soaring pay rises, bonuses and stock options plus benefits in kind such as free golf membership and other perks. The head of an American international chemical firm earned more than a hundred times the $200,000 salary of the then President of the USA, Bill Clinton. It is estimated that shares authorized for management equity-plans are accounting for almost $2.5 billion in America's 200 biggest firms. These are democracy's faithful believers and, as they control the media, they make believe that this sort of democracy is good for the rest of us.

The crisis of the welfare state, from the point of view of job security, insurance pension schemes and assistance safety nets, expresses the increasing pressure and friction between business and society. Because the brain of society is numbed, and its heart frozen, the engine of economics that represents the liver of our collectivity, is in overdrive and overheating. "The business of business is business," Milton Friedman told us in the 1970s, but business does not take place in a vacuum. Ultra liberal capitalism embodies a growing divorce between society's needs and corporate needs; it further contributes to the split between welfare and wealth, a loss of holistic awareness and of shared emotional values.

THE DARK SIDE OF THE FORCE

L'humanisme est périmé! Vous êtes un vieux sentimental ridicule.

Humanism is outdated! You are an old sentimental fool.

 — Ionesco, Rhinoceros

The forces that control the lives of the working citizens of our democracies are not, of course, under their control. Institutions which once policed these forces are now bewildered and incapable of doing so. The digital revolution has linked companies around the world at breathtaking speed. Satellite links can transmit the equivalent of the London telephone directory in a matter of seconds. The devoted believers in cyber-theology burble rapturously about the empowering effect of information technology, hardly noticing that people are left behind. As lenders go digital, for instance, electronic banking will lay off 500,000 bank employees over a five-year period in Europe alone. There are now 350,000 inexpensively available computer engineers in China, and before being fired themselves, Western engineers will design programs as to how best to integrate them in their firm's networks.

Free trade plus microprocessors have launched global capitalism into the ultimate stage of contradiction, that Marx and Engels could not have possibly imagined in their most baroque dreams. Supercomputers and ever more complex mathematical instruments are turning capital markets into a game of highly volatile trillion dollar roulette that will interfere with governments' ability to tax, spend and borrow. Essential aspects of any country's policies are no longer under the control of its elected leaders.

The situation is startling for governments of the First World who had assumed that the relationship with business interests was under control. The alliance between finance and lawyers bypassed national regulations: the Eurodollar market, for instance, grew from $80 billion to $4000 billion between 1973 and 1987. When the Group of Seven major economic nations of the world, the IMF and the World Bank mounted an unprecedented effort to save the Mexican peso, they mobilized the considerable amount of $50 billion. Compare this to the funds controlled by the three big American pension funds, Fidelity Investments, Vanguard Group and Capital Research and Management: $500 billion. Size matters.

The traders and fund managers already 'censor' the decisions of politicians and bureaucrats and by moving around their huge portfolios, they pass judgment on the value of the Mexican peso and of the related rescue package, the US trade deficit with Japan, the survival of the Swedish welfare state or the extent of Canadian social spending. This form of 'voting', i.e., money managers 'voting' by moving money around, influences policies far more thoroughly than the citizen's electoral ballot. And it influences people's daily lives directly as it dictates the value of our money or whether one's employment contract will be renewed. Elected authorities of democratic countries seem less accountable to the voters than to the traders in the international stock markets, now a veritable casino of speculators.

The power of democratically elected governments is therefore severely eroded. An example: when the central bankers of the Group of Seven led a $4 billion coordinated intervention to back the US dollar in June 1994, foreign exchange markets, which routinely trade $1 trillion a day, hardly took any notice. Typically enough, the fate of the 'war on unemployment' declared by President Chirac and Prime Minister Juppe, did not depend on the French prefects, as they were told, or the success of ministerial initiatives, but on the judgment passed by the financial markets. The Popular Party in Spain came to power strongly boosted by the support of the money markets. For those who win the traders' favors, the rewards are substantial but for democracy and social justice the future prospects are less certain.

Monetary sovereignty surely consists in being able to achieve specific results by altering monetary policy. A country may have monetary sovereignty over its interest rates, but in the system of free capital movements, it is the foreign exchange markets that ultimately have sovereignty over its exchange rates and hence over the comparative value of currencies and international terms of trade. Not surprisingly, the G7 emperors have no clothes as they watch their group's failure to tackle the problems of the world economy. The Basel-based Bank for International Settlements, the bank for central banks, soberly observed in its 1995 annual report that "the power exercised by financial markets can only continue to increase." Thus, governments are invited to bow down and undertake "what adjustments are inevitable and to initiate them in a pre-emptive manner." Money thus saved, through fiscal adjustments and austerity budgets, meaning cuts in social services and job losses, can then be thrown into financial speculation. The 1994 turbulence in world bond markets is estimated to have amounted to a capital loss of some $1.5 trillion. The new volatility and extreme price swings in the foreign exchange markets will continue to penalize economically productive operators and reward parasitic financial speculators on a scale never known before.

This survey of trends in the 1990s makes more sense once one knows what happened later. The plunge of the stock market in 2001 and 2002 penalized cruelly small investors and pensioners who invested in the 1990s.

Nothing but a fervent invocation of Adam Smith's invisible hand suggests that investors' driving force is chiefly concerned with society's greatest good or a wider public interest. The pace of life on Spaceship Earth is ever increasing but where is it heading? Our livers and brains are racing; most of us who work, work more for less; but what is the outcome? Indeed, nowhere is the story of the hot liver told more powerfully than in our pursuit of hot money. History is playful: the combination of Milton Friedman, Ronald Reagan and the now almost forgotten Margaret Thatcher, has ushered the market place into a strange new world.

At the end of 1994, some $20 trillion worth of swaps, options and other derivative products were whirling and roaring round on the five continents' markets. They flow in and out of any particular national economy in a matter of seconds, playing havoc with jolted currencies, distributing wealth or ruin, delocalizing factories without care for the workers. This is more than three times the size of the US economy and the movement of this money is impossible to control. Hybrid financial products are bewildering the institutions, which once policed the marketplace, as are complex instruments such as futures, derivatives, junk bonds, mortgage backed securities, currency swaps and multi-billion dollar hedge funds. The potential shakiness of the global market is enormous.

THE DISCRETE CHARMS OF THE WORLD BOURGEOISIE

In the mouth of Society are many diseased teeth, decayed to the bone of the jaws. But society makes no efforts to have them extracted and be rid of the affliction. It contents itself with gold fillings. Many are the dentists who treat the decayed teeth of Society with glittering gold.

— Kahlil Gibran, Thoughts and Meditations

Plato, when he was writing the laws, was of the opinion that the amount of property should be left unrestricted up to a given point; beyond that point, he was in favor of restriction, proposing ... that no citizen should be allowed to accumulate to an extent which would make his property more than five times as large as the smallest property owned by any other citizen.

— Aristotle, The Politics

Are we comfortable with so much wealth in the hands of so few? Is it not an expression of the loss of our social balance? Never in recent times have wealth differentials and income gaps been wider than now, between countries and within countries. The gap between rich and poor in some rich countries goes up to five hundred times. In the underground passage of Geneva Airport an advertising sign for a private banker makes sure I understand where I've landed. It says: "Money talks: wealth whispers." I take the train for Bern. The loud speaker announces: "We are very sorry. The train is two minutes late." I am just back from India where the Mahalakshmi Express was delayed by 24 hours, without apology; I will survive. I relax in a comfortable armchair as the train speedily purrs through a spotless countryside, which looks like one big manicured garden with each tree standing at its appointed place. In the newspaper, an irate citizen is interviewed about a recent mudslide in Brig in the canton of Valais. He tells us that such things should not happen in a country where people pay their taxes. Arriving in Bern, a pretty, ancient Germanic city with a profusion of geraniums in the front of every window, I notice that despite the pouring rain, a vehicle of the municipality sprays water on the road to clean it. Having just arrived from the noisy disorder of Bombay, I feel I have landed in a world of odd perfection. Who can its inhabitants be?

A sage from the East, Engy Oman, once told me a strange tale. All the ancient races from earlier ages, the *nagas* (serpent people), the *gandharvas* (celestial minstrels), *rakshasas* (demons), *asuras* (titans), the elves and the dwarfs of the Niebelungen are now all merged within the human race. In Tolkien's *Lord of the Rings* the dwarfs have an ambivalent nature. They can become good or bad depending in which way they are pushed. But they love cleanliness, alchemy, a good war, living underground and, above all, they love gold. When the late George Brown, Chancellor of the Exchequer in the Labor government of Harold Wilson, coined the phrase "The Gnomes of Zurich," he did not realize perhaps that he was rediscovering the modern location in history of that most industrious and ancient race.

Have a look: the Swiss are maniacally clean and tidy; I saw once a neighbor cutting his lawn with manicure scissors. They developed today's version of alchemy (and LSD) through the big Basel chemical and pharmaceutical corporations. They have a bellicose past and were hired for a price by the armies of the kings and princes of Europe; they still worship their army and maintain underground military airports, fortresses and absurd compulsory anti-atomic concrete bunkers in the basement of every house. Above all, they successfully love gold and sit on a handsome pile of it.

Cozy private banking in Switzerland is doing fine, thank you very much: one private bank in Zurich managed SFr 43.6 billion of private assets at the end of 1994. At the end of the 1990s one in Geneva controlled SFr 100 billion, up from SFr 40 billion just five years earlier. This is many more times the GNP of most developing countries. It is calculated that Swiss banks together have a dominant 40% market share in the select business of international private banking. Goldman Sachs, the US investment bank that came to Zurich in 1993, discovered that people who have a fortune of at least $9 million visit Switzerland from one to four times a year. This financial hub, the brain of the octopus, as Che Guevara used to call it, is exemplary in its smoothness. But is all this in the best interests of the country as a whole? The Swiss writer and sociology professor, Jean Ziegler, emphatically says no. While still a deputy in the Swiss parliament, he was one of the first to point out that the role of the banking system is distorting the policies, economic life and the image of the country.

Switzerland, in the meantime, continues to allow the laundering of the dirty money of the Russian, Albanian, Chinese and Italian Mafias, of the Colombian drug cartels, and of the dictators of the Third World. It has the highest per capita income in the world if we exclude tiny oil producing emirates. It also has among the highest rate of teenage suicides, drug addiction and AIDs. We know, don't we, that owning is not enough. But how fast we forget.

MASTERS OF THE UNIVERSE: THE NEW BREED

Most of the trouble in the world is caused by people wanting to be important.

– T.S. Eliot

The awareness of billions of people becomes the coveted slices of market share for the owners of television or satellite networks. Technological breakthroughs have offered the globe to those who first knew how to go global: people such as Ted Turner, at the time with CNN, Rupert Murdoch of News Corporation Limited or geo-investor Georges Soros, the man who launched the Quantum Funds. The many who exert real power and the army of those who serve them, feel best left alone to exert it freely. The corporation must inherit the powers taken away from the State, something that clearly should not be left to supra-national institutions. Industry captains want all power for the 'free market' for they dominate it. They claim that what is good for them is good for society as a whole and they find people to say it their way.

"The New Deal is dead. We should remove the corpse before the stench becomes unbearable." A member of the Progress and Freedom Foundation professed this funeral eulogy of the Welfare State. The Foundation is one of the new mercenary think tanks that influences policy in the United States Congress under its Republican majority leadership. Its ideology is a detonating blend of puritan fundamentalism, WASP racism and anti-intellectual swearing, dressed in modern garb by technological millenarism. Cyber-space and the 'e-conomy' have become the new frontier for the third millennium, the place of Utopia where mankind will discover happiness. The United States has been the trendsetter for the post-war world and it is worth looking where such trends seem to lead us.

The Republican Congress increasingly seeks the opinion of very reactionary ideologues. The American Enterprise Institute leads the charge against governmental regulations. The Cato Institute advocates withdrawal of the USA from multilateral organizations. The Hoover Institute and the Hudson Foundation seek the dismantling of the tax system. All these influential right-wing think tanks are flooded with big business money from real estate, banking, tobacco, chemical, pharmaceutical and high-tech industries. Congress had previously made the mistake of backing budget cuts in the army, promoting environmental protection and health system reform, all measures considered heretical by these groups.

Powers must be transferred to the deregulated big operators of the market place, who generously pay for this lofty analysis. The Federal State is left to play a security function against those who do not understand the great American Way. Hence budget increases for the police and the prisons are deemed legitimate. Global competition has been erected as a moral imperative for the good people to absorb all kinds of social hardship. This is the return of the predators - Jurassic Park without a fence.

Those who do not understand that Jurassic Park is good for them are largely the losers, the under performers, the poor. We must remember here the radical fundamentalism of the puritan Anglo-Saxon immigrants who founded the USA. They were God's own chosen. Red Indians had no soul and hence could be mercilessly exploited or killed. For all these devoted Bible readers it was all right to build a free country on the basis of genocide: elitism and exploitation go well together. Freedom and democracy are for the elect only. The Ku Klux Klan is not an American aberration but the Southern side of the same equation. In typical Calvinist fashion, the rich are blessed because God loves them while the poor are so because they are bad people and deserve to be. This form of predestination is the kind of theology that business best understands. In this sense, not much support can be expected from the (not so) new right for Federal social programs that help the God forsaken under privileged. Finally, like the Nazis before them, the ultra-right despises 'decadent' culture and intellectuals.

Ultra-liberalism, dressed in populist slogans for public consumption, loves a good ideology. It has been re-theorized by economist icons and the ever-mercenary experts from the techno-structure, who will tell us in twenty years what Robert McNamara, tells us today about Vietnam: "We were terribly wrong." Never mind, they don't know it yet and meanwhile they are having fun! Number crunching and system analysis did not work that well then nor will today's financial mathematical models. But as with Vietnam, those who will pay are not those who played.

Emperor Wilhelm II, von Hohenzollern, who dragged Germany into the First World War, represented the caricatured excesses of military power, sitting like Humpty Dumpy on the wall with a big moustache, all his horses, soldiers and cannons. Might we imagine a caricature of today's power holders, the business overlords, CEOs who award themselves fat seven-digit bonuses while at the same time firing workers by the thousand? What sort of democracy is this?

In the period under review, the 1990s, the $150 billion Savings and Loan bankruptcies and the real estate crisis in the USA, the collapse of the Maxwell holdings and the Barings bank in the UK, the crash of the Credit Lyonnais in France and the Schneider real estate scandal in Germany, have given us a foretaste of what this caricature could be. These are predatory behaviors and jungle practices at the edge of criminality. The taxpayer must pay for the damage. Clearly the thousand or so people who control the mega-networks in finance, information and production are representing the greatest concentration of uncontrolled wealth and power ever in the history of mankind. Boardroom alliances have replaced dynasties while fiberglass and satellites control awareness; hostile takeovers and speculative moves replace the blitzkrieg. But the business overlords have the same desire for power as the Machiavellian Prince who saw the world as a place for him to conquer. Today it is the Barons of the market place who say: *"l'Etat c'est moi."* As it happens, Louis XIV died bankrupt.

Modern democracy was created to control the powers of absolute monarchs and it created a system of checks and balances so that democratic institutions would not be corrupted by a powerful few, but power is a clever fox and always jumps out of the boundaries within which legislators would wish to keep it. This is because the drive for power is the ultimate temptation of the doers, those who strive on the channel of the sun that inspires action. There is a dark side to this force when it is not balanced by an equal influx of energy from the left-side lunar channel that relates to emotions, love and desires.

Over-activity of a cell in the body can lead to cancer. If we consider corporations as cells of the collective economic tissue of our societies, we should try to identify which type of management prevents 'cancerous trends' in corporate activities. Obviously the answer is to be found in a good balance of intellectual (IQ) and emotional (EQ) coefficients. But a good balance is hard to find. Man is losing the boundaries of time, space, and traditions through globalization and the information revolution.

Indeed the pursuit of quick money best tells the story of our hot liver. We might rejoice in the creation of wealth generated by the Wall Street bull market of the 1990s. But we must regret that the fruits of this prosperity have not been spread more widely and equitably. The lack of concern for the worker, the consumer or the kind of ecological scarcity we shall leave to our children reflects the chilling egoism of the ruling thought of one or two generations engrossed in the one-dimensional pursuit of profit.

The fact that the frozen heart of our civilization fails to influence economic behaviors in favor of genuine demand stimulation could, in the end, undermine the very foundation of prosperity. Inversely, problems with the organ of the right side, the liver, fuel in a dialectic manner the hurdles on the left side, that of the heart, briefly reviewed in the preceding chapter. People are too stressed to love.

A 'hot liver' leads to supply side economics and the threat of overproduction leading to deflation and recession. At the same time public services, which are meant to cater to the needs of the collectivity, are impoverished. Restructuring and budget cuts hurt firstly the already vulnerable population groups.

One can argue that the market place is inherently democratic, to the extent that a trader needs a partner to trade with and a producer needs a consumer to buy his product. The entrepreneur has a vested interest in spreading prosperity. But western economies favored oligopolies and distorted the optimal functioning of the market place.

Of course, in recent years, the downturn of the economy has exposed the shortcomings of the 1990s. Can we learn from our mistakes? Many business operators have everything one can own in the material world, and much more besides. Some of them, exploring the concept of corporate responsibility, of knowledge-based processes, have started looking for an expansion of the capacities of their consciousness. Perhaps they should aim at the new frontier, that is, to conquer the spiritual divide. Could they be empowered by spirituality? Would this be difficult for them to comprehend? What is missing?

7. THE ANESTHESIA OF THE BRAIN

The self styled poverty of philosophy, committed with all its concepts to the given state of affairs, distrusts the possibility of a new experience. The Socratic discourse is political discourse inasmuch as it contradicts the established political institutions.

— Herbert Marcuse, One Dimensional Man

WHISPERS FROM THE AGORA

It is no proof of a man's understanding to be able to confirm whatever he pleases; but to be able to discern that what is true is true, and that what is false is false, that is the mark and character of intelligence.

— Emanuel Swedenborg

God, in addition to everything else, also created intelligence and to use it is not a sin. In the words of Herbert Marcuse, the search for the concepts of virtue, justice, piety and knowledge become a subversive undertaking as it denounces the established falsehood. If only we could interview Socrates in the main square, the Agora of ancient Athens, he would probably still be frustrated with the indolence of his fellow citizens. Would he be willing to share with us his secret? How to go about getting the kind of knowledge that makes the difference, how to walk out of the dark cave of uninformed opinion and see instead enlightened reality by the light of the sun?

The teacher of Plato and Aristotle might remind us that there are two types of knowledge: knowledge that enhances the capacity of the human mind ('*vidya*' in Sanskrit, '*episteme*' in Greek), and the so-called knowledge, or opinion, which hampers it ('*avidya*' in Sanskrit, '*doxa*' in Greek). We are experiencing, in its full magnitude, the modern expression of *doxa* whereas access to *episteme* is increasingly restricted.

Episteme is the direct knowledge of reality. We will not argue here with modern philosophers, who claim that such a thing does not exist. I do not need mental computations to find out that fire burns, that information is registered directly on the central nervous system as my finger comes too close to a flame. Similarly, through experience, insight or intuition, the brain can acquire and store living knowledge. Direct knowledge enriches us with cognitive experiences of reality. It generates self-control and a better mastery of our life, a crucial condition for the survival of our species.

Doxa is the darling of modern relativists for whom truth does not exist. For them, *doxa* is mere opinion, a projection that exists only in the hazy pseudo reality of a mental landscape. It creates relative and interchangeable images and it swells, in bits and pieces, with the information we take in everyday. The thought process is bound to circumstances and is subjective. Truth is only a flavor for oneself, from a specific standpoint, and has no reality as such. Modern theories of knowledge have denied that there exists such a thing as true or false, right or wrong. It all depends on your point of view. President Clinton, who said he did not smoke pot because he did not inhale, who was not alone with a female intern although no one else was around, reminds us that truth is a matter of definition - an entertaining way of celebrating the positivism of Ayer and to a lesser degree, Wittgenstein. Truth is what you believe it is. If you do not see the truth the way your boss does, you are fired because you are 'off message.'

Yet, after indulging in these mental processes do we feel enriched, improved or in any way better? *Doxa* influences the course of our actions but it does not enrich us existentially.

This ancient philosophical question today takes on a new acuity. Equipped with cable TV and the Net, we now face an overflow of data, information, designs and concepts, but we have somewhat lost the capacity to navigate in this asteroid field of information. The huge amount of information available is not a substitute for the quality of knowledge. The brain needs a radar system that helps to sort out true from false, appearance from reality and right choices from wrong ones based on poor information.

Should we not be afraid of leading a virtual life? Our development of software will keep us in a virtual vision that is the total illusion of 'techno-doxa,' a battery of opinions, dementedly multiplied by information technologies. The term 'virtual reality' is interesting. It means such a good fallacy, such a convincing falsehood that it replaces the need for the real. It goes hand in hand with our modern virtual democracy where the appearance of power sharing - enshrined in the liturgy of the elections process - is a substitute for actually having power.

The world we think of as real, the world of our daily lives, of our desires, appetites, tensions or contradictions, the world of infatuation and anger, of bipolar stress, that world as expanded by technology, is in fact, a virtual world.

We tend to project into geography our yearning for a place of happiness: the island of Utopia of Sir Thomas More; the famed region of Shangri-La, somewhere in Eastern Tibet. We have used geographic metaphors to project the state of mind we aspire to, the peace of oneness with our self, our fellow beings and the cosmos.

It would be a mistake to underestimate the importance of being real. Even if positivists assume the contrary, truth has not gone away. Reality always comes back with a vengeance.

ZAPPING VALUES OUT OF SIGHT

But for the time being we run away from reality. From childhood onwards we learn how to scatter our attention, how not to focus. For instance, a child is sitting in front of a TV screen, with a hundred plus channels cabled in and the remote control in its hand. It zaps through the programs. Never mind how many scenes of rape and murder it will watch within a typical hour.

Are we going to be twice born on the Internet? Will we achieve real physical fulfillment and satisfaction in the solitary absurdity of cybersex or new interactive erotic video games? Are we becoming wiser by accumulating more and more data? Galaxies of information are floating adrift in the infinity of cyberspace but we are lost without a navigational system and the PC explorer does not find the gate to *episteme*. We walk around in shallowness without depth or focus. The Nintendo children are learning to float, to move, to zap through life: speeding along, destination unknown while the adults, scrambling for 'Nowhere land,' are not far behind.

Our brain needs help from 'Overeaters Anonymous.' It is losing the sense of taste; it misses access to the right menus, led astray by the multiplicity of choice in the overflowing supermarket freezer cabinets. The Federal Administration in Washington DC issued a set of dietary guidelines in which it warned against taking in "too much" fat, cholesterol, alcohol, etc. In a country that spent $3.8 billion on potato chips in 1988, selective eating has become a sort of necessity. Junk food excess becomes a greater concern than malnutrition. And what about junk food for our brains?

The brain of the inquiring man has been numbed, not by a phenomenon of scarcity but by overabundance. Data, information, concepts, goods and services are confronting us with a dizzying wealth of opportunities, alternatives and choices. Nothing is simple anymore. Even the shopping mall has become a challenge, with its diversity of goods and multiplicity of prices. Data floats in a world of relativity, shifting meanings and plastic values. In this context, one may fear the loss of the sense of acuity of the brain, the fading of the sense of discrimination through which we can critically review and analyze the existing state of affairs. Perhaps this was just fine with the established order of things that might not really rejoice in such critical enquiry. Confusion is the order of the day. These are puzzling times of mysteries, complexity and troubles. Without firm benchmarks, we further lose the sense of direction through which we establish strategic priorities. We may cling to half-truths or hide ourselves behind the false security of accepted dogmas, creeds or ruling theories. Alternatively, we may just acquire some sector expertise or technical skills in order to fit neatly into the production system. But none of this helps us much to enjoy life or to get satisfaction.

Where would we learn an alternative approach? Few are the academic institutions that have the caliber to promote a holistic system of teaching or to transmit the needed trans-cultural perspective on contemporary social or economic processes.

Hence, a first suspicion: the brain is numbed because some people have an interest in keeping it so. Who are they? Presumably those who benefit from the fog because their rule is facilitated by our lack of critical intelligence.

The National Cattlemen's Association and the National Pork Council are not keen on the idea of dietary guidelines. They want open and free access to our stomachs. The lobbies of those who, in the name of democracy, want free access to our brains, not minding much about its health or condition, are even more formidable. The 'pornocrats' who swamp the Net with their products, including films of live torture and murder, claim the First Amendment and freedom of expression. Never mind the findings of social criminologists that establish the connections between serial killers, criminal sex offenders and their addiction to pornography.

If I had to explain our predicament to my 8-year-old son who may well have to deal with all this further into the twenty first century, I would put it like this: the stomach is fed through the mouth; the brain through the ears and eyes. It is relatively easy to control what we take into our mouth, much what comes through our eyes and ears. Furthermore, our mind is not unlike white linen; ink can darken it in a split second; to wash it off takes much more time.

Indeed, feeding the brain is no less important than feeding the stomach. It is simply less obvious. Warnings on this matter issued by some of the most distinguished contemporary scholars and scientists have not been heeded; their signals could not pierce the fog.

MINDING OUR OWN MIND

With stupidity the gods themselves struggle in vain.

— Friedrich von Schiller

Values don't always lose out against facts. The 'ought' has something to do with desire. Gandhi did bring about a new fact - no less than the freedom of his country, and the end of British rule - by stubbornly and against all logic and odds, upholding high values. He went on hunger strike to mobilize millions of Indians for the cause of Independence. It worked because the idea of the 'ought' could penetrate the brains of his followers. Their hearts were awake, too. They were sustained in their march towards freedom by their desire for improving the fate of their Motherland. Or better, they could put their hearts into their brains and this made a powerful combination. One can say that in the last days of the British Raj, the khadi-clad Indian farmer proved to be ethically more evolved than the British trader in his three-piece suit.

If Gandhi had been a British subject in the United Kingdom fighting for some lofty social cause, his fate would have been very different. He might have gone on a hunger strike and died, a minor news item, listed on page five of the newspapers.

It is intriguing that these barefoot farmers showed higher awareness than sophisticated intellectuals. Perhaps this is because the Indian cultural context, at that time, was still rating moral and ethical values very highly. The fighters for India's independence tried to turn their desire for a better world into reality and like most revolutionaries who came before them, they unfortunately did not succeed in the long run and their successors fell into the practice of large-scale corruption.

Today's democratic consumerism, lost in the swamp of material gratification, glorifies the 'is.' It does not believe it needs to know the 'ought' type of knowledge of the navigational system.

In the relatively recent past, one philosopher, however, exerted a great influence on the student movement of the 1960s and the early 1970s. A Professor of Philosophy at the University of California at San Diego, Herbert Marcuse delivered a scathing critique of our society, which inspired students on the barricades of Los Angeles, Rome and Paris in 1968. Herbert Marcuse exposed how manipulation of the language leads to blurring the line between authentic and illusory meaning, thereby diffusing a potentially critical analysis of an unjust capitalist society. He notes: "…the therapeutic task of philosophy would be a political task, since the established universe of ordinary language tends to coagulate into a totally manipulated and indoctrinated universe. Then politics would appear in philosophy, not as a special discipline or object of analysis, nor as a special political philosophy, but as the intent of its concepts to comprehend the unmutilated reality." [9]

Marcuse carried the Socratic hope that intellectuals could be the guardians of critical thought and, in this capacity, the vanguards of the revolution. He said that pseudo democracy is taking us for a ride: he exposed the mystification of our mind. The manipulation of language, symbol and the trivialization of values is a democratic commonplace. Democratic rationality i.e., the justification of the capitalist status quo, negates idealism. Hence it silences a potentially subversive search for meaning. Ideology and values are vested in the process of producing goods and services. People are kept mystified in the dull happiness of the quick consumption society and the one-dimensional society is a material world where ideas lose their meaning.

It is the material world where "the material girl" who has taken the name of the Madonna, sings about God also and sells an expensive book with erotic pictures of herself. Between 'good and yellow,' words expressing morality, values or ethics are emptied from their substance. Just listen to a politician on the campaign trail for whom ethics is but a word, sprayed on the political jargon to make the candidate appear more worthy.

In a world made of relative propositions, anything goes. Absolute values have been derided as outdated legacies of an ignorant past. Such a mindset favors the business partner, the politician, the business strategy, the brand logo, product or movie, which dresses its dreams and aspirations with the appearances of reality. The numbed brain does not mind that 'show' counts more than substance, and without the guidance of the heart, the mind cannot any more discern the difference. This is, after all, the era where Coca-Cola was discovered to be the "Real Thing." Emmanuel Kant used to call the real thing *"das Ding an sich."* The Buddhists call it "suchness" (*tathaga*). They did not mean Coca-Cola but something else. Many do not know or remember what, or even care.

Cybernauts and corporate fat cats are thrilled to see the wave of deregulation sweeping the digital domain. One assumes that more information leads to growth of consciousness but as said before, information is not knowledge. Marcuse was fed by a long tradition of thinking. Dialectic thought, from Heraclitus to Lao Tzu, reminds mortals that things are not quite what they seem to be. Everything flows, everything changes, and changes come with a twist. You can never dive twice into the same river. Dialectics understands the critical tension between 'is' and 'ought:' it allows political leaders to measure the established systems - the 'is' - against moral ideals - the 'ought.' Facts confront values. As a matter of fact, our forefathers who dealt with politics were quite concerned with raising their society to a higher level of perfection. Hence, in the *Mahabaratha* epic, the Pandavas under Krishna fought the Kaurava Empire for a just cause, and Socratic discourse contradicted the Athenian establishment. Socrates was a subversive teacher, and loved by his students for his unfailing dedication to intellectual honesty and political justice.

[9] Herbert Marcuse, *One Dimensional Man*, Beacon Press, USA (1966), p.199.

It would seem then that there is no chance to free the brain from its conditioning by the established patterns of language and behavior. Thus, even a pertinent criticism such as Marcuse's becomes, in the end, an innocuous academic controversy, partially funded by the Rockefeller Foundation. Pragmatism, as the new, implicit ideology of democracy, does away with the practical guidance that ethics only can provide.

Some ancient civilizations highly praised wisdom, including, for example, Chinese, Indian, Greek, and Jewish cultures. Its main purpose, at the gate of our brain, was to feed the intellect with real knowledge only. This gift of wisdom involved the capacity to discriminate between truth and falsehood, to see what is actually going on without wearing the tainted glasses of biased perception. Wisdom empowers us with inner sight to witness the plays of light and shadow, to absorb the first and reject the latter. In the world of ancient teachers, the highest ambition of the education system was to build up this capacity in pupils through the teachings of enlightened masters. This is a far cry away from the curriculum of the modern University: courses are now to impart skills so that we may fit as brave little screws in the robotic complex of our mode of production.

Those who could see, the seers, offered their guidance throughout the ages. Leaders with a vision have shown the path to others. Socrates said, "Know thyself"; Christ overturned the tables of the moneylenders and warned against adulterous eyes; Lenin, before being carried away by the nemesis of the revolution he had unleashed, was concerned with the praxis of social justice. George Washington fought for freedom and Abraham Lincoln fought for righteousness. Philosopher-kings, in Plato's view, were optimally qualified to lead society. They were, in a sense, the gatekeepers of our brains, inspiring us to think and act for the greatest good of self and society. Where are such leaders today?

For the current established trend of thought, "Know thyself" means to know matter, not spirit. Christians have swelled beyond proportion the adultery statistics and it was the children of Goethe and Hegel who shouted "Heil Hitler." Marxist-Leninist regimes turned into farcical bureaucratic behemoths before their ultimate collapse. In the land of Lincoln, the word ethics is a mere slogan for the image dressing of the vote getter or the populist claims of Christian fundamentalists. Nevertheless, the profit makers are doing fine: moneylenders sit at the World Bank, ready to save the world, and bill the poor for their services. Bankers in offshore centers have expanded their skills; they became the dirty money launderers behind the bankers' clean white shirts.

To safeguard democracy, paraphrasing William Blake, "Would to God that people were seers." This would make for very different election campaigns. Is the idea of an enlightened democracy a total utopia? Today, the great personalities of the past have no influence on those who fashion our minds. Madison Avenue and cable TV have diffused our attention. We are told that the information super highway and multi-media networks will spread knowledge, but what sort of knowledge, will help us to live a better life and will it be available? We need people to mind their own minds.

THE TECHNOLOGY OF ENTERTAINMENT

The consequences of anesthesia of the brain are becoming apparent when confronted with the challenge of technology. Manufacturers and PC addicts the world over see the multi-media highway as the road to the future. Little do they realize that they are not increasing by one comma the true knowledge, *'episteme'*, that modern society so desperately needs.

Technology is equipping the arm of a society with armor plates, a society whose brain is growing increasingly dumb. Those who profess that technology will solve our problems do not see that it develops the arm of society, not the brain; it expands the branches of the tree, not its roots. What will then happen to the tree?

Technology, like democracy, is ethically neutral, neither good nor bad. But its considerable potential for accelerated ecological and social change raises in a compelling manner the ethical question of the use to which it is put. What forces fuel technological acceleration? Is it man's noble passion for science and discovery? The argument of technology going its own socially irrelevant way has been explored by, for instance, Jacques Ellul (The Technological Society) in France, and in John K. Galbraith's account of the "Technostructure." It is presented, in Toynbee's analysis of history, as the major emerging threat.

The essence of their argument is that one of the most demonic forces in technological civilization is the craving for growth, which is enhanced by countless institutional devices ranging from national prestige to real estate promotion and other forms of commercial advertising. If modern man is encouraged to expand still further his appetite for the products of industry, if he continues to assume that every innovation is worth having and justifies the rejection of worthwhile practices simply because they are old, then disasters are inevitable, whatever improvements may be made in the technological process. Neither wealth nor knowledge can provide effective ways to deal with human excesses. The demons to be exorcised are therefore not in technology but in the minds of men.

What good for society is a technology which puts people out of jobs and throws thousands of vulnerable families into further poverty? The ruling thinkers continue to pretend that technology will solve all our problems and that innovation such as the Internet and genetically modified food will eliminate poverty. We need to be reminded that the electric light bulb, invented in 1870, is still inaccessible to two billion people.

In dealing with ethics and choices, we have to go back to our desires, to our hearts, if traces of this organ can still be found in the brain of our society. If not, we are probably speeding fast down the road where science fiction sees the modern megalopolis ending up: a mechanical monster from whence the Terminator comes back.

Hence destructive trends are not linked to technology itself but to the appetite for continuous growth that technology is serving. Did we not say earlier that desires matter? The field of the real crisis is in our brains; a perception shared by many, now forgotten, writers of the 1970s. The psychologist M. Scott Peck writes: "We are beginning to realize that the sources of danger to the world lie more within us than outside and that the process of constant self explanation and contemplation is essential for ultimate self survival."

One could fill books with quotes of such warnings. The beauty of it all is that in the 1980s, uncontrolled growth and money grabbing reached euphoric summits: "Greed is good!" says Michael Douglas, playing a rapacious corporate raider in the movie *Wall Street*. Unmistakably, the growth and concentration of wealth during America's deregulation years have not served for a democratization of wealth.

It is aptly symbolic that it happened during the era of Ronald Reagan, the president of the USA known as "the great communicator" who had been groomed for the role by his earlier career as a movie actor. Perhaps our leaders perform best before a numbed audience. His act seemed so good that we forgot the social agenda. Yet increasing the income gap within the country goes against everything American democracy is supposed to stand for.

For instance, it is worth remembering that increased crime, drugs, homelessness or the creation of a devastating budget deficit at home did not affect Reagan's high popularity score. In foreign affairs, Reagan's popularity at home benefited from staged high-action entertainment such as the bombing of Quadaffi's own camp in Libya and the invasion of Grenada. He did not always meet success: with, for example, 200 marines blown up in Beirut and a prompt retreat thereafter. This latter episode is to be compared with Carter's ill-fated attempt at rescuing the American hostages in Teheran: where a much smaller number of victims in this aborted secret operation cost Carter his presidency. The difference between the two cases is entertainment: President Reagan could entertain his voters in the great patriotic celebration of "America is tall again," building the image the public wanted to see: God, Freedom and the Flag become melodic lines in the 'White House turned Broadway show.'

CNN coverage of world events translates untold human dramas and sufferings into hot news to grease the wheels of broadcasting power. For the media, bad news is excellent. TV viewers want to be entertained by instant history turned into high tech thriller, marveling at the precision of Tomahawk missiles and laser-guided bombs.

"*Panem et circenses!*" "Bread and circus games," roared the crowd in the Coliseum. The Roman Emperors faithfully minded the advice and used the device: let the people be happy or, more easily, let them believe they are. This understanding of the politics of entertainment is, in Western countries, the best-preserved legacy of the Roman Empire. Definitely, some leaders love a happy dumb crowd. Thus the system pampers its entertainers and the services of the Walt Disney CEO, of Madonna or Tom Cruise are highly prized and rewarded. Do we ever wonder what crucial services they render to society in order to merit such enormous rewards? We hear Mickey Mouse and Donald Duck sing in theme parks, "It's a wonderful world." But, children, the world we'll leave to you is becoming less wonderful all the time. Maybe this is why the incomes of such people are so high. The paymaster wants us to believe, and the entertainers take our minds off what is really going on.

THE CONTAGION OF NUMBNESS

It is hard to free fools from the chains they revere.

— Voltaire

The ruling class loves a happy dumb crowd because it silences the type of enquiries that could challenge the exploitation of the many by the few. No doubt about it, show counts more than substance. The appeal of the Western democracies for developing countries today depends increasingly on its capacity to dominate the communication and entertainment business worldwide. I watch increasingly tedious CNN news in my hotel rooms from Dhaka, Bangladesh to Gaborone, Botswana and in the cities of Central Asia's fabled silk road I see Kazakh and Uzbeck kids dance to rock and rap on MTV programs. Billions of viewers delight in the psychological agonies of Californian or Texan soap operas. Skirts are getting shorter on Indian movie actresses, for the Western fashion leads the way. This goes back to the core of our discourse.

The anaesthetized brain has lost its yearning for objective truth. Instead, it seeks outside the reflection of its own phantasms. It loves a President, a TV presenter or a banker who tells it what it wants to hear, who dresses dreams with the appearance of reality, who gives a shape or an echo to the brain's projections. Reality is as we define it. But, as my daughter said, our belief that the earth was flat did not flatten the earth.

Capitalist democracies of the post-industrial age do not need a 'Propaganda Agency.' There is a pervasive understanding in the communication industry of the type of entertainment mystification which suits the establishment and which suits also their own corporate interests. If this understanding is challenged, the going will get tough for the challenger. In the mid 1980s, UNESCO attempted to assist Third World governments in gaining a better control of the material that is broadcast in their countries in order to promote national aims such as economic development, ethnic harmony and to rid news coverage of excessive Western bias. This move was, typically enough, considered ideological: the USA and the United Kingdom withdrew from the Organization and the Director General of UNESCO, Mr. M'Bow from Senegal, became the target of an aggressive and relentless media campaign. It was deemed imperative that Africans in Gaborone should know everything about *Dallas* or *Miami Vice*, and in the meantime, more satellite dishes on the roofs of Bangalore, Carthagena or Tunis stretch towards the sky, begging for the droppings of our Western junk culture.

Modern entertainment is not necessarily fun but, in its essence, it must intoxicate. Watch the crowd in a soccer game, in a hard rock disco, or take the Space Roller Coaster in Florida's Disney World. Those who promote hard rock discos or nightlong rave parties know that there is a jump-start from anesthesia to hallucination. The beat of the music pounds the skin and pierces the head. A sort of shock therapy for the mistake of existing, Jean-Paul Sartre might have said. If not always a disco, our brain also has become a noisy place and the mind is addicted to outside flight, a monkey stung by a bee as Buddha used to say. But in his day the monkey was not jumping so frantically.

This review has been illustrated with anecdotes from the 1980s and 1990s. The last decades of the Second Age capture some of the problems Adam ran into, at the end of the Christian age, at the end of his lone quest for happiness. Adam is an allegory for a one polarity, male dominated society. With his balance lost, Adam cannot go within to seek inner truth or true desire. He cannot see the truth outside either. Instead, he is entertaining himself with opinions, expectations and love affairs. Our minds create the thick electronic fog of mental activity, which prevents us tuning to the right wavelength.

Silly brain, a Pindaric dream of a shadow, a drunken ship, without the somber beauty of Arthur Rimbaud's poetry. The moorings are lost. We are floating in magnified self-delusion. Mental modernity has ultimately generated spiritual backwardness through perverted desires, misguided thoughts and misled actions.

Trapped within the *gunas*, we experience the state of the unhappy consciousness. Nature, nations, societies and families are under such stress that they threaten to disintegrate. Are we preparing for ourselves the fields of Armageddon, the day of reckoning, for Judgment Day? Few paintings are as modern as Edward Munch's The Scream, where the air itself reverberates in purple agony. Many are screaming with it, "We are not going to take it any more." We have climbed on board a roller coaster. We scream but we can't get off. Is there a way off and out?

8. EQUILIBRIUM POINT

And there are those who have the truth within them, but they tell it not in words. In the bosom of such as these the spirit dwells in rhythmic silence.

— Khalil Gibran, The Prophet

The advent of the Third Age means for most of us that we are headed into uncharted waters and virgin territory. Perhaps, brain research specialists who evidenced the duality of functions in the two hemispheres of the brain (left side, more mental; right side, more emotional) would attribute the limited performance of our mind to the Western bias in favor of left-brain learning. Or, returning to the archetype of the first human couple, this is Adam without Eve, leading to an excessive dominance of analysis over intuition. Scientific studies show that the most successful people in any occupation are those who use both the left and the right parts of their brain. This reminds us that harmony, was the fundamental value in the aesthetics of ancient Greece. This being said, does our present lifestyle permit us to reach this balance; does it help us to strike the note of harmony, and can we still reach in our brain this subtle point of equilibrium between the two hemispheres, where we know truth and experience joy?

BETWEEN PAST AND FUTURE

History is a pact between the dead, the living, and the yet unborn.

— Edmund Burke

One set of statistics speaks for itself: by the year 2010, the populations of Western Europe and North America, both of which are ageing populations, will represent only 5.5% and 5% respectively of the total worlds population. We are facing an era where a minority of older people controls most of the world's wealth and they will be confronted by a vast majority of younger and poorer multitudes. Would it not be sound judgment, self-interest even, to follow the politics of the heart and to enact true solidarity in international relations? Maybe we should spread greater welfare and share more equitably some of this wealth while there is still time. Should we not prepare for the future or must we wait until it is taken away by might, natural catastrophes or fate? Surely, from an economic point of view, if wealth would be more evenly spread, the prosperity of the supply economy could be sustained by a more predictable and robust world demand. Wouldn't that make sense? Alternatively, are we going to look for Malthusian solutions to this population dilemma? Will our pharmaceutical industry continue to fight the availability of cheaper drugs to stem the AIDs epidemic in Africa? Do they mean to re-establish some population balance through the death of millions of HIV positive Africans? Some 27 million people are HIV carriers in sub Saharan Africa alone.

Are we heading forwards or backwards? Societies seem caught between the movements of a grinding mill. The development of the global market backed by monstrous computer power seems to push us fast into the future while the eruption of multiple conflicts takes us backwards into the past. Hutus and Tutsis settle pre-colonial scores; Slavs still fight the legacy of the Ottoman Empire and the Taliban in Afghanistan locked their women away in a sinister nationwide concentration camp. Indeed, violence often manifests the return of the worst ghosts from history: the specter of old wars of religion is haunting Kashmir, the former Yugoslavia and Israel. Fundamentalism, be it Christian, Muslim or Sikh is the murderous way backwards, embraced as it is by communities who feel insecure because of economic deprivation, social disintegration, moral decay and the sheer pace of modernity.

Fear freezes the heart of both individuals and society. The very word security, as in "security forces", itself engenders insecurity and fear. Fathers lose their jobs, kids are shot in their schools, and girls are kidnapped in the streets.

Believing in the future and its technological millennium, or seeking refuge in the past, with its protective cocoon of dogmas, are widespread attitudes. We try to respond to rampant anxieties, but escape into a time loop is not a rational response. Escape never destroys fear and it is imperative that we now find a way to restrain these pendulum movements, to relocate the center of our focus in history. We must achieve the mastery of the present, that elusive point in time where we exist, where we must finally find ourselves. Only then can we truly open our hearts to promote the collective values of solidarity and togetherness, which are essential for the survival of the human tribe.

How to reinvent a project for society? Social democracy had its chance without delivering the required fruit. It is not going to help to yearn after bygone days, to fall into the nostalgia of Rousseau's 'noble savage,' as the hippies did in the 1960s and 1970s. To seek refuge in technology, down the computerized alleys of our future, will not bring the solution. There appears to be no way back and no exit forward.

THE STANDARD BEARER

It is common sense to take a method and try it. If it fails, admit it frankly and try another, but above all, try something.

— Franklin Delano Roosevelt

Our Adam is currently in a disturbed psychosomatic condition and the consequences are potentially disastrous. We need to find a way to create balance in human beings, so that the heart can reassert itself, thence enlightening the brain. In terms of the metaphor that we have been using, the heart needs to be unfrozen and the liver cooled down.

In the sixth book of Homer's *Iliad*, generations of men are compared to generations of leaves, each sharing a passing but common destiny. Generations, reacting to their own past and acting in anticipation of the longed for future, tend to develop behavioral boundaries. As they move through time together and share a common age location on the trajectory of history, members of a generation are basically sharing the same matrix of perceptions and understanding. Their behavior is shaped by age-determined participation in milestone happenings and events. They share their location in time and space with other generations, and these interactions contribute to shaping the mood shifts of history.

In 1996, the first baby boomers born in 1946 turned fifty. When they did, in the USA, they received a cordial greeting in the mail. It announced that they have just been 'guaranteed acceptance for membership' in the AARP. That's the American Association of Retired Persons. It is attitude adjustment time for the 76 million Americans born between 1946 and 1964. It is no secret that elderly boomers the world over will collide with under-funded pension and health care schemes, starting in the first decade of the 21st century. This is one issue where the exceptional size of the Boomer Generation does matter. In America, a straight line mathematical extrapolation of known trends suggests that, by the year 2025, younger workers would have to hand over 30% to 40% of their payroll to provide retired boomers with present day levels of support. The mathematical dead-end in other rapidly aging European countries or Japan is every bit as serious.

How are the many once-spoiled kids of my own aging generation going to face Third Age poverty? According to a detailed analysis of probable generational patterns, the boomers are unlikely to wage the political war necessary to win the right to extract such heavy taxes. Rather, they could gain credibility by enforcing socially responsible policies in response to a global mission for restoring balance to society. The aspirations of this generation reaching retirement will put elderly boomers on a collision course with the younger generations' appetite for ever more consumption.

The Boomer Generation is strongly identified with the cyclical phenomenon of spiritual awakening and self-enquiry. They believe in an inner path to find solutions to the outer world's problems. This generation, through continuous turns and twists and countless oscillations, has shown itself hooked on principles, capable of potentially destructive fervor and obsessed with self-actualization. They charged through pop music, psychedelic euphoria, and New Age sects. They projected a militant vision with a mixture of high self-esteem and self-indulgence, soon to feel sorry for themselves having been cheated by 'angel dust' or the likes of the Maharishi.

From the rage of student rebellion, from the Vietnam War to the complacency of posh suburban affluence, from hippies to yuppies and beyond, the boomers have undergone many a metamorphosis and outlived waves of high expectations. They passed through the 1960s and 1970s in confused spiritualism, smug cultural liberation and grass roots evangelism without having yet found their home and leaving the task of establishing an ethical community unfinished. On the contrary, they exhibited the pathology of deteriorating social trends: suicide, divorce, drunk driving, teenage pregnancy and crime rates mounted with each successive wave of births. This anti-climax illustrates the lack of a tracking system and in their relentless search for perfectibility, the boomers threw their considerable energy into misguided paths, blurring the borderline between freedom and license. They undermined access to this higher morality they were all along yearning for, they misfired, they freaked out, they went dumb, and in the end tried to find solace in the Beatles' *Let it be*. Having failed in the attempt to conquer the inner world, they took on the outer one and launched the great consumption binge of the 1980s.

In the genesis of its expression, the boomers' screaming revolt against the Vietnam War was a revolt against the father, the denial of the 'heated liver' and the aggressive ways of the previous patriarchal, left-brained generation. According to Strauss and Howe, boomers were close to their mothers who, through intense home nurturing, had given them needed self-confidence for their further investigations. In a sense, it was these mothers, then happy to stay at home to raise their kids, who prepared the long quest of their Faustian sons and daughters.

Typically, as a tribute to their mothers, the boomers coming of age would foster the feminine, motherly concern for the collectivity rather than the masculine conquest for individual glorification. Out of the lonely emptiness of modernity, they may now call back Eve and rediscover the deeper insights of emotional intelligence.

As it registers the heat on the sun channel, the *Pingala nadi*, and the freeze on the moon channel, the *Ida nadi*, its brain emerging from self-inflicted slumber, let us bet that this epochal generation will return to the drawing board. Can we hope that the boomer's urge for value changes, that a society-wide effort to recapture communal togetherness and spiritual authenticity will seek to express itself in the wake of the birth of the third millennium, now that this generation is at the helm of affairs? This is also the time when Western boomers are challenged by the decline of the Western economic empire. They will be tempted to build the walls of a more enlightened Polis, protected from the savvy tricks of the more materialistic and streetwise younger generations, which will be spreading into decision-making positions all over the world.

Clearly the great struggle is now to win the hearts of this crusading generation. Which visions will it choose? What revolution, likely to dwarf in significance the French and Russian ones, will carry us to the promised spiritual awakening? The global revolution that this generation must finish can turn into a crisis of apocalyptic proportions. Will this generation fall back into the false security of puritanical, sectarian values? Will it meet fundamentalism with fundamentalism? Alternatively, will it imbibe the global dimension and adopt trans-cultural wisdom to finally complete the journey within and thence redeem society? This is a titanic fight between the bigot and the open mind.

We need to dwell on this. The 1990s were unfortunately a missed opportunity for the West to show solidarity with the rest of the world. The rich countries neglected development aid and environmental cooperation and the combination of poverty and demographic explosion in the third world bred the seeds of growing discontent. Youth without jobs or economic prospects are vulnerable and local politicians exploit such frustrations. In the Arab world, the fundamentalists have used for their benefit this volatile combination, from Algeria to Indonesia. Extreme terrorist movements have labored for years and mounted a scenario of destruction, hoping to take with them Arab public opinion. The purpose of this Jihad, equipped with the perspective of controlling the oil fields, is to bring down the West. Facing this kind of hostility, the West must resist the temptations to regress into its own fundamentalism. It must shun the simplistic Manichean schemes and the logic of violence. While standing strong and using force in self-defense if needs be, the West must build a world coalition around core humanistic values. We must regain the credibility of genuine ethical behavior. The USA enjoyed a moral leadership at the end of World War II by behaving as a magnanimous victor. It built the mechanisms of solidarity through the Marshall Plan, the establishment of the United Nations and the Bretton Woods institutions. We need again men and women with vision.

GOING BACK AND FORTH DOES NOT BRING US FORWARD

Would you tell me please which way I ought to go from here? said Alice

That depends a good deal on where you want to go, said the Cheshire cat.'

— *Lewis Carroll, Alice in Wonderland*

The pull of the past, powerfully carried by fundamentalists, suggests that the bigots will triumph. The push towards the future tends towards a discovery of our universality through a yet unstable globalization process. Oscillations between the poles of the alternatives will merely destabilize world society.

It is to be hoped that the boomer generation will wish to draw the line between freedom and license. To that effect, they may find a new meaning in the concept of The State and choose to re-orient public institutions and laws towards a socially redemptive purpose. Social safety nets, taxes on financial transactions and a new legitimacy for the rule of the law will plant electric fences around the biggest predators.

The Social Forum in Porto Allegre contrasted with the Economic Forum in Davos to pointedly review these issues. Measures aiming at restoring some form of equitable order are discussed to assert the common good ahead of individual short-lived self-gratification. There are encouraging trends. For instance, regional planning, administrative decentralization and coalitions of citizens could bring government closer to the people. Environmental alliances will push for new economic instruments. They would propose incentives for modified personal and social behaviors in relationship to energy use, transportation and consumption. Dependency on fossil fuel would be reduced. Consumer protection will be revitalized and the fashion industry will emphasize quality rather than quantity with a strong preference for hand made products and high value, durable handicrafts.

The new search for morality will aim at Kant's categorical imperative. "Do not do unto others..." Each proposition must be universally valid. The inward unity of a personality will count more than its projection in the outside world. Moral consistency will not tolerate the bracketed weakness of addictions such as alcohol, careless sex, career lust or tobacco and substance abuse; pornography and ego promotion will no longer be cool.

Politicians and business people always want to sail with the wind and they try to see the shape of things to come. Senator Robert Dole started his presidential campaign in 1995 with a pugnacious speech attacking the Hollywood entertainment industry for undermining values. He asked its executives whether they felt good about debasing the nation, attacking children and making money on violent movies and obscene rap music. Sure enough, two weeks after denouncing Hollywood for peddling movies and music rife with gratuitous brutality and casual sex, the Senate majority leader changed his tune and during a debate on telecommunications legislation, Dole urged senators to reject a regulatory plan to limit violence on TV shows. He worked to turn the votes in favor of the media giants.

Selective calls for human rights smack of hypocrisy. What is the moral authority of the West? The moralistic invocation against the ills of fascism did not stop the rise of the far right in France. In an era of rising materialism, the celebration of virtuous citizens, guided by the moral lights of traditionalists, is breeding popular cynicism.

In today's China, far removed from the China of Chairman Mao, the motto is to serve society and to get rich, but the Party ideology does not tell how to choose between the two. Deng Tsiao Ping conveniently assumed, as Calvin did at the beginning of the capitalist age in Protestant Geneva, that the latter goal serves the former. The communist nomenklatura, in the former Soviet Union as in China, is the group best placed to enjoy the fruits of economic liberalization. In the meantime the new role model is not the hero of socialist labor, but the real estate developer with a portable telephone in a Mercedes. From Bombay to Bogotá, from Ulan Bator to Lagos, what makes people tick is the exhortation of Guizot, minister of King Louis Philipe of France whose reign marked the rise of the nineteenth century bourgeoisie: *"Enrichissez vous."* "Get rich." Loftier philosophical concerns are a luxury the youth of the Third World cannot yet afford. Not a fertile ground for an innovative ethical reengineering of society.

Indeed the call for virtue sounds naïve and silly, alas. We should not forget that both Marx and Lenin, initially infused with compassion for the exploited workers, had an intensely ethical vision of society and because they imbibed the aspiration for equal justice, millions of simple-hearted people in China and Russia accepted a life of extraordinary privations and hardships in following the communist ideal. The bankruptcy of the communist regimes is a reminder that morality, planted on the candleholder of power politics, is but a flickering flame.

The preaching of the so called 'developed countries' is just not credible. They play the moralist so as to defend the established politics of wealth and power and they glibly preach to others without any attempt to reform themselves. Ever subtler forms of colonial domination will again be justified by mythical reference to our spiritual roots. The Crusaders pillaged Constantinople and the Spanish conquistadors burned the Inca Atahualpa for the greater glory of God but they didn't forget to take the gold.

The longed-for ethical reform of society is failing because it is not carried through or preceded by an inner transformation.

The outcome of the forthcoming fight between the bigot and the open mind is hard to predict. The bigot is not sure to win. Some hard facts will talk louder than his ideologies. The unprecedented tourism boom looming ahead, for instance, will mix people of various civilizations like never before and challenge the temptations of parochial withdrawal. Tens of millions of wealthy Asians will join the ranks of globetrotting Westerners. The global travel industry will likely employ some 338 million people and push the revenues from travel and tourism to $7 trillion within a decade. People will mix: not only bodies, but also ideas.

On the other hand, the open mind, according to its track record, is likely to lose as every new frontier explored by the inquiring boomers has caused them to lose direction. Pop culture has ended in rap music and psychedelic explorations ended in the hospital. New Age cults collapsed in frauds and sex liberation lost out to HIV syndrome. The electronic frontier might lure many further away from reality, providing escapes for those who cannot cope with the stress of daily living. Moods are swinging. Between the seeking introspection of the 1970s and the extrovert consumption fever of the 1980s, the contrast is well marked.

Going back and forth between the two poles of our accumulated contradictions will exacerbate the pendulum movement. Each apple has its worm and each action its reaction. The Ying flows into the Yang and vice versa. In the words of Viktor Chernomyrdin, the one-time Russian Premier, "We wanted to do it the best way but it came out the way it always does."

THE RULES OF THE GAME

Entertainment is about play and to play we must learn the rules of the game. When we play chess, the knowledge of the game allows us to play, to enjoy the game and eventually, it helps us to play to win. Is there a type of knowledge that similarly helps in the grand game of life?

When people extol the supremacy of knowledge-based economies, they refer to a knowledge that helps us to perform within specific levels of activities and not a knowledge that helps us to live better, in a more fundamental way. It is perhaps overlooked that the way we perform in any given area of our life is related to the state of our being. Hence, in the last analysis, a coherent improvement in our performances would ultimately depend on the knowledge of our being. We play many roles in life: on any given day we may be, at the same time, an investor concerned by the currency fluctuations, a manager who needs to insure the cohesion of her team, a wife who must respond to her husband's expectations and a mother who faces the teenage crises of her daughters. Any specific skill or knowledge in any of these roles does not guarantee that the full range of situations can be addressed successfully. Yet a failure in any of these roles can affect performance in any other one.

Knowledge in the chess game, the market place or the boardroom is a 'win-oriented' power tool. But, mostly, it is only a 'one-win' kind of knowledge; it is likely to bring success only in the specific field it relates to. Thus the brain goes on accumulating this type of segmented or functional knowledge in order to maximize the chances of the individual's coping strategies for multiple challenges. Our expert may acquire PhDs, language skills, and computer proficiency and whilst all this is helpful, and multiplies the chances of winning scores, it is not quite enough. It does not secure the personality's global success, for it does not help him or her to face life in an integrated fashion.

In contrast, knowledge of the actor behind all the roles is a 'win-win' knowledge for it is the type of knowledge, conscious or not, that will help in delivering all the roles and functions in a consistent manner. It is the level of identification with the actor behind these roles, the Self, that can smoothly carry the day. The mastery of the Self (spiritual knowledge, the first Win) means mastery over its protean roles (functioning in the material world, the second Win). This mastery implies knowledge-awareness and not mere knowledge-information. We will illustrate further in the next chapters the workings of 'win-win' responses to the challenges of our environment.

The quality that was meant to keep our brain in this alert, awakened stage was cultivated and highly praised by our forefathers. It was called wisdom. But even if wisdom were to be considered as an innate human quality, it needs to be nurtured, cultivated and transferred. Cultures, ideally, were designed to secure the conditions for sensible values and shared wisdom leading to true knowledge.

Contemporary culture however has thrown us in the whirling worlds of what one might call 'Technodoxa.' Information technology has opened new treks for our attention, it has vastly expanded possibilities of forming opinions and has pushed us into a culture of fiction-based entertainment. Technodoxa has opened the channels of a virtual reality where endless options for escaping the *"hic et nunc"* of daily life takes us further away from the gate of real knowledge. The ultimate temptation is to claim, of course, that fiction is reality. Yet, it is within the present, the here and the now of daily life that we must firm up the processes of self-discovery, contemplation, relationships, enjoying life and having fun.

There is a really no need to swim against the current. We must assume the dynamics of change and we can do so through a holistic grasp of the present environment. We must integrate change with the dynamics of balance and harmony by harmony between the heart and the brain, by reconciling our intellect and emotions. Moreover, to achieve this, should we not reach to the other side of the great divide between matter and spirit, manage this grand transformation and walk through to the other side of the screen carrying democracy with us?

A SPIRITUAL MANIFESTO ON GLOBALIZATION

Conditions may now be ripening for overcoming some key contradictions of modernity as we enter the Third Age of Joachim. Propositions contained in this book assert the possibility of a revolution in human psychology, but they are not fully perceived in the context of the issues that command attention on the international scene. These issues, as illustrated in key instances (Bretton Woods institutions, WTO, Davos Forum) basically relate to the globalization process. The underlying tension zones are seen and expressed in the increasingly violent protests against G7 policies in Seattle, Washington, Melbourne, Prague and Genoa. The wars of the twenty first century, the fight against terrorism or fundamentalism, the combat against natural catastrophes or poverty will take place against a background of global relationships.

This manifesto reflects some propositions that came to mind after the extraordinary encounter with Shri Mataji Nirmala Devi Shrivastava described in the next chapter. It does not argue whether globalization is desirable or not, rather it suggests why experimental spirituality must be understood as a necessary collective development in order to avoid the destructive aspects of globalization trends.

1. Globalization consists of the interaction between information technology, the global economy, the common biosphere and regional cultures. A sharp increase in the rate and level of international transactions in these fields is an easily measurable index of the process of globalization.

2. The scenario: technology, trade, finance and the liberalized economy cast a long shadow on the protection of the ecology and the maintenance of regional cultures. The decay of traditional cultures causes social alienation, instability and the return to simplistic models. Affluent countries are not prepared to change those consumption patterns that contribute to greenhouse emissions in the atmosphere, thereby threatening global climate change with its aftermath of floods, droughts, extreme temperatures and rising sea levels. Climatic imbalance worsens the scarcity of natural resources.

3. Globalization trends seem compelling for income growth but the benefits are not universally distributed nor acknowledged. Increasing discontent in parts of the world community could, in times of recession, roll back the process and leave the global trading system adrift.

4. Concerns about the globalization engine focus on the ethnocentric agenda of the 'haves'. They use the global momentum to perpetuate exploitative relationships with the 'have-nots'. This situation has opened wider socio-economic disparities upon which confrontation and wars often feed. Wider disparities exist within national societies and at the international level. Actually, it can be argued that globalization is doomed to failure if it cannot be substantially adjusted to address the equity issue.

5. The gap between the fifth of the world's population in the richest countries and the four fifths in the poorest countries has widened. This magnitude of inequality is fundamentally unstable and breeds resentment between the young poor and the old or ageing rich in Europe, the USA and Japan.

6. In the context of deprivation, natural catastrophes, resources depletion and environmental scarcity, these factors cause refugee flow or extreme instability within vulnerable regions. Conditions of frustration and despair lead to conflict. Mass migrations and claims on natural resources considered of vital interest, have historically become security issues leading to military action. An alternative scenario for evolutionary - as opposed to confrontational-globalization would call on policies to foster compatibility in the increased integration of societies.

7. International diplomacy must demonstrate that globalization does not become a vehicle for exploitation, and build confidence that globalization is equally beneficial to all. It must act decisively through international policy instruments required to hold a critical mass of Global Equity Equilibrium.

8. Spirituality lies at the core of the great regional cultures of this planet and these have been eroded by centuries of clerical manipulation and by modernization. Only a revival of spirituality can foster a post-materialist, meta-modern society, in which the necessary change in consumers' behavior is at all possible.

9. Sahaja Yoga, as proposed by Shri Mataji Nirmala Devi, reactivates the core messages of the ancient world religions in a coherent manner, through the actualization of the process of Self-realization. Self-realization opens more ethical options to satisfy human needs and demands for happiness, thereby facilitating more solidarity within societies and between nations.

10. Sahaja Yoga can contribute to Global Equity Equilibrium as it calls for mutual understanding and tolerance between world cultures, a more

enlightened and equitable distribution of wealth and the return to ethics. However, this call is only effective because of the unique capacity of Sahaja Yoga to grant the experience of a new individual and collective spiritual consciousness.

11. The connections between spirituality, collective wellbeing and cultural integration have been much neglected. They can be effectively established only when spirituality opens new paths of satisfaction to human consciousness. This is an area where we must make progress to prevent deadly fractures in the global fabric of our race. Positive synergies must be encouraged in the context of policy forums at the highest level.

12. In the light of the above, concerned citizens in every country, non-governmental organizations and public authorities are invited to focus on the potential of the happening of Self-realization to serve as the trans-cultural foundation of a more humanistic global world civilization. This vision was at the unifying core of all religions. To implement this vision in history is the challenge of this time.

PART FOUR

THE SECRET INSTRUMENT

True and lasting solution to present ills can be found only by inner, collective transformation of human beings.

— Shri Mataji Nirmala Devi

There are many strong threads that lead here, important points which should be made clear and not lost. Remember, our brains are numb; we are tired and have the stresses of modern life to deal with, so I wish I could make this easier and more enjoyable for you to read.

The challenge is whether I can make this book interesting, for instance, to consumers of cosmetics. I can mention that meditation is the best cosmetic because it erases wrinkles and re-creates youthfulness better than any product on the market. Unlike many of the claims of the cosmetic and beauty preparation manufacturers, this is true and you can check it out for yourself. Many people who practice, and gradually master the art of Sahaja Yoga meditation, not only look good but radiate from inside, and have a magnetism that no number of visits to the beauty clinic can give.

I also hope that workers and executives will want to read this book because it can be shown that it will help them to succeed. I hope that artists and poets will want to read it as it will open them to the source of creativity and people will love their creations. I hope that lovers will want to read it as it will make them more lovable and loving. I desire that people in pain and those who are lonely will want to read it because their pain might be lessened and the lonely could discover that they are like a drop of water that rejoins the ocean. Can I help make people who are not so good, or who want to be better people, want to read it? I was one of them. Can I give everyone what they are looking for and in a form that is understandable and digestible by all?

I wish I could. Sadly, I am no magician and I feel it would take a great one to communicate convincingly that magic can belong to daily reality. To do so in words, and in a language foreign to me, seems daunting but it should be possible to communicate something, because the key that was offered to us is a master key.

SHRI MATAJI AND THE YOGA OF THE SPONTANEOUS UNION

One has to know what is the ultimate goal of our life. The ultimate goal of our evolution is to become the Spirit, which is the reflection of God Almighty in our heart. That is self-identity and also self-knowledge. Also, one becomes one with the all-pervading Divine power of love. Our awareness is enlightened by the spirit, and divine vibrations start flowing through our central nervous system enlightening our being. We also feel the cool divine love coming out of our fontanel bone area, as well as flowing through our fingertips and our hands.

– Shri Mataji Nirmala Devi

In Chapter 2, I explained how I came to hear about a very uncommon Guru; how I was told that this spiritual guide could actually awaken the energy of the Kundalini. This was a claim that none of the many teachers I had visited before could make. Even more extraordinary was my friend's statement that this event could take place, not only for a few selected individuals, but also for larger groups of seekers. Either such assertions are crazy or they are worth checking. I decided to check.

August is the month of the lion and of high noon hopes. It is also the time for harvesting. Let us go back to that sunny and slightly misty day in 1975 at Hurst Green in the quiet English countryside where Shri Mataji was then living. I knocked at the door, and again, and then I rang the bell. An Indian servant opened it. I entered into the hall and Shri Mataji entered from the living room on the right. She was wearing a white sari. I bowed and offered some flowers that I had bought at the station. My manners probably contrasted with my looks. My hair was a bit wild; I was wearing an old pair of jeans and a US Army jacket with a hole in it. I was quite intimidated because my friend in Berkeley had told me that so many people were holding her in high veneration because of her stupendous spiritual powers. You do not meet every day a Great Master of Yoga. The gurus who had come to the West were always rather remote; I had seen some of them in the past, protected from the crowd by bodyguards and here I was in her home. I remember her hair, very brilliant and black, and her welcoming smile, which was radiant, and her eyes smiled, too.

We moved to a living room decorated in exquisite taste. The sun was coming in through a large window, which overlooked the garden. It distributed shade and color and extended to the feet of a gracious marble statue of Lord Krishna playing the flute. But rather than the beautiful surroundings, it was an invisible quality in the air that captured my attention. The atmosphere was extremely cozy and peaceful, exuding a tremendous sense of security. I felt that I had walked through this door and into another place, leaving the world of noise and troubles behind. I felt it distinctly and yet could not believe that such a state is possible or that it could be for me. It was a bit like reaching a safe place, the hidden abode of Elrond in *The Lord of the Rings*, but being still haunted by the memory of the Black Riders. This contradiction was to keep me company over the following days.

The husband of Shri Mataji, Mr. C.P. Shrivastava, is a distinguished gentleman and also, as I would be privileged to discover later, a most openhearted host and inspiring thinker. He was at that time the Secretary General of the International Maritime Organization of the United Nations, and as he was on a mission and away from home, Shri Mataji was able to take time from her busy diplomatic schedule and related obligations to take care of me. I checked into a hotel nearby and spent most of that week in the company of Shri Mataji. In our conversations, I emptied my mental baggage, piece by piece: why are things in such a mess, why so much evil in the world and is there any way out? But it was not that straightforward and I probably took hours to put the case for those of us who were searching and felt lost, tired, mocked at and empty handed. The discussions were embellished with cups of chai tea and delicious Indian sweets. She listened very attentively and patiently. I found out she covered the most disparate subjects, from metaphysics to medical science and the arcane aspects of psychology with the greatest ease while at the same time, directing repair work in her house that had been entrusted to some English craftsmen who had initially arrived slightly drunk. I discovered to my delight that She was also an exceptional cook and although she had servants in the house, she cooked herself and the food she prepared was, to my sheer delight and amazement, a spectrum of new tastes.

In *The Advent*, privately published over twenty years ago, I tried to describe what happened during the days of this encounter. Shri Mataji led a sort of 'soul therapy.' Her knowledge was all penetrating and she mastered subjects from the most mundane to the subtler intricacies of ontology and cosmology but she did not speak like a university professor; she spoke very simply and directly, as someone who knows. It was fresh, enlightening, ground breaking and full of common sense. I felt that her knowledge was oriented towards us, ordinary people, and that the astounding depth of her psychological perspicacity was carried by a pervading benevolence and desire to comfort, counsel and heal. I also discovered her power to redeem, and with her compassion, knowledge and powers, through various sessions of guided meditation and 'chakra workshops', she awakened my Kundalini. I will try to summarize how I registered this process.

First, I experienced some vibrations flowing in my hands, which first caused a sensation of heat, tingling and a slight sense of burning in the fingers. As Shri Mataji worked on the plexuses along my spine, the flow stabilized, became cooler and it could be described as a light breath. She seemed to work mostly with her attention but also with her hands, making at times some concentric gestures towards the location of the chakras in my body. This took a couple of sessions because I was in a bit of a mess. Progress translated in the relaxation of the thought process, the waves of thoughts calmed down and a soothing silence settled in. Of course, at first, a thought came, such as, "Oh, I am not thinking!" but gradually the space between the thoughts increased, the sweet bath of lucid silence became more enveloping and a sense of ease and lightness spread in my body. I saw successive curtains of light moving and rising within my closed eyes but these movements of lights quietened down after some time. Finally a cool breeze emitted from the fontanel bone at the top of my head. "You've got it!" Shri Mataji said and she looked very happy indeed. This condition is intimate in its obviousness, in its direct sensation of physical and psychic wellbeing. When it deepened, it turned into a very tranquil force, a wonderful joy.

This experience was repeated over the course of the following days. In the same way that I know that fire burns and that water is wet, that is, through the sensations of my central nervous system, I, without particular skills or merits, experienced on my central nervous system the rising of my Kundalini leading to Self-realization.

Far from the auto-hypnotic attempts or psychic manipulations that I had witnessed previously, this experience was permeated by the joy of a higher reality, the reality. I came to understand that Shri Mataji had introduced me to that state of consciousness of *sammadhi* where existence, bliss and truth melt in one integrated and glorious condition of being. I finally had met someone who had the knowledge and could transmit the access code.

I remember a fine morning in August 1975, sitting on a suburban train between Hurst Green and London where we were going to join a small group of yogis. Shri Mataji Nirmala Devi was sitting in front of me. I had spent such intriguing and mind-boggling moments in her house during the days before, having felt levels of consciousness and bliss it is quite impossible to describe. I was fairly puzzled and asked quite simply: "Shri Mataji, who are you?" She responded by saying something like: "Open your hands, close your eyes and ask the question again," suggesting that I should ask through my meditation. I did so. A vast, expanding silence pervaded every aspect of me. "Dom-dom, dom-dom," the noise of the train was now coming to me from very far away. In that deep silence, it was as if I, myself was expanding. But it was sort of multi-dimensional and I felt that I had grown so that I had no size left. At the same time I had settled into a state of peace, which was almost tangible. After some time - I do not know how long it was - I opened my eyes again. Shri Mataji was smiling; she said "So?" I responded, "Nothing, Shri Mataji, just the silence." She said, "I am the silence." We arrived at Victoria Station and for the rest of the day, I had the feeling of being so light that I was literally wondering whether my feet were touching the ground; the quality of wellbeing throughout this day of shopping and meeting new friends in London was ecstatic. These states of higher awareness were simply beyond doubts. The perception was direct and the feeling was clear and intense.

So, who is Shri Mataji? Caiaphas asked Jesus: "Are you the Son of God?" When Jesus replied affirmatively, the Pharisees sent him to Pontius Pilate and to the Cross. Sometimes people ask and do not want to know; sometimes people ask and do not want to believe. But if we ask because we are genuinely interested and honest, then only in meditation can we get close to the answer, in a living and experimental manner. All else is mere words, and words are just that: ambivalent and unconvincing. The history of spirituality shows that spiritual masters are fought by the mainstream establishment when they are alive and worshipped when they are dead, in order to take advantage of their legacy. My advice to those who would like to know the truth about Shri Mataji's unique and historical advent on this earth is to get access to Self-realization through the proven techniques of Sahaja Yoga and to go deeper in meditation where responses unfold.

I must be candid about where I come from. There is something about diving into this chapter that may take the reader by surprise but I must honestly confess it. It is the depth of experience from the rising of my Kundalini that has made the whole picture very clear to me and I owe this experience solely to Shri Mataji. Of course, many teachers and religions say that theirs is the way and their converts are out on the streets telling others to join them. How is Sahaja Yoga different and why does it so deserve our attention? How do I persuade people from other religious traditions, atheists, agnostics, scientists, businessmen, people in pain or in a hurry to pay attention to this?

I do not know the answer. I can only share what my experience taught me. The good news is that there is a way, and a destination, and both are within each of us. The even better news is that I met this unique teacher who has the know-how and the power to transfer this knowledge to others. Millions have now felt this experience, with different shades of beauty and intensity, depending on the condition of their inner system. The bad news for me, at that time, was that I had been pretty damaged by my previous lifestyle and my chakras were consequently weak, my Kundalini wounded. I absolutely needed some 'tender loving care' to begin repairing my system. It was lucky for me that the guru was a mother. When the light of truth turns its blinding light, the spots hidden inside are exposed and I could only say as did the poet Tukarama: "It is Thy glory to be called Savior of the sinful; O preserve it for Thy own! The saints will call Thee the Lord of the helpless; when I heard this I took confidence. Make me not hopeless." [10]

I was not meditative by temperament but instead rather prone to action. I could easily become impatient and, sometimes angry, notably with myself. I also felt rather inept on the sainthood front and as a matter of fact, sometimes, in Shri Mataji's house, I was torn between my hopes and my apprehensions, doubting that I could make it. Having discovered that this higher state indeed existed did not mean I could stay in it all by myself, and this led to a truly spectacular moment.

I was about to leave England and had come to say goodbye. I must admit I was feeling quite dejected, as I did not know when or whether I would see Shri Mataji again. As I've mentioned, I worried as to how I could possibly maintain myself in the realized state. Shri Mataji sat in front of me, perhaps a yard away. She was observing me and must have followed the course of my disturbed thoughts and the rising of my self-doubt. I was holding my hands towards her to feel the vibrations, which I could not, at that moment, perceive very clearly. Then she just moved her hand and it all started.

The vibrations coming from her increased and felt cooler but soon my attention was taken by another sensation. The top of my head was coming alive and I had the sense of it opening, and it felt like the outpouring of an incredible liquid awareness. I became drenched in an inner lake of joy, which then coagulated into something that I can only describe as a solidified state of bliss. My eyes were closed and gradually, slowly, the cup overflowed and bliss started flowing down from my head into my whole body, filling every nerve. It was both a state and a sensation, both spiritual and physical. O my God! I could not even utter these words; but I was just the awareness beyond the words: It was a flow, a river of beatitude; something that literally and completely, in the parlance of the time, blew my mind. What I had known of

10 *The Poems of Tukarama*, Tr, J.N.Nelson and K.B. Fraser, Motilal Banarsidass, Delhi, (1881), p. 166.

the intensity of physical love seemed only a tiny inkling, a spark of this. It was a sacred moment, completely beyond description. No matter how little prepared or purified my inner system had been, I felt washed, healed, cared for and loved by the touch of this divinity within. This condition, as I say, was unlike anything I am capable of describing accurately but if I were to try to characterize it, I would say that it was, at its core, the sensation of being completely, absolutely real. Was it a stream of consciousness, a liquid joy, a nuclear bliss? Indeed, as it happened, I did not know yet, at this time, the words of Saint Jnaneshwar: "Contact with this bliss removes from the mind even the memory of desire. This bliss, which is the aim of Yoga and which is the final goal of all knowledge, is attainable even though encumbered by the body." [11]

When I opened my eyes Shri Mataji was smiling encouragingly and said something like: "You should not be sad." I realized She knew exactly what had happened within me. She was both majestic and so beautiful, her eyes full of warmth and love. I should not be sad, I understood, because I was leaving her house but taking this treasure within that she had revealed to me.

The taxi ride to Gatwick Airport and the flight back home were enveloped in a deep, soothing and regenerating silence. I was looking at places and people with a feeling of detachment and compassion. I was feeling rather humble and quiet, a bit like someone who is awed by the mystery of being alive after experiencing a mighty healing process. I had more confidence now that I could manage my recovery but I also knew that I needed to take care of myself, too. I had been given a chance and I did not intend to miss it or squander the opportunity. I could not possibly take this incredible gift for granted. For the world outside had not changed during these few extraordinary days in Hurst Green and I still needed to interact with it.

I remembered the old mythologies of India, where the demons fought the gods to win the elixir of ecstasy, the amrit or ambrosia. So, it was all true, it had happened and it could be felt. There is within us, the mechanism by which we can taste ambrosia, the drink of the gods. And if an ordinary person like me could access this experience, why not all those who would desire it? The striving of generations of code seekers for a higher consciousness was not irrelevant, utopian or to be ridiculed and it was all about a state that really did exist. This made a big difference for me. To look for something that exists, even if most of us would not find it, is not the same as looking for something that does not exist. I felt that all of us who had tried and failed before were vindicated. I really wanted to tell them all, including those who'd taken substances, drug addicts and alcoholics, "Please listen, there is a way," but I did not know how I could possibly say it.

I must say I find merit in quoting, in this book, some almost forgotten texts written hundreds of years ago. Modern men lost interest in them for they thought they do not make sense. Well, they do and after these events in England, I went many times to India, partly to find out more about those who knew about this. For instance, in his masterpiece of *Advaita Vedanta*, non dualist philosophy, entitled the *Vivekachudamani* or The Crest Jewel of Discrimination, the great Saint and Guru Shri Sankaracharya had this to say:

[11] *Jnaneshwar Gita*, Manu Subedar, SSM Trust, Ahmedabad, 4 ed, p. 57

"By this sammadhi are destroyed all desires which are like knots, all work is at an end, and inside and out there takes place everywhere and always the spontaneous manifestation of one's own real nature." [12]

I did understand that the "Everywhere and always" Shri Sankaracharya was talking about was not quite for me yet. Great saints, who prepare themselves and get their *sammadhi*, receive a definite experience and, I suppose, do not move from this stage. This is because they have already cleansed their inner system by years of practices. That purified inner system sustains the strength and permanence of the realized state. But the majority of those who receive the gift of Self-realization in these modern times did not have the opportunity to do so. They come to the experience, like I did, with the impact of all the hurdles and shortcomings of their life still captured within their inner channels and centers of energy. The realized condition can be accessed, which is an indescribable blessing and breakthrough. Shri Mataji explains that, "This is the experience the Buddha received under the boddhi tree but you are not the Buddha." We can receive this gift at this critical moment in time, space and history but depending on the state of the individual, some considerable meditation and yoga practices will be needed to restore the health and purity of our inner subtle system. We will come back to this in subsequent chapters.

I had to travel many roads to reach the front door of the house in Hurst Green. Not everybody needs to do so and some may even solve the puzzle while sitting in the comfort of their home. Perhaps those who kept their sanity in their search for God, or whatever we call Him, are going to be lucky. Many people, from common folks to scientists, may well have a feeling for God. Nature lovers may not be consciously seekers but they often strongly feel in their proximity to nature and their enjoyment of this world's tremendous beauty, the touch of its artist. Scientists, more aware of the universe's amazing dynamics and order, often feel the aesthetic mastery of a great architect. Those who keep the simplicity and the spontaneity of children in the sincerity of their prayers are and will be guided to the door of their own Self. They are surely closer to this lofty goal than those 'religious people' characterized by conformist dullness, insane and irrational devotion or fanatical outbursts of religiously motivated violence.

Naturally, in the years that followed, I desired to know more about Shri Mataji and her teachings known as Sahaja Yoga. Even if it challenged rational certainties, I had to be intellectually honest. I had to see the full implications of my experiences in Hurst Green. She had done it, she had delivered the highest initiation, she had proven to me to be this Master that all those who pray for guidance hope to meet one day on earth. And it was such a relief to discover that a Master of this caliber was also a very caring Mother, full of compassion and understanding.

Shri Mataji Nirmala Devi was born in 1923, at noon on the 21st of March in Chindawara in the center of India, in a Christian family of noble descent. When she was a young girl, Mahatma Gandhi recognized her deep and special qualities, and she often stayed at his ashram. Later she studied

---

[12] *Shankaracharya , Vivekachudamani or The Crest Jewel of Discrimination*, Swami Madhavananda, Indian Press Ltd. 9th ed, Calcutta (1974), p. 138.

medicine and took an active role in the movement for the independence of India. In 1947 Shri Mataji married Mr. C.P. Shrivastava. She then led for many years the life of a householder and mother. They have two married daughters, four grandchildren and two great-grandchildren.

On May 5th, 1970, at the seashore of Nargol, a beach near Mumbai, India, Shri Mataji witnessed in an extraordinary vision - the rising of the Primordial Force, the Adi Kundalini in an event that marked a milestone in the history of evolution. She recalls: "The experience was like this. I saw my Kundalini rising very fast like a telescope opening out and it was a beautiful color that you see when the iron is heated up, a red rose color, but extremely cooling and soothing."

By the early 1970s, Shri Mataji had evolved a unique system and the few first disciples got their initiation. These experiences were documented and recorded, sometimes by medical practitioners. Not only could the subtle feminine energy called Kundalini be spontaneously awakened, but also it could rise in the central channel of the spine through all the psychosomatic centers and pierce the seventh center on the top of the brain. Henceforth, in response to Eve's ancient curiosity, the serpent-like energy delivered indeed the secrets of the Tree of Life and of its fruits.

During all this time Shri Mataji also devoted herself to the education of her children and, from the 1970s onwards, she played host to the diplomatic community in London when her husband was elected to be head of the IMO. Mr. C.P. saw it as his mission to bring members of his organization together and to forge a consensus in support of dynamic new policy initiatives. The Queen of England knighted him and he received numerous orders, distinctions and international awards in recognition of his services. All the while, Shri Mataji was investigating the contemporary status of spiritual research, visiting preachers and gurus and developing through her then secret yogic powers a methodology to open the seekers' access to their secret instrument.

The name Sahaja Yoga means 'inborn union,' and it describes the natural and effortless manner in which the inner awakening occurs. What is amazing is that the same process can be passed on from person to person, and so to the whole world. Shri Mataji comments cheerfully: "As an enlightened candle enlightens another candle."

Hence Shri Mataji devoted her life to imparting this historic discovery as widely as possible. She has traveled the world in a punishing schedule of public addresses, programs and seminars that have resulted in the growing practice of this advanced meditation across all five continents. It is typical of her style that the many spiritual events she encouraged express a rich cultural diversity: high quality music festivals, theatre plays and dance, all displaying beautiful creativity and facilitating a tangible, deeper enjoyment of the spiritual self.

Every field of knowledge, at one time or another is covered by her attention and interest. But mostly she gives advice to assist us in developing the practices of meditation and introspection, the two pillars of yoga.

"What makes a guru great? Perhaps the most remarkable fact about Shri Mataji is that, not only does she 'deliver the goods' spiritually by granting Self-realization, but further, that she gives to all, at no cost, the guidance and knowledge to develop the very same powers which she possesses. In essence a great guru wishes the disciple or aspirant to become the best they can be."[13]

The positive changes that manifest in the individual from the practice of Sahaja meditation demonstrate that we truly have within ourselves the means to transform our lives. Thus Shri Mataji is confident that the human race can turn back from its destructive ways. In this respect, she tirelessly warns us of the pitfalls of our modern lifestyle, denounced in her brilliant essay on 'meta-modernity'.[14] The glance she casts on some of the prevailing trends in our society is very sharp indeed, yet full of humor, and her analyses are grounded in a refreshing, no-nonsense common sense.

More important than identifying problems, Shri Mataji proposes practical solutions. At the core of her message is the manifestation of collective en-masse Self-realization. The mastery over such a yogic feat obviously denotes the presence of a very high master. In fact, the followers of Shri Mataji worship her as an Avatar, that is, an instructor of mankind of divine descent.

Erich Fromm said once that giving is the highest form of potency and countless numbers of people have had extraordinary Kundalini experiences or extraordinary occurrences linked to her presence (*darshan*). Some recalled their past lives, some saw the future unfolding, many were healed and many more have documented a long series of miracles. But she is best likened to a mother and her patience and compassion that permeates her style and her work is permanent evidence of the genuine feelings she has for people who desire to progress on the path of inner improvement.

While New Age gurus are noted for picking the type of followers who will advance their cause, savvy operators and people with money and connections, Shri Mataji has visibly and completely ignored such considerations. Her followers come from all walks of life. Her 'organization' worldwide, such as it is, is lean and informal, relying on a word of mouth network. Its lack of material resources is in stark contrast to the economic empires, the considerable wealth and possessions accumulated by the false prophets of the last days of the Second Age. Hers is a genuinely grassroots movement and she was often seen sitting for seven consecutive hours on the same chair, in humble Indian villages, attending to huge throngs of devotees and healing the long procession of villagers seeking her comfort and blessings. Shri Mataji insists that the spreading of spiritual knowledge, as a matter of principle, cannot be sold or purchased and she relies exclusively on the work of volunteers to assist seekers reaching the gates of Sahaja Yoga. She has also encouraged charitable work and educational activities, notably for the benefit of lower income and destitute groups in India. At times, dogmatic rationalists, atheists or religious fundamentalists have joined hands in an odd partnership to find fault with Sahaja teachings. When this has happened, she has been completely unruffled, seeing these episodes as unavoidable, given the magnitude of the consciousness breakthrough that she proposes. Beyond the non-violence that would be expected from a person associated with Mahatma Gandhi, Shri Mataji believes in love as a force that can redeem societies, here and now. But how shall we learn to express our love?

[13] Geoffrey Godfrey, *The Divine Mother*, Life Eternal Trust, New Delhi (2000), p. 47.

[14] HH Shri Mataji Nirmala Devi, *Meta Modern Era*, Vishwa Nirmal Dharma, Bombay (1995).

WHAT IS TO BE DONE?

So now, O sons of the thought, listen to Me, to the speech of the Mother of your mercy, for you have become worthy of the mystery hidden from the beginning of the Aeons, so that you may receive it.

– Trimorphic Protonnoia, Gnostic text from the Nag Hammadi library.

Shri Mataji Nirmala Devi says: "You cannot know the meaning of your life without being connected to the power which created you." Villagers in India are not rejecting electricity because the man who discovered it, Thomas Edison, was an American foreigner. Are we going to ignore spiritual progress that results from discoveries made by an Indian woman? Can we accept that this is the age of cross-cultural fertilization in our global village? We need to dwell on this. Today, Shri Mataji's enormous contribution is being increasingly understood and her method has brought to spiritual knowledge the principles of scientific enquiry. Her work on Self-realization includes both the laying down of a scientific hypothesis and the verification of the hypothesis through experimentation. Self-realization is a phenomenon that happens and moreover, the experience of it is easily communicated.

This exceptional teacher has revealed in the mid-1970s a practical access to spiritual transformation. It relies on the spontaneous (sahaja) activation of our hitherto untapped spiritual potential. Her method has been trendsetting; today, she is a recognized spiritual figure worldwide whose message is focused on en masse Self-realization. For Shri Mataji, as for so many philosophers before her, the actualization of the Spirit within us is the goal of the human adventure. But she sees it in the most practical terms. "For what are you preparing my children, what are you seeking? It is your own growth that is important to you. Not what others are doing. What matters to you is your own development."

The state of the condition of our inner system, our behavior, relationships, mode of interactions with people depends on a complex and subtle coding stored in our chakras. Before the happening of realization, we are of course unaware of this, and we simply undergo different mental states and nervous conditions without understanding how or why they arise. We act and react but we are not in full control of ourselves.

Shri Mataji asserts that we have already within us an instrument ready to be awakened, to switch us into a deeper understanding of reality. Its purpose is to deliver our transformation, the access code indeed to the higher consciousness of which it was said in parabolic terms: "Verily, verily, I say unto thee, except a man be born again he cannot see the kingdom of God. Except a man be born of water and the Spirit, he cannot enter in the kingdom of God. That which is born of the flesh is flesh; and that which is born of the Spirit is spirit." (John 3:3.5.6).

The psychosomatic and spiritual instrument, (*yantra*), through which we experience our second birth, is not an arbitrary structure and all the code seekers can gradually learn and use the corresponding inner technique (*tantra*). It was built and pre-positioned in us for a purpose.

In other words, what is to be done is to obtain Self-realization. The possibility for mankind to get Self-realization is a threshold in the evolutionary process. It relies on the spontaneous activation of untapped spiritual potential. Self-realization is the moment when we can perceive directly this divinity within ourselves and connect with the Whole.

We have finally identified the likely location of the gate to the other side of another dimension of existence, but what is the rite of passage? Shri Mataji demonstrates how, after realization the human microcosmic computer is wired to the cosmic program, and the data starts to flow in our nervous system, to be felt as vibrations. The personality, even the destiny, of each human being depends on the quality of the relationship between his or her spiritual instrument and the cosmic archetype.

But what is the Whole? Is the cosmic archetype a kind of First Model or, as proposed in the *Bhagavad Gita*, a living entity, the Integrated Primordial Being called Virata in Sanskrit, of which the human inner system would be a reflection? It was reported that the Virata encompasses everything that exists. We could perhaps say, by analogy, that it is to the universe what an operating system is to a computer.

As a matter of fact, the knowledge of Sahaja Yoga reveals the link between the microcosm and the cosmic. In each of us, the Tree of Life is the replica, perfectly miniaturized, of the Virata, a first imprint or Gestalt. This primordial archetype is venerated in different ways by all humanity. It is called God and He intervenes in history, but He does so mostly through the movement of evolution, from lower to higher forms of awareness. He does so through 'software,' stored within us, which is a projection of His own attributes. Order and change in the cosmos depend upon the interactions between different forms of a higher energy that our ancestors, in their wisdom, perceived as Divinity.

The *Bhagavad Gita* of the *Mahabharata*, the central Hindu epic, relates how Shri Krishna revealed to his disciple Arjuna the awesome vision of this Primordial Being, the Virata. It can be imagined in the Platonic sense as that which pre-exists this material universe that we know. It is the original Gestalt, that is, the reference framework from which all shapes, rules, and meanings flow. It is also a totally holistic entity integrating all global processes; it is the absolute software and mainframe, storing all knowledge and information. The greatness of the First Age, the age of the Father, recognized in Platonic thought, can be said to have revealed the Virata.

In the *Gita* there is a description of the functioning of the Primordial Being or Virata which matters to us because it reveals the very functioning of what we call God but also it reveals an important secret: man's inner psychosomatic system in some mysterious way reflects that archetypal structure. In other words, according to Shri Mataji, the original cosmic structure of the Virata is completely reproduced at the microcosmic level, in each one of us. Even more amazingly, this interior instrument of our inner improvement delivers the second birth. According to Gnostic teachings, we carry in us the filigree image of the cosmos; and the design of our Creator is imprinted in our soul. We are each a miniaturized Gestalt of the Virata and we carry within us the interior instrument for the transformation of our awareness.

"Allah Hu Akbar!" God is great, God is One, affirm the great religions, and the monolithic aspect of this unity is symbolized in architecture by sacred stones: by the *lingam* of Shiva in Pashupatinath near Katmandu or the black Kaaba stone of Mecca. However, seen under a super microscope, a stone is seething with the activity of trillions of atoms and in saying, "God is Energy," we remind ourselves that energy is convertible; it may be used in manifold ways. Unity does not exclude a plurality of manifestations; universality contains the particular. A single human body contains hundreds of billions of cells, organized into numerous organs in order to carry out multiple tasks. The human being that dwells therein is even more complex in the many forms of his or her mental and emotional life.

In the same way, the idea of the oneness of God does not imply that He only has one aspect or attribute, or that He only exercises one function. In the Hindu tradition God is both male and female and projects countless manifestations (*avatars*). In the Christian tradition, God is embodied in three forms (the Trinity of the Father, the Son and the Holy Ghost). In Islam or Buddhism, God is formless (*nirakar*).

He is not a static Being. Shri Mataji describes: "Him who is omnipresent and omniscient, who controls all things, who is at once smaller than an atom and more vast than the Cosmos, He is infinitely more complex than Man in His manifestation while remaining perfectly integrated." And "when the One started to manifest His multiple aspects, the Creation was set in motion." And "the material universe that we know is only a momentary glimpse of this manifestation."

We can symbolize history by an elliptical motion, drawing away from an initial point only to return there. This means that if, through the creation, God moves from the infinite, (Himself) to the finite, (His creation), one can conceive a contrary motion, that the finite might, in its turn, return to the dimension of infinity. Human Self-realization would then mark this turning point on the ellipse as well as the opening of the Third Age. The message that spirituality is a matter of personal experience comes out clearly as the paradigm of the Third Age.

That is what all the different religions of the world tried to show, as their founders wished to prepare man to participate in this scheme and receive Self-realization. At a certain stage in evolution, highly evolved saints, having become conscious of the greater potential of their brains, proclaimed their own aspiration to the 'great return,' echoing the *Aranyaka Upanishad*: "Send me to the world which I desire. Send me to that world. Send me towards the All." The period of the Last Judgment, as explained in Chapter 18, is the turning point.

The Virata is not a purposeless personality. His desire is to share His bliss and love with His creation. If hell is a state of mind, heaven is not. It is reality itself, as C.S. Lewis claims in *The Great Divorce*. The problem is: how to access the heavens? This is where mistakes start. The most common one is the attempt to force the narrow gate, or to sing in the manner of Frank Sinatra's rendition of *My Way*. 'My' way is the way of ego. We must do it 'His' way, the way of Reality.

Playing at the game of recognition is a bit like surfing on a wave off a Hawaiian beach, knowing how to ride the wave and not forcing one's will on it. We may join the game but we cannot control it. We must tap into a greater store of knowledge, an infinite supply of energy and not impose our finite perspective. Humility is the key to the door. The great religious traditions emphasized the need for man to learn how to let things happen. Zen teachers derided the futility of voluntary attempts and the Beatles sang, "Let it be." What is to be done is just to let it happen. If we can just do that, the realization of the age-old prophecy of the advent of the Golden Age, a time of enjoyment and blessings, will be brought much closer.

KNOW THYSELF

To see a World in a Grain of Sand,
And heaven in a Wild flower,
Hold Infinity in the palm of your hand
And Eternity in an hour.

– William Blake

I am enjoying seeing my teenage children grow and am fascinated by their process of self-discovery. My younger daughter observed the other day: "It is strange, I do not know who I am." She sounded puzzled. The emerging preoccupation of teenagers with themselves and the definition of their identity may, at times, appear narcissistic, but it is a beautiful expression of their capacity to wonder. My son feels he is on the way to meeting someone and looks interrogatively at that person in the mirror of his bathroom. A live curiosity is healthy and discovery is an adventure; it is a play and we must find the rules. What makes some adults so boring is their acceptance of self-ignorance, no vision, no blessed little grain of folly to challenge the systematic dullness of a world seemingly under control. You cannot tell such people to get a life for they do not know they do not have one. The guy who shaves in the mirror wondering: "What am I doing here?" is in tune with the *Kena Upanishad* and Socrates: this is a question worth asking.

Spirituality is man's quest for understanding himself and his environment more deeply, recognizing his origin and identifying its destination. It is because spiritual knowledge is strategic for society that powerful rulers or clerical leaders so often confiscated it and neutralized it through simplified dogmas. It is because it is so strategic that modern man, or better, the meta modern man must make some sense out of it. It would be most paradoxical that man should have developed his mastery over all provinces of knowledge but would accept being stuck in the shallowness of half revealed truths and unfinished teachings corresponding to conditions of societies long gone, that he would give up looking for the answers to questions such as, "Who am I?" or "What is to be done?"

In the *Bible*, God said, "Let us make man in our image, after our likeness." (Genesis 1, v. 26). The protector of Voltaire, King Frederic II of Prussia mused about it: "One speaks a lot about the fact that we, kings, are the very image of God on earth. I thus examined myself in a mirror and am obliged to say that I am really sorry for God." Frederic the Great was not that great a reflection because human reason does not reflect His image but project its own shape. It is the silence of meditation that creates the mirror. When

Socrates went to find out exactly what the Delphic Oracle knew on the subject, the answer came back: "Know thyself." Socrates was the first psychologist and prominent guide of Western thought to suggest that spiritual, and indeed most other answers, can be found by looking inside. This must be compared with the message of the world's most ancient civilization: the cornerstone of a Hindu's faith may be taken to be the achievement of the beatitude of merging in a World Soul, or rather a soul of all the universe, *Paramatma* the Supreme.

Spirit or Atma, it is reported, is the spark of divinity in man, and spirituality is about lighting it. The spark to enlighten the flame of the Spirit must be more than just the sincere desire to reach our deepest reality. Religious, philosophical and Gnostic traditions emphasize that experience, and not just faith, embodies the description of a cognitive happening, a moment of initiation, which opens to us the gates of a higher spiritual knowledge. It is called *'sammadhi'* for the Hindu, *'satori'* for the Zen Buddhist or the 'second birth' Christ mentions to Nicodemus. Today, it is commonly referred to as Self-realization. Self-realization must be understood in two ways: it is the crossing of a key threshold in the process of self-improvement. It is also a breakthrough in the collective evolution of mankind. Self-realization opens vast provinces of experience whose beauties have been sung by ancient poets. Let it suffice to say here that it marks the entry into a state where we grasp better, enjoy more and become more effective.

10. HOW DOES IT WORK?

He who knows others is wise; he who knows himself is enlightened.

— Lao Tzu

The greatest thing in the world is to know how to be one's own self.

— Michel Eyquem de Montaigne

The conception of Spirit involves its being regarded as inherently, intrinsically universal. It is not the individuality of the subject that is revered but that which is universal in him; and which among the Tibetans, Hindus and Asiatic generally is regarded as the essence pervading all things.

— G.W.F. Hegel

Saint Thomas is famous – or infamous – for having said: "I'll believe it when I see it." If I were to meet with Thomas, I would have to admit some sympathy for him. Skepticism can be a healthy thing and when Rajesh wanted to give me my initiation in the meadow above the observatory of San Francisco, I didn't really want it and preferred instead to check it out myself at the source and hence took a plane to London.

This tale would, maybe, provide material for a nice piece of fiction but I assert again that crossing the movie screen of our perceptions and getting Self-realization is not a fiction, it really can be done. This is not based on just a few days in Surrey but on everything that has happened between then and now. When Sahaja Yogis work on me to help clear catches, i.e., obstructions on the chakras, I feel almost instant physical relief. We can even feel this relief in the company of realized children who have the force but do not even know about it. The areas of tension in my being melt away, I enjoy a pleasant feeling of relaxation, and then the blissful silence indicating that my Kundalini has risen above the sixth center. Being in the midst of a crowd of realized people, I find myself at times, in an incredible tornado of happiness and love. The other day, when my secretary brought her newborn baby to me, I went immediately into thoughtless awareness. I was enjoying the purity of the vibrations of this beautiful little girl, born realized. It may sound odd if at this stage, you don't yourself know if she is or if she isn't. My skeptical friend may not wish to listen nor want to know or even to desire this. But the description of the difference in a life protected by the Grace and a life that may be visited by emptiness, confusion, numbness and fear, without awareness of vibrations, has already been sketched out in Part Three.

What is explained in this chapter is the fruit of direct experience through a combination of approaches consisting of meditation, introspection and working on the chakras with the techniques of Sahaja Yoga; the resulting know-how and discoveries build up an experimental body of knowledge. We also have access to the considerable amount of knowledge communicated by Shri Mataji in countless lectures on audio and videotape. The content of these teachings can be verified by one's own response and by one's own inner awareness. All this amounts to a sort of psycho science that is not subjective. Many others, similarly endowed with the new awareness, can independently verify it.

I will just give my dear friend, the skeptic, one more example. One day in London, in one of the countless sessions that she granted so benevolently, Shri Mataji was working on a Sahaja Yogi and there was a blockage on the finger corresponding to the right side of the throat chakra. We were sitting around him, all feeling the same pressure in our corresponding finger. Shri Mataji told him: "Your father must be down with a bad dose of bronchitis." At the end of the session, somewhat intrigued, our friend picked up the telephone and called home to Scotland. His mother came to the phone and told him, word for word: "Your father cannot come to the phone; he is in bed with a bad dose of bronchitis."

Sahaja Yogis are those who have entered collective consciousness. They are sensitive to the condition of other people, in ways mostly closed to the rest of us. In this particular case, the young man was feeling in his own system the impact of the condition of his father, hundreds of miles away. The advantage is that we also learn how to free our chakras from such interferences. Medical science has not yet reached the level where it can register such psychosomatic phenomena but that does not mean such phenomena do not exist. As shown in the book by Dr. Marlo Morgan, recalling her experiences in Australia,[15] the indigenous Australians, the Aborigines, still have sensitivity to subtler vibratory phenomena. They can communicate over considerable distances in a telepathic manner, find the location of water underground, heal with the hands and use vibrations to select which plants and animals to eat.

THE TREE OF LIFE

Sell your cleverness and buy bewilderment.
    — Jalal Ud-Din Rumi

Shri Jnaneshwar is acknowledged as one of the greatest teachers in matters of spiritual yoga. In his commentary on the *Gita*, Shri Krishna is reported to have told Arjuna: "Under the tree of Yoga are lying millions of fruits in the form of salvation. The Lord Shiva himself treads the path of pilgrimage to this tree. In the first instance, numerous ascetics wander in the byways of their hearts, but by constant practice, they reach the proper path. When the high road of the wisdom of Self is seen, the yogis leave all other paths of ignorance and pursue it. The big sages have followed this path. The wise men as well as the great teachers have all reached attainment on this path. Reaching this path, a man forgets hunger and thirst and does not even remember the difference between day and night. Wherever he sets foot, he strikes a mine of liberation. Even if one strays from this path a little, the bliss of heaven is at hand…. It is no use talking about this. You will experience this yourself."[16]

The French poet, Paul Valery, observed that man is not an exact solution to the problem of existing. Mythology, religion, philosophy, psychology, and even the exact sciences are different avenues by which human research seeks the solution. Our forefathers studied the different levels of manifestation of the elusive primordial reality, aiming at a global understanding of life and thence discovering successful approaches for managing it. However, in the past, each civilization or culture tended to single

[15] Marlo Morgan, *Mutant Message Down Under*, Harper Collins Publishers, New York.

16 Shri Jnaneshwar, The Gita Explained, Manu Subedar, SSM Trust, 4th ed, Ahmednagar, (1972), p.54

out one particular aspect of such manifestations to the neglect of the others. Only now, benefiting from ongoing research, can we attempt to answer the enigma of the Delphic Oracle and to find the relationship between the complete morphology of a Divine Primordial Being and man's psychosomatic structure. Thus spirituality moves towards science. In a very concrete sense, enhanced mastery of spirituality means enhanced mastery of the material world in which we move every minute of our lives.

In the Indian cosmology, God means: Generator (Brahmadeva and his power or wife Saraswati); Operator (Vishnu and his power Lakshmi); and Destroyer (Shiva and his power Parvati), although Shiva is also Existence and Love. We are more concerned here with the 'Vishnu principle' that is, the aspect which operates the cosmos and guides evolution. In an incarnation of Vishnu worshipped in India as Shri Krishna, God showed to the disciple Arjuna his full Being as Virata. As said earlier, we may translate this as the integrated form of the Whole: the Virata whose structure, as we shall see, is reflected within the human microcosm.

Taking as a hypothesis the proposed link between the original cosmic structure and the psychosomatic support of our everyday life, we shall now try to describe these linkages in more detail. Figure 1 is an anthropomorphic depiction of the Virata within us. In this figure we distinguish three energy channels (*nadis*) and the seven energy centers (chakras), a coiled spiral in the triangular sacrum bone (representing the Kundalini energy), and a flame, located in the heart, representing the Spirit (Atma). Each of these four elements of what can be defined as the 'subtle system' will be briefly discussed below.

Of course the Virata transcends our dimensions and limitations, existing in a state of energy-consciousness, which we cannot conceive. However, consciousness makes experiments, and it is the way of evolution to lead us thus along the path of experimental consciousness. We can summarize by saying that, in many spiritual traditions, before creating the material Universe in which we live, the Primordial Divine Energy created the Gestalt of the Virata, which integrates and manifests the different aspects of the highest reality. On the cosmic level, this archetype directs the universal evolution, and on the microcosmic level, it controls our inner becoming.

The three channels can be viewed as the central operating system of the Virata, and the seven centers of energy as the main pillars of its evolutionary program; that is, the iterative scheme in store for the cosmos and the microcosm alike. The program is gradually implemented as the Kundalini passes through the various chakras on the central channel, triggering new steps of evolution. This process is an actualization of the primary objective of the Virata: to project through the creation a gradually more focused and accurate picture of itself. This understanding of the purpose of creation and of the destiny of our race corresponds to a resolutely optimistic sense of history, because the encounter with such a reality is a promise of excellence and superior wellbeing. *Sattwa Yuga*, the Age of Truth, is in sight. Human awareness and society is undergoing a tremendous process of change to join in this play of self-actualization of the Virata in history. According to the hypothesis presented by Shri Mataji Nirmala Devi, the mechanisms which structure the cosmos are reflected and reproduced in Man.

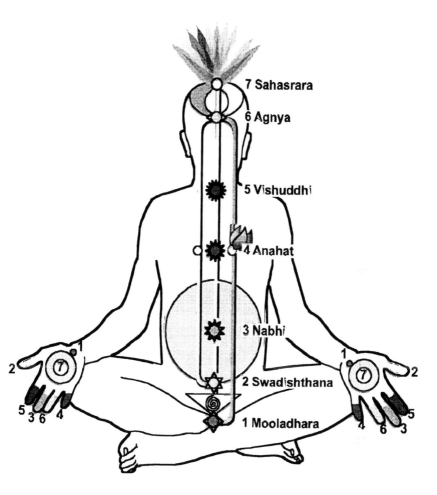

1. Mooladhara Chakra	*Innocence, wisdom*
2. Swadishthana Chakra	*Creativity, aesthetics*
3. Nabhi Chakra	*Peace, harmony*
3a. Void (Bhavsagar)	*Knowledge*
4. Anahata Chakra	*Security, love*
5. Vishuddhi Chakra	*Collectivity, diplomacy*
6. Agnya Chakra	*Insight, forgiveness*
7. Sahasrara Chakra	*Integration, union/yoga*

Figure 1. The Cosmic Structure

Forming the center of the trunk of the Tree of Life, the *nadis* or channels carry the triple forms of energy. The *Sushumna nadi*, the central channel, caters to the growth of the tree. The *Ida nadi* on its left carries the energy of the earth from the roots to the branches, flowers and fruits; the *Pingala nadi* on its right carries the energy of the sun that is absorbed by the leaves to the whole tree. The *Ida nadi* is existence, desire and emotions, the *Pingala nadi* is doing, creativity and thinking, and the *Sushumna nadi* is sustenance, wisdom, peace and the balance that opens the middle path of Lao Tzu and Confucius.

In this analogy, the roots of the tree represents our deeper spiritual and mostly invisible dimensions within. The inner yoga (Antar yoga) caters to the health of the roots and insures that this spiritual dimension nourishes the leaves, our actions, and the fruit that represents our achievements. The branches, leaves and the fruit represent our manifestation in the world, our more familiar and visible dimensions within the material world. The yoga of action (Karma or Krita yoga) makes sure that the product of our actions does not just fritter and dissipate away. But our actions and interactions with family, co-workers and society further contribute to a continuous investment in our own personal growth. The first movement of yoga, from the roots to the branches, is contemplative and constructs our vertical dimension, the inside, and builds our being. The second movement, from the leaves to the roots, is creative and expands our horizontal dimension, the outside. It manifests our being. Both movements contribute to the harmonic growth of the tree. The beauty of Sahaja Yoga is that these energies circulate spontaneously, because the serpent that was previously coiled around the trunk has now risen to catalyze and harmonize the process.

In the past, it was extremely difficult for practitioners of yoga to achieve the right balance between these movements of energy, that is, between contemplation and action. A tree without leaves represents an ascetic who tries to grow by taking care only of the inner dimension, and his goal will elude his efforts. A tree with branches that are too large represents a man totally invested in external action, with a shallow spiritual basis. The overgrowth of the branches is likely to make the tree unstable and cause it ultimately to fall down. Shri Mataji applied this analogy to society itself: "It is extremely difficult for me to write about the problems of western life. It is like a tree, which has grown outside. This is now to be pushed down to the roots and made to grow inside. It is only by going deep inside that we can find out what the problems of western civilization are." [17]

---

[17] HH Shri Mataji Nirmala Devi, *Meta Modern Era*, Vishwa Nirmal Dharma, Bombay (1995), Preface, p. 1.

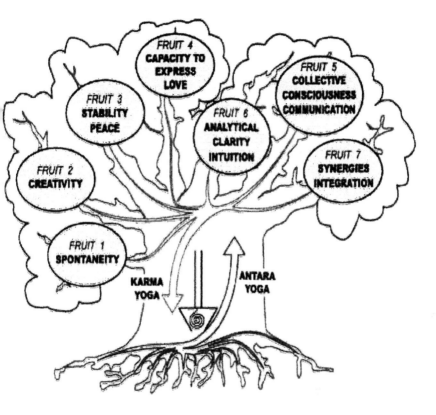

Figure 2. Tree of Life

The Tree of Life (Figure 2) is more often represented poetically in another fashion whereby its mystical fruit and flowers are represented by the chakras, although the representation is not as precise as in Figure 1. There are seven main chakras in the human microcosm. They correspond to:

• A specific aspect of the Virata that is reflected in our subtle system. The reflection of the quality of the primordial being within is improved when the chakras are cleansed by the Kundalini. We will come back to this in the following chapters.

• A particular adaptive and energizing function in the everyday life of the individual. When the spiritual energy of the chakras is awakened by Kundalini, the chakras start emitting positive energy with beneficial results at the physical, mental, emotional and spiritual levels.

• A specific degree of actualization of our evolutionary potential. The growth of our capacities and awareness depends upon the gradual opening of our chakras. Through our many incarnations we are on this course for the long haul, and the only memory we store of our past lives is unconscious to us because it is stored in the chakras, in the Kundalini, and not in the brain. The gradual expression of the subtler qualities contained in the chakras contributes to draw on all the lessons learnt and provide for the manifestation of a higher, transformed personality.

After realization, the qualities of the seven energy centers are activated. The Kundalini spontaneously labors to perfect the conformity of these qualities with their perfect essences contained in the centers of the Virata. We might say in more abstract terms that the Kundalini works to increase the vibratory resonance between the primordial chakras of the cosmos and the corresponding chakras in the human being.

This hypothesis of the relationship between the nervous system of the individual and the cosmic structure of the Virata is only confirmed after realization. The practical implications are many. Firstly, most people who have gone through the experience of Self-realization gradually have found that their inner system had been already damaged by the lifestyle they had led. The accumulated consequences of all our errors, sins and good deeds are recorded on the chakras and this information is known by the Kundalini. All of us make mistakes, of course, and the damage at the inner spiritual level is expressed through their outer manifestation in our every day lives. These may have caused health problems, troubles associated with psychosomatic malfunctions. Sahaja Yogis find that meditation practices can restore the condition of the chakras. The different chakras respond to the utterance of prayers, invocations or mantras to their controlling principles or Deities. Healthy chakras maintain our psychological and moral integrity.

Perhaps a useful way to introduce the relevance of the chakras in our everyday life would be to discuss the all too common conditions in which we find ourselves when the chakras do not function properly, when they are constricted by the pull or push from the lateral channels. Damaged chakras cause dysfunctional behavior and make us vulnerable to various types of subtle aggressions. We may refer here to what our ancestors called the six enemies of the soul: lust, anger, greed, attachment, jealousy, and vanity. In short, these enemies represent some forms of psychic addictions. Perhaps therapists who focus today on the visible damage done to mental health by substance addictions do not always realize that psychic addictions traditionally played a formidable role in hampering man's perfectibility. Modern 'workaholics' for instance, are more likely to experience a breakdown than a breakthrough. Parents who are workaholics, for example, are responsible for many broken families and frustrated children. It is a consequence of over-activity of the Swadishthan chakra that will ultimately lead to health problems. Meditation can restore balance to the chakra and thus improve the corresponding behavior and related problems.

The positive impact of Sahaja Yoga meditation is not just hypothesis; Dr. Ramesh Manocha, at the Royal Hospital for Women in Sydney, Australia, is one of the scientists that has proved this in clinical tests. His work has shown positive results using Sahaja Yoga on a variety of conditions as disparate as stress, asthma, migraine, menopausal symptoms and Attention

Deficit Disorder. In fact, IBM is now using his methods in Australia as a means of coping with Executive Stress.

Thanks to the manifestation of the inner instrument, our attention becomes aware and can focus on our inner moral condition and psychosomatic constitution. The Holy Koran warns: "On that day you will be exposed to the full light of day; not one of your secrets will remain hidden." (69;V; 18) In her penetrating analysis of Islam, Flore Descieux comments: "The Book of Action held by the two angels is the subtle body, records all our actions, good or bad, through our former lives up to the present date. During our present life the angels continue to record the products of our behavior, the signals which appear on our left and right sympathetic channels as well as on other chakras." [18]

She quotes Shri Mataji's teachings in explaining the roles of Gabriel (known as Hanuman in India) and Michael (known as Bhairava in India), the great Archangels, who act as facilitators on the *Pingala nadi* and *Ida nadi* respectively.

Connotations of Judgment Day are threatening for Christian and Muslim alike but when the Mother is the inner judge, she, as the Kundalini, mercifully erases the tapes of our negative conditionings and bad karma. Rather than bringing a punitive judgment, she helps us to face ourselves, that is, to face this inner judgment. Her day is the day of redemption!

THE WHEELS OF LIGHT

We shall briefly describe here the chakras. The prophet Ezekiel saw the chakras as wheels of light that move about. Kabir tells us, "Within this earthen vessel, the body, are gardens and groves, and within it is also the Lord; within this vessel, the body, are the seven oceans and countless stars." Guru Nanak (1459-1538) speaks about mysterious self-fulfilling flowers inside us.

This book does not attempt a full presentation of the science of the chakras and this table is extremely schematic and simplified. In fact, each chakra gradually manifests a full range of qualities and the opening of the different chakras develops combined or synergistic effects. It would take a separate book to adequately describe these processes. On the other hand, the malfunction of one or more chakras generates psychic disorders as well as possible medical consequences. Targeted meditation practices, based on the knowledge of the inner system, can thus achieve a fundamental recovery of the whole personality and deploy a variety of therapeutic effects. For many of us, bruised in life by a bumpy journey, managing our own recovery on a sound basis is a first priority.

The relationship between the chakras and health is a rich topic for further study and for future books. The healing process can be understood as follows. When the chakras are connected to the *Sushumna nadi* through a condition of equilibrium, they supply the energy of the parasympathetic system to all the parts of the body and play both a supply and regulatory function. When excessive behaviors disconnect a chakra from the center, these functions are hampered. For instance, in a person who is active, the

[18] Flore Descieux, *The Light of the Koran*, Ritana Books, New Delhi (1998), p. 114.

107

THE CENTERS OF ENERGY (CHAKRAS)

	Sanskrit Name	Place in Central Nervous System	Physical Organs Controlled	Emotional and Spiritual Qualities
1	Mooladhara Chakra	Pelvic plexus, coccyx	Sexual and excretory organs	Spontaneity, innocence, straight forwardness, magnetism, wisdom,
1a	Mooladhar	Sacrum bone		Kundalini; pure desire, power to evolve
2	Swadishthan	Aortic plexus, adrenaline glands	Liver (part), spleen, kidneys pancreas	Creativity, mental abilities, art, aesthetics
3	Nabhi	Solar plexus	Liver (part), intestine	Consciousness, peace, well-being, sense of morality, satisfaction
3	Void		Stomach	Capacity to guide and teach, knowledge, gravity
4	Anahata	Cardiac plexus	Heart, lungs	Selfless love, confidence, sense of security, joy
5	Vishuddhi	Thyroid gland	Throat, mouth, ears, nose, arms, hands	Communication, diplomacy, detachment, collective consciousness, vibratory awareness
6	Agnya	Pineal and pituitary gland	Optic chiasma, vision organs	Clarity and purity of vision, analysis and intuition, power to forgive
7	Sahasrara	Fontanel bone area	Brain	Realization, integration, liberation, truth

Swadishthan chakra moves to the right side (*Pingala nadi*) and disconnects from the center. The supply of energy from the *Pingala nadi* is gradually drained out. The Swadishthan chakra no longer supplies the energy from the *Sushumna nadi* and this process is then accelerated by the intense mental activity of planners or thinkers. Indeed, Shri Mataji says, this chakra supplies energy to the grey matter of the brain and because of this chakra's displacement and of the channeling of energy to the brain, which makes the heaviest demands, the supply of energy to the other parts of the body controlled by the Swadishthan is insufficient. Our engine then starts heating up, so to say, without lubricant. This heat can travel to the lungs and cause asthma; to the spleen, where it triggers blood cancer; to the pancreas, where it causes diabetes; to the kidneys, where it causes the failure leading to dialysis with possibly fatal consequences.

The curative principle of chakra therapy is extremely simple. The meditation practice of a realized soul reconnects the chakras with the *Sushumna*, thereby accessing the energy store of the Kundalini. It re-establishes the proper balance of energy flows. A range of meditation techniques and specific methods apply to address the problems of various chakras, depending on the psychosomatic symptoms of the illness. A number of physicians are presently doing research on the subject and have reported positive results, which have been scientifically monitored by controlled experiments on various groups of patients. It has been reported that the incidences of cures are higher in the sample of patients following the curative principles of Kundalini awakening than in the control groups.

THE RIVERS OF ENERGY

I am I can I wish.

— Gurdjieff

The triple expression of the primordial energy, which controls the three modes of operation of the Virata also control, on a grosser level, the three parts of our autonomic nervous system. The left sympathetic nervous system is controlled by the power of existence, the *Tamo guna* or *Ida nadi*; the heart is the chief physical organ sustaining it. The right sympathetic nervous system is controlled by the power of creation, the *Rajo guna* or *Pingala nadi*; the liver is the main organ sustaining it. The parasympathetic nervous system is controlled by the evolutionary power, the *Sattwa guna* or *Sushumna nadi*, and the brain is the principal organ on this channel. Thus the entire complex primordial structure of the Virata is imprinted on our human microcosms, waiting for its realization.

The whole structure of the Virata is ordered around its principal energy channel, the *Adi Sushumna*, which represents the way of becoming, the energy of evolution, with its presiding Deity, Mahalakshmi. It is flanked on the left by the *Adi Ida*, the primordial channel of emotional energy, the presiding deity being Mahakali, and on the right by the *Adi Pingala*, the channel of creative energy, the presiding Deity being Mahasaraswati. And so it is for us. The three main energy channels (*Ida*, *Pingala*, and *Sushumna*) represent the three principal modes of operation of the energy within the Virata. They are said in the *Bhagavad Gita* to correspond to the moods (*gunas*) of the Virata, to its three principal qualities. Let us summarize:

1. The channel of Desire, the *Ida nadi* in the Virata (*Tamo guna*, mood of stillness, passivity of the Virata) is related, within ourselves, to the heart and the power of emotions. In Chapter 5 we surveyed the consequences of the malfunctions of this channel, in terms of the sorry state of modern families and societies, and the degradation of the environment.

2. The channel of Action, *Pingala nadi* in the Virata (*Rajo guna*, mood of creation, activity of the Virata) is related, within ourselves, to the liver and the power of the intellect. In Chapter 6 we sketched the consequences of the malfunctions of this channel on our work place, professional context and economic system.

3. The channel of Evolution, *Sushumna nadi* of the Virata (*Sattwa guna*, mood of harmony, revelation through evolution) is related, within ourselves, to the brain and the evolutionary power. In Chapter 7 we tried to show how the malfunctions of this channel have an effect on our awareness and analytical abilities, on the media, advertising and entertainment industries.

The three *gunas* can be superficially characterized as follows:

Tamo guna represents the desire of existence, which pervades the entire cosmos and controls the right side hemisphere of the brain. It is found in the nucleus of each atom, electromagnetic forces in matter, and the vital force in plants, animals and in man, where it controls particularly the emotional being and determines the orientation of our desires. In philosophical writings we find it again as the thesis of Hegel's *Phenomenology of Spirit*, the Yin of the Taoists, nature as opposed to culture, and so on. In the history of art, we see that baroque architecture, romantic literature, poetry, and music express the *Tamo guna*. Temperaments that tend to approach knowledge through the sublimation of this field are said to be more emotional and intuitive. The negative side of *Tamo guna* is darkness; the force of inertia, which opposes self-improvement; or an excess of passion.

Rajo guna represents the will for action and creation and covers the left hemisphere of the brain. It manifests that aspect of the Virata which engenders the causal essences, the elements, the material universe including the constellations, and our solar system. At the theoretical level this field was perceived as the Yang of the Taoists or the antithesis of Hegelian dialectics. It is expressed as culture or civilization as opposed to primitive nature, and it characterizes the ordered, classical, and cerebral aspect of western aesthetic sensibility. Man has magnified this field by his rationality, which has produced law, social organization, science, and technology. Those who try to approach knowledge through this field are said to be more rational and analytical. The negative side of *Rajo guna* takes the form of agitation, aggression, oppression, domination and dry sterility.

Sattwa guna is the dimension through which the Virata aims to reveal itself gradually in the cosmos, determining the universal evolution and the growth of consciousness to guide mankind along the middle path. It is thus the state of balance, of integration and revelation, above and beyond the oscillations between *Rajo* and *Tamo gunas*. It is the Hegelian synthesis, expressed by man as musical harmony, and in the great rhythmic masterpieces of art and architecture. Each manifestation of balanced and mature behavior expresses the coefficient of *Sattwa guna*. In this mood, the subject is contented and exerts a benevolent influence on his environment. Perhaps the only negative aspect of *Sattwa guna* is that, in this contented state, the drive for higher achievements might be lost. When the Kundalini rises it attracts the attention of the individual into the *Sushumna* where the potential for ascent and fulfillment is actualized.

The presentation of this system was already contained in the *Bhagavad Gita*, one of the oldest sacred scriptures of mankind. What is new is the possibility of doing something concrete with this information, something we can bring to use in our daily lives.

THE SERPENT OF FIRE

When the sleeping Kundalini is awakened, by the grace of the Guru, then all the lotuses (the chakras) and knots (granthi) are pierced.

 — Hathayoga Pradipika, chapter 3 verse 2 1893

Like a young serpent bathed in red pigment resting twisted around itself, this small serpent power, the Kundalini, is asleep ...in three-and-a-half coils. She is like a streak of lightening or a flood of flame, or a polished band of pure gold.

 — Shri Jnaneshwar, The Jnaneshwari Sixth Chapter

Western writers dealing with eastern spirituality have focused on the process of bipolarity, discovered mostly through the teachings of the Chinese sage Lao Tzu. They know less about the existence of the chakras, which was known in Ayurvedic medicine and by some contemporary practitioners of alternative medicine. Even less is known about the existence of a Kundalini in the universe. C. G. Jung covered extensive ground in his quest to uncover the secrets of our psyche and he wrote, "The idea of transformation and renewal by means of a serpent is a well substantiated archetype. It is the healing serpent representing the God ... probably the most significant development of serpent symbolism as regards renewal of personality is to be found in Kundalini Yoga." [19]

Over the last thirty years, Shri Mataji has delivered literally thousands of lectures explaining its functioning. The primordial Kundalini must be understood as the residual energy of the Virata, an awesome storage of untapped pure energy, which triggers the various phases of the evolutionary process and thus pushes ahead the dynamics of universal history. The Kundalini is a virgin power, says Shri Mataji, and this again can be related to Jung's research. In the innermost of the hierarchy of Greek gods, he observes, it is not Hera, Zeus' spouse, not even Aphrodite, goddess of love, who stands at the pinnacle of worship; it is the virgin, Pallas Athene, and she carries the emblem of the serpent on her scud. Another goddess, Artemis, is also a virgin. "The Kore (Maiden) Goddess throws light on the old mythological idea in its budlike capacity to unfold and yet to contain a whole compact world in itself." [20]

[19] C G Jung and C Kerenyi, *Science of Mythology*, Ark Paperbacks, London (1985), p. 218.
[20] C G Jung, op.cit, p. 106

Within man, the Kundalini is likewise the power of catharsis and transformation and when she rises within the *Sushumna nadi* located within the spine and pierces the seven centers of power in the limbic area at the top of the head, she grants the experience of Self-realization. As such she must be considered a mother of the twice born, a feminine, motherly power whose pure desire is to bestow the blessings of inner growth on her own child. The Kundalini remains dormant in the sacrum bone until the moment of its manifestation. Over the millennia, very few people achieved Kundalini awakening and this is why knowledge of it was shrouded in mystery and secrecy. The Kundalini was protected down the centuries from the curiosity of the masses by a strict esotericism, but nonetheless it would take hundreds of pages to cite all the initiatory texts which have glorified her, and to present the symbols through which she appears in art and architecture across many cultures.

It would seem that the masters of the Order of the Templars, back from the Crusades, knew something about it. This is probably why the Catholic Church and the King of France accused them of sorcery. Some magi of Egypt and South America probably had access to one aspect or another of the technique (*tantra*) for the awakening of Kundalini; they acquired diverse magical powers (*siddhis*) but they do not seem to have approached the Kundalini herself. As a particularly explicit symbol of the Kundalini we may cite again the serpent Agathodaimon of Hermes Trismegiste or Mercury. According to the Gnostics it was the alchemical symbol of the process of psychic metamorphosis: it specifically represented the spinal column and the Rachidian Bulb. Today, this serpent is the emblem of our pharmacies and we buy our pills without knowing what it stands for. Other symbols for the Kundalini recur: volutes of clouds or water which frame the stairs of the Forbidden City in Beijing; the burning bush or tongues of fire as referred to in *The Bible*... Artistic references to the Kundalini and its three-and-a-half coils can be found in pre-Christian Ukrainian pottery, pre-Colombian handicrafts, or at Newgrange, just outside Dublin, Ireland, a site thought to be the oldest known manmade structure in Europe, revealed by carbon dating to be at least 500 years older than the Great Pyramid of Giza.

The spiritual masters of Asia considered the existence of the Kundalini and her interior path to be the most precious knowledge, which they would only transmit to a very few selected disciples who were deemed worthy. But, down the centuries, even some non-realized beings got wind of the secret. Some lamaic and sexo-tantric sects deformed the tradition, confused the serpent of fire with the sexual impulse and perverted the cult. In some tantric temples of India, virgins were raped in awakening rituals and gradually the pure tradition vanished. In modern times apprentice sorcerers and phony gurus confused much about this secret knowledge. The field appeared to be new and accurate knowledge hard to come by. Most books currently available on Kundalini Yoga recommend exactly the opposite of what is actually to be done if one wishes to preserve one's chances of attaining Self-realization. They describe Kundalini awakening as a frightful experience, generating tremendous heat, consuming the marrow and the water of the body and similar to the bite of a thousand scorpions.

Shri Jnaneshwar, one of the greatest world Masters of yoga, took his birth in Maharashtra, India. In his comments on the *Gita*, called the *Jnaneshwari*, he wrote several pages on the Kundalini. Such texts can have been tampered with through the ages but the description is consistent with what is experienced by the practitioners of Sahaja Yoga. For instance: "The cask of moon nectar situated above tilts on one side, and the nectar begins to flow into the mouth of the Kundalini. The nectar fills her and then spreads to the whole body and is soaked therein by the help of prana. As wax placed in a red-hot mould melts and fills it up, so the body looks as if luster, covered by skin, has descended in the human form." [21]

This language is typically consistent with the overwhelming experiences and the bliss that I myself discovered as my own Kundalini arose. I felt the stream of nectar flowing from the top of my head in my encounter with the Maha Guru, the Great Master, Shri Mataji. Reference to this bliss is indeed described in more poetic terms by Shri Jnaneshwar: "It is like a picture of delight, or a form of great happiness, or a full blown bush of contentment, or a bud of gold flower champak or a bust of nectar or an orchard laden with tender leaves, or like the moon embellished with the autumnal dew, or like a statue made of luster sitting on a seat, when the Kundalini drinks the moon elixir." [22]

The Kundalini enters the centers of energy and activates their dormant properties. Each chakra corresponds to a planet of the solar system, a note of the musical scale, a color of the spectrum and a specific quality of the mind, and the Kundalini, in her ascent, awakens in us a multitude of powers and global correspondences. It would be futile here to attempt to describe them all, but the principle is basically this: through our Kundalini, our chakras enter into contact with those of the universal unconscious, the Virata, that reacts to us. It listens to our desires and this connectivity unfolds multiple beneficial consequences. Desires originating from the left or right sides come closer to the center and those from the *Sushumna* are endowed with more collective qualities. More *Sattvic* personalities seek achievements for the greatest happiness of the greatest number.

Once Self-realization has occurred, it is logical to expect changes in the pattern of desires. The Kundalini has the property of consuming our burdens, burning in us all lower hankerings from ego and superego, overcoming cravings, addictions and our more futile wants. We drop the desires for fleeting, elusive or marginal satisfactions and focus instead on pursuits more likely to bring solid, genuine fulfillment. When these lower desires are overcome, whether they be the expressions of individual weaknesses or of the influence left by the surrounding society, there is a sensation of heat in the sympathetic nervous system and the ensuing vibrations are perceived as hot. When the Kundalini regenerates and heals the nervous system, the vibrations are felt to be cool. The Kundalini may be a fire, but its flames burn with coolness and freshness.

---

[21] Shri Jnaneshwar, *The Jnaneshwari*, M R Yardi, Bharatya Vidya Bhavan, Pune (1991), p. 127.

[22] Shri Jnaneshwar, op.cit, 256-260, p. 127.

In a very practical and effective manner, the Kundalini is our inner mother, guide and the inner reflection of the motherly protective power. This protective power of the mother was also worshipped, once upon a time, in European countries. It was embodied in the Holy Virgin Mary. In the words of the twentieth century Saint Bernard of Clairvaux:

Ipsa temente non corruis	She holds you by the hand: you do not fall
Ipsa protegente non metuis	She protects you in person: you fear nothing
Ipsa duce non fatigaris	She guides you in person: you are not tormented
Ipsa propitia parvenus	She takes care of you: you reach your goal
Si insurgant venti	When the winds are rising.

The power of Kundalini is such that it releases the dynamics of love as it passes through the Anahat (heart) chakra, even if our heart has been bruised and burnt by past experiences. One of the great insights of Sahaja Yoga is the realization of the symbiotic relationship between the heart and the Self. The Self is physically located within the heart organ and when the Kundalini pierces the seventh chakra at the top of the brain, she does so at the very spot that corresponds to the location of the heart chakra within this all-encompassing super-center, the brain. Bliss then flows from this center and hence the Kundalini establishes and regenerates in us the flow of the energy of love, the capacity to feel, and to enact compassion.

BEING IN VIBRATIONS

Of what avail are words then?

— Shri Jnaneshwar

Mild, creative breeze, a vital breeze which traveled gently o'er things which it had made.

— Wordsworth, Prelude 1'43-45

When I met Shri Mataji, one of the first perceptions I felt was the cool vibrations coming from her into my hands like a gentle breeze. In my case, this did not happen at once. I'd feel it and it would disappear, or I would feel heat or some pain in a finger corresponding to a specific chakra. Shri Mataji later commented that I had damaged myself too much in my quest. Overall, I did feel the cool breeze and denial was impossible. The wind of the vibrations and the blessed silence of thoughtless awareness are the first indications of the Self-realized state. They seal the stamp on Selfhood.

I had heard about the Kundalini before but I did not connect the cool breeze to the Kundalini as she is described as a serpent of fire. Only much later did I read the *Jnaneshwari* where the High Master clearly described such a connection: ".... then the Brahmarandhra readily opens. There is another great region resembling the calyx of a lotus, in which the Self resides aloft. The supreme Kundalini then enters this abode of the Self and offers him the victuals of her luster. She indeed offers intelligence as a vegetable dish to him and does it in such a way as to leave no trace of dualism. The Kundalini gives up her fiery complexion and remains in the gaseous state. You might as well ask how she looks at that time. She dissolves herself in this gaseous form and keeps aside her garment of golden stripes."[23]

---

[23] Shri Jnaneshwar, op.cit, 291-295, p. 129

The Brahmarandhra refers to the seventh chakra, the Sahasrara, which is located on the top of the brain. While the translator uses in English the words "gaseous state," it becomes clear, a few lines later, what is meant: "although she is called *Shakti*, she is still in the form of gas (*vayu*)."[24] *Vayu* is indeed the God of the wind and this becomes still clearer: "The earth is dissolved by water, water by fire, and the wind dissolves the fire in the heart. Then the wind alone remains, but in the form of the body; and that too becomes absorbed in the sky of the Brahmarandhra. Now she is not known as Kundalini but takes on the name 'windy' (maruta). Then leaving the jalandhara bandha and breaking open the end of the Sushumna nadi she enters the cidakasha of Brahmarandhra."[25]

These lines of the *Jnasneshwari* describe the amazing feat of Shri Mataji. Yogis of yore and Tibetan lamas were weary of awakening the serpent power. Dissolving the earth and water elements of the body corresponded to the dangerous path of initiation that was followed under earlier masters and these steps of the process in the lower parts of the body were also alluded to by Jnaneshwar: "O Arjuna, this serpent power eats up all the solid stuff in the body and leaves nothing of the watery part also. When she eats these solid and liquid parts of the body, she becomes satisfied and remains calm in the spinal cord."[26]

But Shri Mataji short-circuited the process. She conceived a jet Kundalini to meet the challenges of a precarious time when hurried people do not have time to dwell on their own salvation. Indeed, the way she conceived the granting of Self-realization found its roots in the heart and thus she could manifest at once the latest stage of the Kundalini's splendid movement, from fire into wind. This is possible only because the heart is the chakra of love.

"Can you understand total love?" Shri Mataji once asked. "It is with this totality that the Spirit is watching you." Ontology is the province of philosophy, which deals with Being, the Spirit, or, in Sanskrit, the Atma. Thomas Aquinas, the towering figure of scholastic thought, declared that Being is Good, Beautiful and True. On this basis, Thomists over the ages described what Jacques Maritain calls "the metaphysical intuition of being" as the highest cognitive experience man can achieve. It is an experience described by the mystics as suffused with bliss. Thomas did not write a single line after his bewildering experience of reality in the night of Saint Nicholas. Blaise Pascal exclaims, "*Joie, Joie, pleurs de Joie*" (Joy, joy, tears of joy) to celebrate his meeting with his God. These great souls experienced the direct awareness of their inner Being, as it stood revealed in the almost brutal light of their Self-realization.

These ecstatic moments expressed the meeting of the Kundalini with the Spirit in the seventh center at the top of the head: thus the Spirit stood revealed. "In the heart resides the Atman, the Self. It is the center of a hundred and one little channels...in these moves...the breath."[27]

[24] Shri Jnaneshwar, op.cit, 296-300, p. 130.

[25] Shri Jnaneshwar, op.cit, 236-240.

[26] Shri Jnaneshwar, op.cit, 236-240

[27] Prashna Upanishad - commentary by Shankaracharya, Paris (1984), p. 32

According to the *Upanishads*, sacred texts of ancient India, the Spirit is the consolidated state of Truth, Consciousness and Bliss (*Sat-Chit-Ananda*). Parmenides, Aquinas or Heidegger said the same. As such the Spirit is the reflection of God. The philosopher E. Gilson said: "To conceive God as the pure and primordial act of Being, cause and end of all other beings, means at the same time building a theology capable of doing justice to whatever truth would be contained in other theologies." [28]

Plato held some ideas about man and God, which were substantially akin to the claims of Indian thought. But Plato did not go as far as the Hindus, who contended that our spirit was a part of God, indeed was God itself. The Platonic contemplative soul was 'like' the form but did not merge in Him. Yet the right attitude, for Plato or Adi Sankaracharya, was not to believe in God but to experience Him.

Hence this tradition suggests that there is the possibility for any individual to reach the Universal, the Virata, through introspection, the way within. Through the realization of his spiritual nature, man accomplishes the purpose of his destiny. That is to say there is no contradiction between the infinite One and the finite multiplicity since the multiplicity is only another level of manifestation of the One, another vibration of the primordial energy.

Could it be that the happening of Self-realization, powerfully manifesting the qualities of the Spirit in the transfigured awareness of the twice born, introduces us to the turning point of history? In the brilliant introductory chapter to his *Philosophy of History*, G.W.F. Hegel observes: "Universal History is exclusively occupied with showing how Spirit comes to a recognition and adoption of the Truth: the dawn of knowledge appears; it begins to discover salient principles and at last it arrives at full consciousness." [29]

I admit, Nazis, fascists and communists alike misused Hegel but maybe it is time to rehabilitate the vision of the original thinkers when he said: "Such are all great historical men - whose own particular aims involve those large issues which are the will of the World Spirit. They may be called heroes, inasmuch as they have derived their purpose and their vocation, not from the calm, regular course of things, sanctioned by the existing order; but from a concealed font - one which has not attained to phenomenal, present existence - from that inner Spirit, still hidden beneath the surface, which, impinging on the outer world as on a shell, bursts it in pieces, because it is another kernel than that which belonged to the shell in question. They are men, therefore, who appear to be drawn to the impulse of their life from themselves." [30]

Agreed, this text was used to justify fascist Caesarism in the twentieth century but I would submit that, perhaps after all, German Idealism was on track, albeit one century and a half too early. If indeed the World Spirit, *der Weltgeist*, is actually the Holy Ghost at work, and if "Spirit in its self-consciousness must become an object of contemplation to itself," [31] it follows that the Hegelian heroes are not megalomaniac despots but you and I, all women and men who are willing to cross the threshold of consciousness into

[28] Quoted by J. Maritain, *Le paysan de la Garonne* Desclée de Brouwer, Paris, (1966), p. 199.

[29] G.W.F. Hegel, *The Philosophy of History*, J.Sibree, Dover Publications, New York (1956), p. 53.

[30] Hegel, op.cit, p. 30.

[31] Hegel, op.cit, p. 53.

Selfhood. For it is our seeking that bursts open the shell of established certainties.

Self-realization is a holistic moment that can be accessible to you. In the same way that this meeting (in Sanskrit, yoga or union) would reveal the qualities of your Spirit to your consciousness, it would also reveal your Kundalini to you. Through her, the cosmic energy of the Holy Ghost is revealed as Her inner form within you.

Your Self would not then recede in withdrawn contemplation. As the reflection of the Spirit in man, it carries outwards its jubilant dynamism, creativity and compassion. Hence Self-realization triggers a score of constructive social attitudes and behaviors. The Kundalini is felt on the central nervous system. As the ancient *Book of Job* (4:15) records: "The Spirit can make itself felt as a soft breeze." Each finger and specific location in the hand corresponds to a specific chakra, and sensations in the fingers decode the messages coming from the corresponding chakras. We read in the *Koran*: "On that day We shall seal their mouths,Their hands will speak."[32]

Your hands can speak. If he gets his self-realization, our skeptic will feel the cool breeze of the Holy Ghost on his very own hands.

The Kundalini is the inner manifestation of the Goddess or Holy Spirit. The Breath is, so to say, its outer manifestation. In his translation of the *Bible*, Andre Chouraqui quotes John in this famous discourse between Christ and Nicodemus: "What is born of the flesh is flesh. What is born of the Breath is Breath. Do not marvel at what I tell: you must be born from above. The Breath blows where it wills and you will hear its voice but you do not know whence it comes or where it goes. And so it is for those born from the breath."(3.5)

Shri Mataji's words confirm ancient teachings. She says the Breath of the Holy Ghost is called *chaitanya*: "*Chaitanya* (vibrations) is the integrated force of your physiological, mental, emotional and religious selves." It is the sensation offeeling the breeze, the gentle vibrations of energy (*chaitanya*) that marks the connection with the All. Spirit and vibrations, *atma* and *chaitanya*, are the great discovery of the Third Age. The symbol of the Aquarian age is water, a symbol for vibrations, and these vibrations are mostly perceived as a cool wind, blowing onto the hands from a specific source. It happens when the individual is in a state of awareness corresponding to the position of the Kundalini in the seventh center. The vibrations are all-enveloping and in the words of the *Isha Upanishad* (5.10):

"It moves. It moves not.
It is far and it is near.
It is within all this,
And it is outside of all this."

Being and Energy are the two sides of the spiritual equation. In matter itself, we identify these two principles as particles and waves. This teaches us something about the nature of God. If we take a step towards Him, it is said that He will take a hundred towards us. *Jnaneshwar* tells us that the Kundalini and the consciousness become merged in the bliss of Brahman (God):

---

[32] *Holy Koran*, Verse 36.66, Penguin Classics, India (1956).

"Just as the seawater is transformed into clouds (by the process of evaporation) and the clouds, pouring down into the rivers, ultimately rejoin the sea, in the same way, the embodied self, by means of the human body, enters the abode of Brahman and becomes united with it."[33]

All this happens with and within a human body and it is really important that we realize we must respect our body and not deny it in the manner of ascetics or corrupt it as did those of us who led a licentious life. As a student at the time of the 'free' generation, I was fully enrolled in the second category. Thus despite my good fortune in meeting Shri Mataji herself, my ascent has been rather a slow process. My Kundalini was wounded and I kept losing the realized state. We later realized that many people were in a similar condition but fortunately for us, we could learn Sahaja Yoga's meditation and healing practices. It took me quite a bit of time to settle down but the end result turned out to be more than worth it.

[33] Shri Jnaneshwa, op,cit, 306-310, p. 130.

11. PLUCKING THE FRUITS OF THE TREE OF LIFE

Experience is not what happens to you; it is what you do with what happens to you.

— Aldous Huxley

Zen masters used to tell us to stop thinking and talking and that there is then nothing that we will not be able to know. My talking through this prose and the thinking that may arise in your mind as you read these lines are not the answer to the questions. I cannot satisfy the object of your curiosity and if words could, it would be proof that I have failed to convey the message that is central to my discourse: Self-realization is an experience. However, understanding helps put ourselves in a receptive frame of mind for this experience to occur and it is in this spirit that I would pass on to you a description of the inner mechanisms of our transformation.

THE SHELTER OF THE TORTOISE

As water rains upon rough ground
Runs to waste among the hills,
So he who sees qualities separately,
Runs to waste after them.

— 4.14 Katha Upanishad

The oldest question of spirituality has been how to perceive the underlying unity of reality instead of splitting our attention and desires into the fragmented splinters of its manifestation. Answers did not come easy:

"I saw an ant carrying a grain of rice,
And then she spied a grain of pulse,
She was puzzled how to carry both.
Kabir says, she cannot.
She must take the one and leave the other.
As so must a devotee choose between the Lord and the world."

— Kabir, The Divided Mind

For all those who do not fancy asceticism, these lines are not inviting, although such warnings have been repeated down the centuries: to reach God, first renounce the world and its temptations. The snag is that the vast majority who tried liberation through renouncing worldly pleasure failed in the end to reach their goal. They did not reach the higher plane and retained a nagging attraction for the lower ones. But I would read more into the struggle of Kabir's ant: if I only have the capacity to carry one item, or one category of perception, how do I possibly switch from one mode to the other? My category of perception relies on the five senses: hearing, smelling, touching, seeing, and tasting. The senses, invariably, bring my attention outwards. Can I switch mode in order to turn my attention inwards?

The tortoise is the animal associated with the goddess in the ancient temples of India, for the blessing of the Kundalini is to grant the power to turn the attention inwards, as with the tortoise that takes refuge under its shell. Control of the sense organs was always deemed to be the precondition to a higher awareness, but turning the attention inwards is exceedingly difficult for the common man.

The parasympathetic nervous system is beyond the reach of our willpower; through it, we breathe, we perspire, we excrete, we perform all spontaneous functions. Kabir sings poetically about a strange tree which bears fruit without blossoming, the Tree of Life that can be seen on the stained glass of the Chartres Cathedral and in many medieval paintings. The *Sushumna* and the chakras - traditional themes of esoteric poetry - are the subtle homes of the energy which control the parasympathetic. The parasympathetic is, in fact, our 'terminal,' through which we communicate with the cosmic computer, our window on the infinite. The parasympathetic pumps the vital energy, which the sympathetic consumes; the former dilates the chakras; the latter causes them to contract. When the *Sushumna* opens anew before the rising Kundalini, the parasympathetic nervous system starts to absorb the vital energy (*Pranava*) with which it recharges the chakras. The rising of the Kundalini is the happening that sucks the attention inwards.

From then on, the qualities of a new dimension start to manifest. An optimal adjustment is made spontaneously in our energy network, our health improves, our diverse faculties such as clear judgment, concentration, relaxation, etc., heighten. Such realized beings, as described by the master Kuang Tzu, "Become sages in their placidity and kings in their activity." But he who can taste the fruit of the Tree of Life is the one whose Kundalini has been awakened by someone who knows the correct protocol. On the contrary, attempts to awaken the Kundalini by amateur teachers or charlatans, out of ignorance or greed, turn out to be positively dangerous, physically as well as spiritually. Books on the subject warn against the risk of unauthorized Kundalini awakening.

The sixth chakra, also known as the Agyna or the Third Eye, guards the entrance to the city of the Sahasrara. When the doors of that gate open, the noises of ego and superego are expelled from our field of awareness. The space, which then opens between two waves of thoughts, is that of silent consciousness, *Nirvichara sammadhi*, which Shri Mataji calls thoughtless awareness. When one penetrates further and deeper into the silence, one discovers the intensity of the awareness of Being. The new utopia, meaning, etymologically, the new place of happiness, is not Sir Thomas More's utopian island in the ocean; it is a spot in the limbic area of the brain. But even before realization, this process of settling in thoughtless awareness can take years; those whose mental processes are entrenched or who are emotionally unstable have to be patient. After all, this is the age where human attention is drawn outside like never before.

During her ascent, the Kundalini awakens the powers of each center of energy she traverses before she attains the seventh heaven of Sahasrara at the crown of the head. This movement can take place in a fraction of a second. Nonetheless, thousands of people who have had the experience have been able to follow its progression and in some cases, it can actually be heard through a stethoscope. In the event that the force of the Kundalini is insufficient to open a blocked chakra, its pulsation can be seen with the naked eye on the back of the subject at the level of the obstacle. In her method for spontaneous union (Sahaja Yoga), Shri Mataji proposes various techniques to clear the obstacles.

Sahaja Yoga restores the meaning to a host of rites from many religions, because it connects them with the subtle energetic phenomena which they support. Beyond the beliefs of benighted zealots, the activity of the parasympathetic allows us to penetrate into the City of God with neither enrollment in a register, nor collection of money, nor even meditation courses for that matter.

The seventh, the royal chakra, is the citadel of silence and the bliss of the union (yoga) of the individual conscience and the universal consciousness, which is the consciousness of the Virata. The silence, the Void, the unconscious, is the ancestral theme of oriental spirituality. Bodhidharma, the father of Zen Buddhism, said of the unconscious that it effortlessly fulfills all our desires and makes us access a state of absolute freedom.

One important element that must be stressed here is that man cannot use these energetic phenomena for evil ends. We recall that realization comes about spontaneously through the awakening of the Kundalini. This mobilization is possible only when a certain propensity to good in the subject maintains the balance of his energy around the *Sushumna*. An evil being, perverse or tyrannical, is technically incapable of receiving his realization, since his interior system is already out of action and malfunctional.

Moreover, since we are talking about the parasympathetic nervous system, any voluntary or deliberate attempt to provoke one's own realization would start in the sympathetic nervous system and remain there, artificial and even dangerous. This subject must therefore be approached with the right attitude. We are not speaking here about a province of knowledge to conquer with the brilliance of the intellect but a kingdom to be approached with wisdom and common sense.

In the words of Shri Mataji: "If one introspects, and says with humility of heart: 'I do not yet know the truth, but I have to find it'," then, in time, this humility may be rewarded and one may achieve one's ascent. If this happens, the person's attention comes into the center, neither on the left nor on the right; that is, neither dominated by his conditionings from the past nor by the orientations of his ambitious ego. Now such a person is very well suited for Self-realization by which he will know the truth in its absolute form.

THE BREAKTHROUGH

By making the mind all motionless
From sloth and from distraction freed,
When unto mindlessness one comes
Then that is the supreme state!
So long the mind should be confined
Till in the heart it meets its end.
That is both knowledge and release!
All else is but a string of words.

— 6.34 Maitri Upanishad

Self-realization manifests at the exact moment that the Kundalini pierces the fontanel membrane at the top of the head. Some feel the waves of grace, which flow from the Sahasrara into the left and right channels while others simply enjoy the silent consciousness and the physical perception of the vibrations, which mark the integration of the central nervous system and the spiritual awareness. The fusion of the human and cosmic planes takes place instantaneously. From the instant of realization, the nervous system becomes conscious of the autonomic system. Auto, in the sense given by Shri Mataji to this term, means the Self. The awareness of the Self or Atma, which is a spark of the Self of God (Paramatma) is dawning in our conscious mind. Straightaway the new spiritual sensibility manifests on the physical level. The cool breeze of the vibrations conveys the message of the unconscious.

Therapies, which try to mobilize different energetic phenomena, have essentially approached only one aspect or another of the system. For example, acupuncture and reflexology have identified the network of the *nadis*, which distribute the energy of the sympathetic nervous system, and they operate on this limited basis. These practices cannot reach the parasympathetic nervous system, heart of the network and receptor of the vital energy. By way of contrast, the mobilization of the parasympathetic nervous system through the Kundalini can, in consequence, cure even cancer. What exactly is cancer? It can be seen as being caused when the over-activity of the sympathetic nervous system succeeds in dislodging a chakra from its place in the line of the *Sushumna* and cuts its connection with the parasympathetic nervous system. The chakra can then no longer transmit through the network of the *nadis* the organism's evolutionary code, which maintains the cohesion of the cells. The cells can no longer decode the instructions sent to them, via the chakras, by the organizers of life, the Deities. The chakras themselves continue to emit energy, but, in the absence of regulation by the parasympathetic nervous system, the energy becomes destructive. This leads to the formation and proliferation of cancerous cells. The science of the chakras states that if they can be brought into health early enough in the process, this can extirpate the primary cause of cancer by restoring the connection of the damaged chakra with the *Sushumna*.

But all efforts to become aware of the unconscious entail conscious efforts that mobilize, evidently, the energy of the sympathetic nervous system and hence one perpetually slips outside the domain that one is trying to attain. To become aware of the universal unconscious, it is necessary to become aware of our individual unconscious. This, represented in us by the sleeping Kundalini, is simply a part of this universal unconscious. The mobilization of the parasympathetic through the ascent of the Kundalini allows our conscious attention to immerse itself in our individual unconscious and then to access the universal. From then on, having penetrated into the very tissue of the real, we can then begin to recognize it. We enter into relation with *das Ding an sich*, which Kant declared in his *Critique of Pure Reason* to be properly unknowable. We recognize reality through direct perception and no longer through the opinions, reconstruction, or other processes of our mind. In Shri Mataji's terms, "The breakthrough into the unconscious removes the barrier between limited human awareness and reality." The unconscious is also the global pool from whence come the sounds of the Zen drum, the primordial Platonic images and inspirations, the intuitions through which art and science progress.

Consciousness without thoughts, *Nirvichara sammadhi* or thoughtless awareness, is the first stage of the path towards the union with the unconscious. From then on, the one who masters the art of meditation penetrates deeper into a state which is called doubtless awareness, or *Nirvikalpa sammadhi* in Sanskrit; then reality, above and beyond the slightest doubt, is an evident fact.

So the impact of the Kundalini on the parasympathetic nervous system allows our vibratory system to absorb new frequencies from the vibratory body of the unconscious, and even to use the vibrations to diverse ends. This capacity of accessing and activating primordial powers is one of the most ancient dreams of humanity. But in the past, man, unable to know his vibratory reality, has tried to portray himself as the instrument of the unconscious by activating his ego and the ensuing results were not convincing. The signs and messages of the unconscious are befuddled by the parasitism of the ego and superego in the receptor of the subject. Before realization, we cannot fully understand the underlying impulse from the unconscious, which is at the roots of so many institutions, customs, and language structures.

The unconscious works in quite a different fashion in a realized being. There is no grand design, no mental decoding; it is always susceptible to the ego's influence, but it has a spontaneous connection with the mainframe. Not only the receptor of the unconscious, the realized being also becomes the emitter. He or she can use vibrations on their surroundings, cure a sick person of disease and even awaken the Kundalini of another. The more a realized being progresses on his or her evolutionary path, the more effective is the spontaneity with which they emit the vibrations of *chaitanya*. And, without acting, they act upon their environment. To do this, they must remain alert to the incursions of the sympathetic nervous system into the attention, because the ego tries hard to regain control of that from which it has been dispossessed. The transformation of the present time is evidently a matter of collective emancipation. It opens the gate to a social spirituality or to spiritual democracy. Typically, Shri Mataji does not show interest in the solo ascension to the top spiritual pantheon of a few superstars; she sees emancipation as a grassroots movement.

One of the subtle effects of Self-realization is connectivity. In the space of freedom created by meditation, one enjoys a new and fantastic proximity with nature, rediscovering perhaps what our ancestors, as well as, for example, indigenous Australians and some Native American Indians knew all along, that there is some form of awareness in everything that is living. We can touch it. At times, nature responds very directly and to illustrate this, I shall mention one example, something that happened to me, ten years after I had had my Self-realization.

In the Amboseli National Park in Kenya, I was with a group of tourists in a Volkswagen van with an open roof. We were well off the beaten track in order to increase our chances of seeing game. We stopped to watch a herd of elephants taking a mud bath. At some point, a family of elephants passed by, about thirty meters away from us. One baby was following his mother and he was really cute. I targeted him with my attention and extended my hands so as to give him vibrations. After a couple of seconds, the baby elephant turned his head and stopped, he looked at me, left his mother and started walking towards the parked van. The other elephants stopped to see what was going on. The tourists became quite excited, brandishing their cameras and their zoom lenses. I was more than a bit emotionally affected by this, and I was curious too: did he really feel it? I kept sending him vibrations with my hands and the baby elephant eventually stopped just two meters away from the van. He stared directly at me, we met eyeball to eyeball, and he then raised his trunk in salutation and as if he was smiling too. Then he turned away and ambled off to rejoin the other elephants who had started walking away. It was so simple and straightforward. By this point, I was floating far away from my ecstatic neighbors who, by my side, had unloaded the content of their film cassettes on to our young visitor. What I felt was a wonderful, joyful love swelling in my heart. Once more I had realized that, after realization, we are wired to a deep undercurrent of love that exists in everything God has created. It is that undercurrent that makes lovable whatever is lovable. And to connect to it, whenever we can, is so, so blissful.

Of course there is more to the subject than communicating vibrationally with baby elephants. The Self in me and the Self in you are one. If we turn our keys together to access the Self, we shall realize a collective Being. In that case, solidarity will come as a measure of Self-help, not as an act of charity towards the neighbor.

Integration and synergies are the key words here: integration of the individual in the group or the organization. Synergies between various contributions will bring about a result, which is more than the sum of the parts. This is also why the synchronization of a large number of people getting their experience of *sammadhi* matters.

Societies that foster a culture of integration will be putting into place various levels of safety nets and they will better cope with cultural shocks and social transition. They will be able to absorb the predictable decline in payrolls and pension funds through an actual increase in the quality of life, measured on a new index of living standards no longer exclusively confined to materialistic values.

The code seekers are the progeny of Adam and Eve and they have inherited the quest from their adventurous ancestors. It is theirs to complete and at the grand moment they will chose to get their Self-realization; they will, in full synchronicity, turn the key in the lock. They would then open for the human race the secret passage to the other side of the limit, beyond the unhappy consciousness trapped within the *guna*. They shall then access the one thousand codes of power contained in the limbic area of the human brain, and as this happening takes on a collective dimension The Third Age begins.

THE MOTHER WITHIN

Holy spirit, quickening life
Moving all things, the root in all creation,
Who washes all things of impurity,
Removing sins and soothing wounds
Who is shining light and laudable life,
Wakening and reawakening things.

— Hildegard von Bingen, Symphonia

Second birth, like the first, presupposes the gift of life from the mother. We do not come into the world through our own action. Someone else delivered us. Most religions acknowledge that someone else must also give us our second birth. These traditions contain such notions as the role of the Master; the gift of divine grace, and the necessity to surrender to it; the availability of the Divine; and the capacity to let things happen without interfering. In the words of Kierkegaard: "When the sea combines her efforts and recollects her forces she cannot reflect the image of the sky. But when she rests tranquil, deep and calm, the image of the sky sinks into it."

"Those who know are still," proclaims the *Tao Te Ching* (56). When the sea becomes deep and calm, one bathes in the void of silent awareness, which is the manner in which the Self perceives itself. It means that the energy-attention rests in the *Sushumna* without giving way to the solicitations of the sympathetic nervous system. We read in the *Hathayogapradipika* (Ch2, v42): "When the breath flows through the Sushumna the mind becomes steady." Keeping oneself in this condition is one of the most difficult exploits. The great Zen master Ringai Gigen, who died in 867, told aspirants that the whole phenomenon is comparable to the spark made by the hammer as it strikes the steel: it is lost in the blink of an eye.

Indeed, in the past, very few individuals at all achieved their realization. Those who did, like the twenty-six Zen masters, were the precursors who had pulled themselves up between the left and right sympathetic nervous system, like mountaineers who buttress themselves between two walls of a chimney to ascend. Arriving above the Third Eye, the grace of the Kundalini propelled them eventually into the Sahasrara. Most of us could not reach the state of fulfillment to which we nevertheless aspire. Hence the revolt of twentieth century existentialists which represented a last gasp of the ailing western philosophy. But today, in the light of the most advanced teachings available to us, we can propose that this contradiction can be overcome. Observations, experiences, and their results, confirmed again and again in the most diverse circumstances, have shown three important facts:

- The parasympathetic nervous system has the potential to be the agent of transformation of awareness;

- This potential is actualized through the Kundalini awakening which happens when the subject is bombarded with the vibrations of *chaitanya*;

- We now live at a time in the evolutionary process in which this experience is made available to the majority of people who desire it.

In other words, and however intolerable this may be to those who would like to believe that they took birth by themselves and not through a mother, the Kundalini creates the conditions in which we can be born into the Spirit. She pours out the water of life of which Christ spoke to Nicodemus, and she represents the catalytic factor indispensable to the manifestation of man's own spiritual power. She enables us to pass on the experience because the enlightened being is also the one who enlightens. When a candle burns, does it not burn with its own flame? But nonetheless, it was first necessary for another candle, already lit, to enlighten it. A child is born from his mother. A twice born is born from the Kundalini. She is the Mother too, the Goddess within.

12. THE RISING OF THE KUNDALINI

The Kundalini uncoils herself, shakes off her lethargy, and stands erect, she then reaches the palms...creating a draught, the life wind emerges... and creates a cooling sensation in the body internally as also externally.

— Jnaneshwar, Jnaneshwari 6:14

ABSOLUTE TENDERNESS

The child to whom his mother smiled is worthy of the couch of the Gods.

— Virgil

Why are you all so worried, for the Auspicious Goddess is a wish–fulfilling tree. Dwelling in the jeweled Island as Ruler of the Universe, She is ever attentive.

— Vishnu speaking to the Gods in The Devi Gita (15th century)

Several writings reached the west describing Kundalini awakening as a frightening ordeal, generating tremendous heat (Tibetan lamas) or as causing pain similar to the biting of scorpions. Such experiences are due to the misguided practices of uninformed and unauthorized individuals. This is particularly true in India where sexo-tantric approaches to Kundalini awakening have regularly misfired and have harmed the practitioners.

Let us learn more about the true nature of the serpent of fire. In his reflections on how to awaken the Divine within, Carl Jung states: "To activate the unconscious means to awaken the Divine, the Devi Kundalini - to begin the development of the suprapersonal within the individual in order to kindle the light of the gods. Kundalini, which is to be awakened in the sleeping Mooladhara world, is the suprapersonal, the non-ego. For this reason Kundalini is the same principle as the Soter, the savior serpent of the Gnostics."[34] The Kundalini can be compared to a cable coiled in on itself made out of numerous interweaving fibers. She rises and unfolds her coils, piercing each chakra at the center. The thickness of the Kundalini, that is to say the number of her fibers, starts to diminish if the chakras through which the Kundalini passes are constricted or only partially opened. Her force is reduced correspondingly. If the lower chakras are properly dilated, the Kundalini progresses. If the upper chakras are blocked, only a few filaments will reach the Sahasrara.

Kundalini does not force a path for herself; she progresses with full understanding of our problems and her touch is pure gentleness. She is not going to hurt her only child. First she regenerates the damaged chakras, awakens their active principles (Deities), and repairs the flaws in the different dimensions of our being. But clearly if the lower chakras are blocked, the Kundalini will not rise with any strength.

Let us now follow a slow-motion film of the rising of the Kundalini, although in a very highly evolved spiritual being, Self-realization manifests in a split second and maintains itself indefinitely. When her progression happens without obstructions through the first five chakras, the Kundalini arrives at the Agnya chakra and diffuses throughout the lower part of the brain as a sort

---

[34] C.G.Jung, *The Psychology of Kundalini Yoga*, Lecture 4, October (1932).

of cloud that brings with it a slightly numbing feeling of softness and drowsiness. We could say that to begin with, the mother of our second birth sings a little lullaby to relax us fully. Then, given optimal conditions, one feels the vital energy of Kundalini melting and flowing downwards into the *Ida* and *Pingala nadis*, as though the cloud of energy was transformed into a rain of wellbeing. The two channels carry this shower to the Nabhi *chakra* where it is joined by a new impulse of Kundalini. (During this time, the head becomes somewhat lighter, as though discharged of old and heavy loads.)

The renewed force then advances with a greater velocity on the *Sushumna* channel and opens the Agnya chakra. The pupils of the eyes start to dilate and the lightness of the head changes to a feeling of refined perception, of complete lucidity. One starts to feel the silence of Sahasrara. The pressure of the accumulated force of the Kundalini increases progressively with the opening of the seventh center. At this culminating moment of the baptism, the person starts to feel the cool breeze of the divine vibrations penetrate into him or her, and the subject is then Self-realized.

If the Kundalini does not rise higher than the Agnya chakra, the subject is 'awakened' (*jagruti*); and will have, for example, curative powers but will not be able to remain in the silent awareness of *Nirvichara sammadhi*. However, with time, the regenerating activity of the Kundalini, now active, will bear fruit. Ultimately, the twice born will be able to reach the stage of deeper awareness called *Nirvikalpa sammadhi*, 'doubtless awareness,' where there is no longer the slightest doubt as to the true nature of God, the Self and their interconnection.

Highly evolved individuals have found the experience both immediate and definitive. Some felt coolness, almost like having balls of ice in the centers of their hands, which seemed to melt into their forearms and then into all of their being. Others felt a powerful wind blowing over their bodies and a river of energy rushing through their nervous system, the coolness broadening away from their spinal columns. But not everyone has such a clear experience of realization and if the Vishuddhi chakra is contracted or somehow distorted, one does not feel the vibrations despite the fact that the Kundalini has risen to the Sahasrara. However, with the growing silent awareness, one is bathed in a placid lake of inner peace. We can read in the *Maitri Upanishad*: "When thoughts become silent, the soul finds peace in its own source. This is the mystery of Eternity." [35] When Shri Mataji gives realization to many people at once in a public meeting, the atmosphere is filled with a silent and vibrant intensity of joy. In recent years, she has chosen to proceed swiftly. In the past, she followed systematically a progression from chakra to chakra, watching over the points where, due to psychic causes, the energy is blocked. All the time she is leading these reservoirs of energy towards their catharsis of redemption, and giving instructions to her audience. For instance, here is a partial transcription of one of Her programs: "The feeling of guilt which you have is the result of conditionings which have accumulated in the ego and superego. Tell yourselves that the one who committed the mistake was the ego and not yourself. Tell yourself, 'I am not guilty.' It does not matter whatever you may have done or which chakra may be blocked. You simply have to correct them. Do not condemn yourselves. Be the Self. And to do this, the best method is to forgive. This will open your

---

[35] Juan Mascaro, *The Upanishads*, Penguin Books, p.102.

Agnya. Ask God humbly for forgiveness; this will bring your attention back into the heart ... Dignity and serenity will take their place within you when you realize that your nature is that of the Spirit."

The experience of *sammadhi* is filled with an indescribable feeling of wellbeing as if the whole body is caressed inwardly by the tenderness of our inner spiritual mother. In Shri Mataji's own words: "We have the Mother within ourselves, in our hearts, and if She is awakened, She is going to look after us. She is going to give all the protection that is needed. And there is nothing to be frightened of. Kundalini cures you, She improves you, She bestows all the blissful things upon you. She takes you away from the worries of the grosser level."

Far from being harmful, Kundalini has a definite healing dimension. In his work of new insights into vibratory awareness for holistic health care, the late Professor Doctor U.C. Rai [36] has reported on therapeutic programs conducted with patients suffering from epilepsy, hypertension, and bronchial asthma, migraine and ischemic heart disease. He rightly observed that the field of psychosomatic medicine is expanding rapidly and offered preliminary evidence of the significant contribution made by Sahaja Yoga to the field of mind-body holistic therapy. More medical research has been pursued in various parts of the world, notably at a dedicated clinic near Mumbai in India; at Novosibirsk in Russia; and as previously mentioned, in Sydney, Australia. Findings illustrate improvements in the health condition of the sample of patients who follow the meditation techniques of Sahaja Yoga. Generally, records on the physical condition of realized souls, suggest a stronger immune system against diseases, a higher than average capacity to deal with stress and a slower aging process. However, others are more qualified than I to present evidence in the medical and scientific domains.

FREEING ADAM

The history of the world is none other than the progress of the consciousness of Freedom.

    – G.W.F. Hegel

Hegel goes on to say, "The final cause of the world at large, we allege to be the consciousness of its own freedom on the part of the Spirit, and ipso facto, the reality of that freedom." [37] "Resurrection is the core of Christ's message," says Shri Mataji.

Why do we break eggs at Easter? To answer this, let us try now to relate the awakening of Kundalini to the development of our cognitive faculties. Whereas animals are spontaneous, but unaware of the force at the base of their instincts, man is aware of being conscious, but is not spontaneous. Effectively, he programs himself using the rational mind through the activity of the *Pingala nadi (Rajo guna)*, whereas animals are confined to the *Ida nadi (Tamo guna)*. In his normal state of consciousness man perceives himself as an irreducible individual, a distinct and separate person. The shell over his Sahasrara calcifies and this state permits him to develop his ego, which is necessary to overcome the tutelary conditionings of

[36] Prof. Dr. Umesh C. Rai, *Medical Science Enlightened*, Life Eternal Trust, New Delhi (1993), p.188

[37] op.cit, p. 19.

the superego. The 'egg-man,' or ego type, is a myth, but the myth is indispensable because it allows the instrument of perception to develop by which the sense of being the real Self will arise. In the meantime, of course, believing that he has mastery of himself and all matter, he attempts to control history, to manipulate and control both creation and destruction and thus becomes Regent of the planet.

The 'egg-man,' as you might have guessed, is the state wherein which the Kundalini is enclosed in the triangular bone of the sacrum. The psychic life of man and his cognitive faculties depend on the interactions of the sympathetic nervous system, and on the possibility of approaching the equilibrium point between left and right. The 'egg-man' enjoys at first the liberty, which his autonomy implies, and he feels himself to be sole master within his shell, but actually this implies limits, which he starts to feel as his awareness sharpens. Aware of being finite, he cannot entirely ignore the infinite dimension within and without, nor can he ignore the fact that he is condemned to desire the Self without being able to attain it; it is in these terms that Sartre expatiates in the pages of *L'Etre et le Néant*. The breaking of the shell of the egg represents the opening of the fontanel membrane at the top of the head by the awakened Kundalini. Now the chick can learn to fly. The new state is called *'dvijaha'* in Sanskrit, a term which means both bird and twice born. This then is the true meaning behind the rite of breaking eggs at Easter. It is about the breaking of the shell that keeps us separate from true reality. Contrary to what we may think, the non-realized condition is not one of autonomy and freedom, for in it we are under the permanent influences of ego and conditionings. Breaking the shell means both awakening of the Self and gaining contact with the outside world, the collective consciousness.

Jacques Maritain, one of the leading spokesmen of the twentieth century's attempt at Catholic revival, observed: "The pursuit of supreme contemplation and the pursuit of supreme liberty are two aspects of the same pursuit. In the order of the spiritual life, man aspires to perfect and absolute freedom, and therefore to a superhuman state. The men of wisdom of all times have given evidence of this."[38]

Wise they may have been, but they could not communicate the know-how and only too often had to quit society in order to survive. Ultimately we would like to suggest why it would be good for all citizens to acquire Self-knowledge. This would enable us to ride the roller coaster of dialectic contradictions. It would open us to a happier and more enjoyable art of living. Last but not least, it would allow the twice born, including business people, to master the understanding of the basic morphology of social processes. Realized women and men would then be able to bring balance to economic decision-making and management skills. They would be able to build the kind of sensible and equitable commonwealth that is constantly eluding us. From the mastery of our own spiritual fundamentals flows the natural manifestation of our genius, and this is a basis for building a better world.

[38] Jacques Maritain, *What I Believe*, ed. Mark Booth, Firethorn Press, New York (1984), p. 53.

13. LEARNING TO PLAY THE LUTE

It is not because things are difficult that we do not dare; it is because we do not dare that they are difficult.

— Seneca

THE MASTERY OF THE OPERATING SYSTEM

Stop thinking and talking about it and there is nothing you will not be able to know.

— Zen Koan

There are only two kinds of people in the end: those who say to God 'Thy will be done' and those to whom God says, in the end, 'Thy will be done.' All that are in Hell choose it. Without that self-choice there could be no Hell. No soul that seriously and constantly desires joy will ever miss it. Those who seek find. To those who knock it is opened.

— C.S. Lewis, The Great Divorce

Zen masters were fond of reminding us that lute players must maintain their strings in a harmonic condition, neither too tight nor too loose. They meant to say that we need the same skills with which to tune our own nervous system. Through the sympathetic nervous system, we direct our everyday life; our destiny is articulated with respect to the state of our sympathetic nervous system. The *Ida nadi*, the left sympathetic nervous system, mobilizes the energy of desire, (emotional) and the *Pingala nadi*, the right sympathetic nervous system, that of action (physical and mental). This operating system, proceeding by action and reaction, unfolds contradictory but auto-regulatory feedback processes. It will eventually give rise to relative syntheses, moments of balance, which initiate a further cycle of dialectic progress. The psychologist Jean Piaget, apparently unknowingly, takes a Taoist stance in observing that auto-regulation seems to constitute both a characteristic of life and a general mechanism, which is common to organic and cognitive reactions.

As Einstein used to say, imagination is more important than knowledge. Let us have the courage to imagine a world where we would be truly living in reality. When the psychic movements arising from the two side channels are more or less in balance, one develops a mature personality, which favors the awakening of the third channel, the *Sushumna*, as a prelude to Self-realization.

The left sympathetic nervous system uses the energy of the lunar channel. The network of subtle nerves fed by this channel presides over the psyche's subconscious life, and discharges into the superego, in the right hemisphere of the brain. All past experiences are stored there and when the attention dwells in the left side, we immerse ourselves in our emotions, the past, memories, and other affective states. People are intuitive, sensitive and sharing, and perturbations of this channel give rise to emotional problems of the superego, which expose the psyche to many kinds of tensions, from the comparatively benign to cases of schizophrenia. People whose temperaments are rooted in the left sympathetic nervous system tend to develop habits, and to be submissive and suffering. Such people are conditioned; they follow the leader, and accept the aggression of others.

The right sympathetic nervous system uses the energy of the solar channel. It feeds our active consciousness and discharges into the ego in the left hemisphere of the brain. When our attention activates the right side, we project ourselves in mental activity, planning, organization, and all provinces of intellectual achievement, oriented towards the future. Such people are builders and achievers and of course, the West has rewarded and praised this male dominated paradigm, where being 'tough,' being 'a winner,' are the distinctive signs of quality. But the pitfalls are many and should the usage of energy on the right sympathetic nervous system become excessive, there is a surcharge of current on the network. It may afflict all those pursuing power, the typical temptation for action-oriented temperaments. The overdose manifests in stress symptoms such as mental agitation or exhaustion and extreme cases end up in paranoia. Of course, the ego can get out of control and in the worst cases, right-sided temperaments are control freaks, domination oriented, and the cost to society is considerable as seen in the exaggerated cases of Genghis Khan, Hitler and Stalin.

Of course, everyone has ego and it serves a useful purpose, but when the combination of right and left sympathetic nervous system is unbalanced, it creates numerous problems for all of us, even if we are not aware of the way we function in consequence. The individual driven by ego has a strong tendency to impose his views, talk too much, pass judgments, do too much planning and in all endeavors, seeks his own promotion even if he pretends to follow altruistic motivations. He is quick to turn his aggression against others if they get in the way of his auto-glorification and will be scheming and ruthless. It is worth elaborating on this type, which is unfortunately most common in the upper echelons of the corporate world.

The type of people dominated by ego cannot see things in their reality, the *"Ding an sich"* of Kant, because their intellectual capacity, remarkable as it may otherwise be, is not guided by the wisdom of the central channel where truth is sought and found. They create their own truth: they elaborate new theories to justify their ends. This leads us to the beginnings of orthodoxy, fanaticism, racism, or authoritarian management styles. Without truth, rectitude (dharma) cannot exist and rules of ethical behavior are ignored. Without even noticing, the ego type can be adulterous or cruel. "Why not? I like it." The egoist oppresses his spouse and destroys the harmony of the home, which is the source of wellbeing. He is not interested in others, except when they are instruments for attaining his ends. The ego type will be jealous of competent colleagues who may challenge his position; he will take decisions serving his own interests even if they run against the interest of the collectivity. Competitive, running after success, such people are often seen to be expert manipulators, befouling others with their charming manner, rationally justifying their slightest whims. The overdeveloped mind controlled by the ego is content to rationalize what happens. Any dogma, any behavior, however depraved it may be, can thus be legitimized through impeccable analysis.

At this point, the extremity of the ego joins with the extremity of the superego to produce a destructive type of personality. The ego type aggresses and destroys at once himself and others. Individuals with inflated egos are often found at the helm of affairs, in politics, economics, and administration. With consummate skill they pass off the projections of their egos as being for the good of the public, while scoffing at the latter, whose guardians they are. Since they use the resources of the *Pingala nadi*, the mental channel, they often appear extremely prudent and astute; tactful; and generally solemn, preening their social façade the better to impress those they abuse. Eternal Pharisees and politicians, they rejoice in portraying themselves as defenders of the very principles they betray. Yet because of the extreme tension on the right side, they need release on the left. This means a glass or more of whisky or, as documented by surveys of prostitution, a leaning towards sado-masochist practices.

In the eyes of a balanced (*Sattvic*) personality, the swelling of the ego appears in its true colors: it is a palace of cards, a balloon of vanity. However, the ego of a quite subtle person who operates on the *Pingala nadi* (known as a *Rajo guni*) can be as invisible as it is effective. On the vibrational level, they succeed in emitting microwaves, as it were, which capture the attention of those who tend to operate on the *Ida nadi* (known as *Tamo gunis*), identified as they are with the opposite pole, the extreme of superego. A club of sado-masochists thus formed in the bars of Bavaria and culminated in the Nazi apparatus. The combination between these extreme types of the ego and superego can, and in the case of the Nazis, did, form a collective monster. It is frequently found in the charismatic leadership of terrorist organizations. But it is usually not necessary to go so far as to attack the whole of human collectivity. Modern ego types easily and willingly destroy the laws which maintain the integrity of the family and of social cohesion.

A familiar plot of an extreme *Rajo guni* is to legitimize their anger and appetite for violence by taking the mantle as self appointed instruments of God's doom. The elite Nazi storm troopers, the SS, had inscribed on the buckle of their belt: *"Gott mit uns,"* "God with us." This is also the psychological background for the resurgence of these fatal fantasies in the context of Al Qaeda terrorism. But far from reaching God, whose door is on the central path, these characters that kill, either others as *Rajo gunis* or themselves as *Tamo gunis*, run on the wrong tracks, leading into dead ends and regression.

BEYOND THE UNHAPPY CONSCIOUSNESS

There is one good thing about the mind that it will go where it finds pleasure. Therefore one should try to see that it delights in striving for Self-realization.

— Jnaneshwar, Gita Explained

In Part Three we illustrated the conditions of the modern era, trapped in an unhappy consciousness within the *gunas*. But there is a way out and to illustrate the interactions between *Ida* and *Pingala*, let us consider the following sequence of events. When the newborn child emerges from within its mother, it experiences a trauma of separation, which is recorded in the subconscious *(Ida nadi)*. Its noisy protest confirms it in this new existence and proclaims its individual ego *(Pingala nadi)*. Like a bank of magnetic recordings, the infant's subconscious notes all reactions to new situations; fed by information from this store, the ego affirms itself. With the increasing activity of the child, the ego and superego, in the two hemispheres of the brain, start to swell like balloons and eventually completely cover the fontanel membrane, which then starts to calcify. This calcification marks the rupture of the connection with the universal unconscious. A new microcosm is born and the human being is cut off from the subtle divine energy which it was absorbing through the top of its head, which, as said, becomes calcified, and the individual becomes a being separated from the All. Its psyche becomes the field of the tension between ego and superego.

With the growth of the individual, the development of the mental and creative faculties swells the ego, while the superego grows as it adds daily to the stock of experiences and conditionings. The ego and superego create a sort of film of illusion (*maya*), which prevents our attention from becoming immersed in the reality of the seventh center. Only the Kundalini can pierce this web of illusory consciousness but so long as the central channel is closed, the energy of the sympathetic nervous system is cut off from the parasympathetic and our attention is identified with the sympathetic nervous system. It cannot penetrate past the equilibrium point of the sixth center - the Third Eye, the narrow gate, which is the opening to higher awareness. The attention oscillates from left to right and from right to left in a constant elliptical movement.

The flow of energy also oscillates between the two poles, coming to rest from time to time near the equilibrium point of the channel of evolution. The stability and maturity of a person are inversely proportional to the amplitude of the oscillations. The more these become balanced, the more the personality becomes integrated. These movements of energy, between the two opposing *nadis*, exercise a decisive influence on our behavior and on our inner evolution. Far too often they bring us to a reactive mode and we fall into the moods of the *gunas*. This is why the lute player said to Siddhartha Gautama (Lord Buddha) that one could only find the correct pitch when the strings of the instrument were neither too tense nor too slack. This advice helped the Buddha to his enlightenment. When my strings are too slack (over-activity of the left sympathetic nervous system) I compensate by tightening them (activating the right sympathetic nervous system). This process controls not only the progress of our daily life but also that of the cycle of rebirth. Thus Jung observed that every psychological extreme secretly contains its opposite and is found in some way in a close and essential relationship with it. He concluded that the psychic life is controlled by "The regulatory function of the contraries," which Heraclitus called *enantiodromia*. The same movement, perceived as dialectics, controls history. The *nadis* control and balance each other; it is better to have a cool head and a warm heart rather than a cold heart and a hot head. Popular language expresses the fact that the heart needs the warmth of the opposite sun channel while cerebral activity generated by the right side needs the cooling effect of the opposite moon channel.

The archetypal play between the *nadis* of the Virata pervades the matter of the universe and our conceptual models as much as it does our nervous system. How does this auto-regulation function in the human body? When one side of the sympathetic nervous system is overused, the other is then affected. To give a rather extreme example, on the physical level, we can say that a person of too dominating a temperament, with an overactive right sympathetic nervous system, is liable to fall victim to a heart attack, the heart being controlled by the *Ida nadi*. Whereas someone too much affected by the pressure of conditionings on the left sympathetic nervous system will develop mental troubles, the attention being controlled by the *Pingala nadi*.

But well before one arrives at such a state, the organism of a healthy individual has already sent out danger signals, sensing that the movement of energy and thus the two channels are going out of balance. There are various symptoms of physical illness or psychic pathology, which express the over-activity of the left and right sympathetic nervous system. More interestingly, after self-realization the patient, with a little training, can decode the symptoms and cure himself.

Commenting on the relationship between ethics and Self-realization, Shri Mataji states that the art of *Sattwa* is to maintain, through moral rectitude (dharma), the equilibrium of the lateral movements between the Channel of Action and the Channel of Desire. Then, the attention becomes collected at the central point of the middle channel. At this junction, the *Sushumna* offers us an alternative to the horizontal movement between *Ida* and *Pingala*, opening the vertical evolutionary dimension of *Sattwa guna*, through which the attention evolves and becomes finer. Spiritual growth is not possible without respect for ethics. This mastery, sought by sages down the ages, has been brought today within the reach of the masses. We may understand at last that being moral is good for us; it represents the adherence to a sort of evolutionary code, which is broken at our own costs.

When the energy does not deviate from this point of equilibrium, the chakras are not at all under stress and we find 'The Way' of ancient Chinese wisdom. Thus *Sattvic* individuals tend to lead lives of maturity and harmony. In this condition, simple people live in contentment. Philosophers, scientists and seekers of knowledge will have a propensity to receive intuitions from the unconscious, which lead them to success in their field of research and managers strike the right balance between creating wealth and sharing it. Artists express in their work the aesthetics of the truth. The vibrations of such people are cool and they receive realization without difficulty, because the *Sushumna* offers a free and unrestricted passage for the rising Kundalini. Children in their innocence and young people who enjoy a happy family environment often belong to this category of people; their parasympathetic keeps the *Ida* and *Pingala* in balance. *Sattvic* individuals show a psychic maturity without losing themselves in the cerebral convolutions or melodramatic infatuations, which tend to be the norm today.

The realized soul gradually becomes free from the influence of the three *gunas*, even from *Sattwa guna*, which implies a seeking of balance, wellbeing and wisdom, since the Kundalini integrates and then transcends the *gunas* as she moves from her state of latency into one of action.

We have said that contradictions exist on the level of the *Tamo* and *Rajo gunas* of the Virata and on the microcosmic level of our left and right sympathetic nervous systems. Now, it is all very well to become aware of these, but it is even better to be able to overcome them and as we have seen, being trapped within the *gunas* is altogether a dangerous condition. Are the strings of the lute too tense? Be sure not to slacken them too much. But how do we tune them? In practical language the question becomes how to stabilize the perpetual motion between the left and right sympathetic nervous systems? In other words, how to overcome the process of action and reaction? Our reactivity rocks our psyche between ego and superego in such a way that our attention cannot become connected with the Spirit.

The answer to this question cannot be a theological or intellectual one, because it involves the awakening of the potential energy of the parasympathetic nervous system, the Kundalini. The answer is a happening. One cannot awaken her by thinking, by discussion, or by joining some spiritual movement. But what can one do? This is indeed the Zen enigma, the ancient dilemma, which has posed so many difficulties in the human quest for reality, the limit beyond which we cannot pass. The conscience of *homo sapiens* is completely encased by the ego and superego and gives the illusion of the individual separateness.

Let us then consider our dependence on the sympathetic nervous system. In the superego, I am affected by external conditioning; in the ego I am affected by my own projections. In a sense I am lost in the cocoon of a virtual reality where I float astray in a world of arbitrary representations and opinions. Hence I am alienated from my real identity, from the Self, from Joy, Consciousness and Truth. The standard psychic state is thus a state of alienation, the unhappy consciousness. The existentialists indeed define the human condition as such alienation since *homo sapiens* cannot avoid acting mainly through the sympathetic nervous system, that is to say, through the system which cannot be immunized against reactivity, deviations and mistakes, and which cannot rejoin the plenitude of the Self. So *homo sapiens* spends most of the time in a state of alienation, of which the individual is not conscious because there isn't the *Sattvic* capacity of discrimination which would allow identification of conditionings and the ability to destroy artificial identities. "I am" a leader, an expert, a CEO, a hippie or whatever;" the individual person is neither happy nor fulfilled, but most of the time they do not even know it, as they do not have the capacity to perceive and break identification with such appearances. They act and react from these standpoints, becoming embroiled in a deepening web of illusions.

If we consider it abnormal that mankind should be programmed by phenomena and mechanisms that we neither understand nor control, we can go so far as to say that the standard psychic state, which we have hitherto considered normal, is in fact abnormal. Within this anomaly lies the root of all human suffering, as the world created by the standard psychic state, the projection of ego and conditionings, is an unreal world. It is the fruit of an unknown and not very benevolent programming. The good news is: *homo sapiens*, like it or not, is not the final outcome of evolution.

Contemporary psychology is based on the study of the psyche of modern man, menaced as it is by the over-activity of the sympathetic nervous system. It has tried to identify its psychic contents, but psychology cannot go beyond a discussion of the symptoms. Classical psychotherapy would mobilize the conscious part of the psyche to identify and thus exorcise the shades of the subconscious, the repressed feelings and images. It would use the techniques of the *"diagnostische Assoziationsstudien,"* the diagnostic study of mental associations and the analysis of dreams, which tend to discharge a perturbed psychic state through verbalization and speech analysis. In this way the subject has the possibility of disengaging from a prior identification with a false identity and can thus be liberated through a discriminating act of the conscious mind. There is nothing wrong with this in principle, but it can only lead us so far because even if the subject succeeds in withdrawing from a false identification, what is there to stop him or her from falling straight away into another, and possibly more pernicious, misidentification?

The reader will have already recognized that contemporary national or business leaders might possibly not have overcome the contradictions of the standard psyche. Thence, when the blind leads society, it may well end up in the ditch, as in the famous Breughel painting describing just such a scene. This old proposition finds its dramatic expression today because technology has multiplied a hundredfold the power of action - unenlightened action - of the ego type. Its destructive trend has thus an ability to interfere in human affairs on a scale that has no historical precedent. Are we heading towards a great renewal? Or towards the twilight of our era? In the view of the British historian Arnold Toynbee, the end of the Second Age was the final act, proceeding towards its climax: either the annihilation of life, or a new ethical parting, a bifurcation towards a new epoch of human history.

One can sense it: the work is not completed yet; the Virata is still at work, driving evolution through the ascent of the Kundalini. The reader may have guessed that this ethical bifurcation, which the English historian presents as an evolutionary necessity, could well correspond to the kind of consciousness breakthrough we have described. The option for man to mobilize the parasympathetic energy of the central channel allows us to transcend our imperfect mode of perception. The present driving style of Adam is limited to the brake of the left sympathetic nervous system and the accelerator of the right sympathetic nervous system. Gradually, the integrating impact of the parasympathetic makes itself felt on the *gunas*. The left sympathetic nervous system ceases to be a potential source of psychic instability. The right sympathetic nervous system is no longer the instrument of aggression but expresses a confident and constructive identity.

But human society is not yet there. The process of spreading Self-realization takes time. We resist. While hundreds of thousands of men and women discover with delight the passage to the other side of the screen and the opening of a new dimension of life, there may be many more who oppose the move. It is said that when a truth is introduced to the world, it is first ridiculed, then opposed, then finally accepted. Teachings such as those of Shri Mataji have, at times, met with resistance, and sometimes, outright hostility. The club of negation includes some established sects, dogmatists, rationalists scared of the unknown, and even a few failed disciples who could not hold to the high standards of personal morality and ethical behavior that Self-realization implies. Others are simply afraid of the unknown because, as Dostoevsky reminds us, taking a new step is what people fear most. Mephisto says in the Faust: *"Ich bin der Geist der immer verneint,"* "I am the spirit that always says no." In the next chapter we shall see why it is time to say yes.

PART FIVE

THE IMPACT OF SELF-REALIZATION ON HUMAN BEHAVIOR

They call this 'loveliness-uniter' (samya dvama), for all lovely things come together under unto it. All lovely things come together unto him who knows this.
— Chandogya Upanishad 4.15.2

One way to have fun is to laugh at our problems. To recognize the illusion is to gain freedom and what really matters is our relationship with what is real. This is how, without changing, the whole thing changes. There is something crisp about born realized people, something fresh, and it has the taste of a blessed simplicity. So much love flows in and between such people and it gives to the person in the vicinity of such beings a feeling they do not remember ever having before. What kids can be like this, loving each other, helping each other, children growing into adults without losing their inner beauty? This is more than just saying, "I believe in God." We are drawn to people like that for every moment is alive and beautiful. Each person is so intensely caring and gracious, so fair and so aware. It is a beautiful thing to realize that this is what spirituality really is, not the talk of priests or rabbis but the qualities within us that manifest outside and make us happy just to be.

Many people wish for the experience of enlightenment but do not always realize that the flowers and fruits on this path are completely connected to our daily lives and indeed to our own families. Born realized children are handsome, kind and mostly successful in school but they are not pretentious. Such children just praise God by being, for they reflect exquisite qualities and other people recognize and want some of what they have. We live in love and confidence, under the glow of innocence so that we all trust. In God we trust, yes, but this means we trust in ourselves. A successful businessman may have had three marriages and may have five homes but none feels like home. Being home inside oneself, with a house maybe, and with a mostly wonderful marriage within which to share daily fun and affection, is the lot of so many realized souls whom I have met in the twenty last years.

14. FROM HOMO SAPIENS TO HOMO SPIRITUALIS

The best way to make your dreams come true is to wake up.
  – Paul Valéry

GETTING CONNECTED

As all the spokes are held together in the hub and felly of the wheel, just so in this Soul, all things, all goods, all worlds, all breathing things, all these selves are held together.

  – Brihad-Aranyaka Upanishad 2. 5 .15

Great spiritual pioneers of the past have announced the tremendous potential of our cognitive faculties. Shri Ramdas (1608-1682) wrote: "The ecstatic condition of mind in which it realizes Brahman, is called the 'umana' state. The active mind can never comprehend that state. Complete merger of the mind with the Brahman is the highest bliss. This is also known as Sahaj sammadhi. Men with such experiences are rare indeed."

Ignorant of the morphologic correspondences between the Virata and the creation, modern man arrogated to himself the job of hanging judge of the creation. "Man is suffocating inside a conceptual cocoon of his own making," says Shri Mataji; he does not perceive the real issues and simply revolts. With vain pride he ties himself up in an absurdity of his own creation, which he believes to be the essential nature of existence. The awakening of the Kundalini proves that man, far from being marginal or solitary, is indeed connected to the great sources of divine energy and to the different aspects of the Primordial Being, the Almighty God. It proves also one central experience, Self-realization, as the key to the absolute unity of the great religions of the world.

The great religious teachers of the past tried to open the communication channels through which the principles on the chakras of the Virata transmitted their program to humanity. Their teaching formed the parts of the mystic body of spiritual knowledge, revealed by the Virata with the passing of the ages, to guide humanity in its pilgrimage. But today, at the dawning of the Third Age, this body has been dismembered by religious fanaticism. Again and again, the ayatollahs, bonzes, lamas, popes, and Brahmins fight over the dead remains of religion, on behalf of their sects and cults, mostly claimimg exclusive rights over the whole. Dogmatism and totalitarian enforcement of religion block the flow of energy and the sense of evolution. Only enlightened tolerance will open it again.

Before the experience of the cool breeze of the Kundalini (Holy Spirit), it is hard indeed to distinguish between true and false. "It is hard to come out of the illusion (maya) created by my *gunas*," says Shri Krishna. *Homo sapiens* cannot feel the vibrations from the Virata and tries to compensate by mental projections. Reaching reality with thoughts is as likely as reaching the moon with a bicycle. Guru Nanak, the master of the Sikh religion comments: "Though I think a hundred thoughts of God, thought alone cannot reach Him."

Only the manifestation of the Kundalini reveals to the *homo spiritualis* the true unity behind all world religions. All the true masters of the past are different aspects of the one Being. In fact, a Deity rules over each chakra and denial of any one of them by an aspirant creates difficulties in the integration of his own inner system, since the chakra whose Deity he rejects - or indeed the chakra of any Deity he worships exclusively, denying the others - does not open.

Realized beings have acquired considerable experience in such situations and it has often been shown, for instance, that the Kundalini will not cross the space between the vagus nerve of the parasympathetic nervous system and the solar plexus if the Primordial Master is denied in any one of his manifestations (Abraham, Moses, Confucius, Lao Tzu, Zarathustra, Socrates, Guru Nanak, Mohammed, etc.). Fanaticism constricts the chakras while vibrations confirm the authenticity of all the great instructors of mankind. When the first chakra, which is ruled by Lord Ganesha, is affected, the Kundalini's strength is weakened. The saying of the mantra for the principle of innocence of the first chakra brings results, and the Kundalini starts her ascent. If the sixth chakra is blocked, the person is asked to forgive or to say the Lord's Prayer for this chakra which is under the control of Lord Jesus Christ. The person reports that the head clears out and the process of thoughts calms down, a sure indication that the Agnya has been crossed. This is the way, through meditation and vibration therapy workshops, that we have been able to identify the relationship between chakras and the Deities, as the original source of corresponding energies located in the holistic structure of the Virata.

The rising of the Kundalini takes us beyond the limited and contradictory belief system of *homo sapiens*. The Primordial Master, for instance, controls the area of the Void, around the Nabhi chakra. He is the archetype of the master who has incarnated many times, as stated above. For the Kundalini to maintain itself above the Void, we will have to accept the Prophet in all his incarnations. Hence conflicts between disciples of the various manifestations of the same incarnation are shown to be merely the fruit of ignorance as to his true universal nature. Admittedly, fanatics will be blocked at this level; the Kundalini will not rise and they will have missed their chance.

When a person is linked to the cosmic program by vibratory awareness (chaitanya), they start to discover and test the reality of Shiva (the blessedness of absolute existence) or Christ (the crystal light of truth). To the realized soul, as Theilard de Chardin sensed, Deities express a particular quality of the enlightened consciousness, whose grace we start to feel with the opening of the corresponding chakras. Socrates knew that the knowledge of the Self was the key to knowledge of the entire universe.

We have reached that stage of our evolution where homo spiritualis will be able to develop this new vibratory type of perception, which guides us into a new cognitive kingdom. It may be that the positivists of today will go on ignoring it but they will lose their claim of following a scientific approach. Indeed vibratory awareness opens a new field of empirical investigation: the hypothesis, contained in this chapter, can be tested by an experience - the raising of the Kundalini - which can be felt, replicated and passed on. To make the most of it requires that we adopt a new method and a new attitude. Marx declared that all that preceded the revolution was prehistory, which is not entirely false, but his own revolution has now joined that same prehistory. The true revolution for the meta modern era is that which turns our attention towards the interior through the identification with the Self.

Should I describe how life is different for an enlightened being, once the chakras have been cleared out? How his daily experience differs from another? How his path and destiny are different? How he is and where he is different? Again, I think it would take a much better writer, or a poet in order to do justice to the subject. Imagine that life is free and fresh. It is free because the web of stress generated by the *Rajo guna* is disappearing and it is fresh because the web of boredom generated by the *Tamo guna* is also disappearing. Imagine that you feel real. It is as if we currently live our daily lives with just with a small proportion of what we really are. Many people change places or partners, go on holidays or do sports, just to have this little existential kick that makes them feel really good, existing more intensely. With Self-realization you feel the kick sitting in your living room. Just imagine that you feel connected, loneliness is gone, even if you happen to be alone. Connection is established with nature, plants, animals and art, for love is in everything and can be felt in everything. Imagine, more and more people are now sharing this feeling; imagine that nobody and nothing can take it away from us because this is not what we have. It is what we are.

VERTICAL AND HORIZONTAL GROWTH

As birds resort to a tree for a resting place, even so, O friend, it is to the supreme Atman that everything here resorts.

– Prasna Upanishad 4.4

Let us go back to our analogy of the Tree of Life with its roots, trunk, branches, leaves and fruits. We can look at it from a different angle - the circulation of the sap and the movements of energy within the tree. This tree is the symbol of our identity and its potential. The roots are our deeper spiritual dimensions, the trunk is our constitution, the branches are our abilities and skills, the leaves represent our actions and the fruits manifest our achievements. Self- realization creates, in the words of an ancient poet, the living forest of marching, self-fulfilling trees (*kalpataru*).

Spontaneous union brought forward by the Kundalini integrates two types of yoga: the inner yoga, the union in contemplation (Antar yoga) and the external yoga, the union in action (Karma yoga). The first movement expresses introspection. The second movement is of manifestation and both are necessary for the unfolding of our complete potential. Introspection reveals what we really are, and, by manifesting it, we share our spiritual qualities with others. It is the movement of the attention towards the roots. The roots capture the energy of our deeper Self and send it through the *Ida nadi* to the branches and the leaves. The purpose of the inner yoga is to access the supply of energy from the earth. Meditation comprises the movement of the attention inside, a phenomenon which is fully possible only when the awakening of the Kundalini sucks the attention inwards.

Action denotes the movement of the attention towards the outside universe. The leaves capture the energy of the sun and send it through the *Pingala nadi* to the whole tree. The purpose of the external yoga is to access the energy of the sun. These energy flows are necessary for harmonious growth. The balance between the two movements is important. If the branches grow too big, the tree loaded by the overgrowth of the ego will be uprooted at the first storm. If the roots do not grow, equally the tree will die. But if the tree grows tall and strong, it is lord of the landscape and gives shelter to all the creatures of the forest.

Homo sapiens draws energy chiefly from the outside dimension of existence and its creation, the modern world, threatens to be uprooted. Antar yoga grounds our attention and identity in the vertical dimension of our spiritual inner being. Meditation fosters the vertical growth of our being, reaching ever further into its unfathomable depths. It corresponds to the retractable movement of the tortoise and subtracts our sense organs from the influence of the surrounding world, the horizontal dimension. In the case of *homo sapiens*, our being imbibes the outside world through constant sensations, impulses, impressions and conditionings. The outside world is the water, the inside world is the sponge. With *homo spiritualis*, however, the inner world and its energy, catalyzed by the rising sap of the Kundalini, is much more powerful. It is emitted from the personality of a realized person on the surrounding world and it subtly, yet effectively, influences the outside. The inner world is the water, the outside world the sponge.

At the core of the inner world resides the Self, which is approached through a loving heart. Saints were represented with an aura around their heads. This is because the twice born can have a transforming, soothing and positive impact on their environment. The capacity to channel deeper spiritual energies towards the outside world manifests the horizontal growth of such a personality who is charismatic and spontaneously emits love. It generates togetherness and companionship and a realized soul, be it a composer such as Mozart, Vivaldi, Bach or Handel, or an artist such as Michelangelo or Leonardo da Vinci, or a writer such as Dante, Goethe, Shakespeare or Victor Hugo, is invariably excelling in creativity. Realized souls create an atmosphere of serenity, manifest healing powers, and now, through the advent of Shri Mataji, can themselves raise the Kundalini of others. Such souls call for instinctive reverence among animals, who can perceive their aura. They can even, at times, influence weather patterns. There were good reasons in the past that true saints were revered.

In the same way, the tree needs to feed both from the earth and from the sun; *homo spiritualis* needs to balance both Antar yoga and Karma yoga in a holistic manner. He is different from the saints of the past in his dual relationship with contemplation and action. Formerly the saints would devote themselves to Antar yoga, withdraw from the world, as ascetics, saddhus, monks or anchorites, busy with their inner life only: without proper foliage, the tree would not manifest its full strength. *Homo spiritualis* is also beyond the more frequent prototype of our standard materialist, a diseased tree producing dried leaves and rotten fruits that are not properly nourished by the inner sap.

The symbiotic relationship between the horizontal and vertical movements has a most far-reaching implication. *Homo spiritualis* develops a spontaneous tendency to share with the outside world the benefits of the realized state, to transfer the experience of Kundalini awakening, because sharing is an essential part of the spontaneous yoga. Spiritual sharing expresses the synergy between Antar and Karma yoga. It means the birth of collective consciousness, a truly mind-blowing dimension that will completely revolutionize social psychology. All the spokes are connecting to the hub.

These possibilities become actualized after the first initiation. It is remarkable that the Swiss psychologist, C.G. Jung, could see the truly cosmic potential of Kundalini's awakening: "From the point of view of the gods, this world is less than a child's play. It is a seed in the earth, a mere potentiality. Our whole world of consciousness is only a seed of the future. And when you succeed in the awakening of the Kundalini, so that she begins to move out of her mere potentiality, you necessarily start a world which is a world of eternity, totally different from our world."[39]

---

[39] C.G. Jung, *The psychology of Kundalini Yoga*, Carl Jung Lecture 2, October (1932), Princeton University Press (1996), p. 26.

15. DUALITY, SYNTHESIS AND BEYOND

UNDERSTANDING DIALECTICS

In the scientific theories of the last century, traces of the operating system of the Virata are seen through the complementary aspects of the wave and particle models of matter as described in the quantum mechanics of Bohr and Heisenberg, and in the interplay of matter and energy of Einstein's theory of relativity. Indeed, the world as portrayed by modern physics has come more and more to resemble that of the cosmology portrayed by the oriental theory of the three *gunas*. The exploration of the atomic and subatomic worlds reveals the "constant flux of transformation and of change" of Heraclitus.

Thinkers seek to isolate the movements of this eternal becoming which reflects the circulation of energy between the three principal channels of the Virata. As we have said before, in Hindu mythology, Lord Shiva, the God of Existence and Love but also of Destruction, reigns over the *Ida nadi*, the channel of desire. Lord Brahma rules the *Pingala nadi*, the sun channel, as the Creator. Lord Vishnu, the moderator, leads evolution on the *Sushumna*, the third channel. One of Shri Vishnu's thousand names is *Sahishnu*, meaning beyond the duality of hot and cold. From the mythological songs of the *Vedas* to the pairs developed in Spengler's philosophy of history, almost all civilizations have tended to identify the poles of the cosmic bipolarity, whatever the names: nature and culture, *Dionysian* and *Apollonian*, etc. Naturally, through intuition of the interactions and tensions between these two poles, diverse conceptual models *(Weltanschauung)* were produced such as the impermanence of phenomena in the Buddhist world. Closer to us, the Hegelian and Marxist dialectic with its interplay of contradiction and identity refer to the same set of processes.

The sequence is as follows: the movements of energy between the opposites, *(Ida* and *Pingala)*, arrive at a point of balance *(Sushumna)*, which represents a higher and more subtle synthesis, the basis for the next evolutionary stage. But in history, the latter is much harder to perceive than the process of contradictions. Contradictions exist, in effect, on the global level of the Virata, between the *Pingala* and *Ida nadis*, the *Rajo* and *Tamo gunas*, and between the Yin and Yang of the *Tao Te Ching*. These contradictions are reflected in the material world and have been recognized by science. They are also to be found on the microcosmic level of the human being, between the left and the right side sympathetic nervous systems which control, respectively, the right and left hemispheres of the brain.

For *Lao Tzu*, the bipolarity principle of Yin and Yang rules the world of mind and matter endlessly, unless and until it is transcended by the return to the primordial Oneness of Tao. The same perception of the forces that shape human destiny has been permeating Western philosophy. Action engenders reaction: in our psychic life, in behavior, in the succession of happenings. The flow is continuous; it carries us all. *Heraclitus* surfs on the eternal river of change. Marxist dialectic puts bipolarity into motion: it sees in "the law of contradiction" the spiraling movement that fuels history's necessary march forward. Mao must have seen in Lenin a Lao Tzu with a

Russian beard. Again, Hegel inspired Marx. In his *Phenomenology of Consciousness*, and in his *Philosophy of History*, he sees the same principle at work. Through thesis and antithesis, consciousness makes its way towards the synthesis, seeking its purpose within history. One two, one two, one two - this is the state of the unhappy consciousness *(das ungluekliche Bewusstsein)*. Man must run a difficult balancing act between tensions and opposites.

Bipolar contradictions must eventually be overcome *(aufgehoben)* by reaching the third movement, the synthesis - one, two, three. To draw again from *Lord Krishna* in his teachings to the warrior disciple *Arjuna* on the battlefield of the Kurukshetra: the Blue Lord unveils the intricacies of the cosmic hide and seek play, and in so doing, he reveals the same Trinitarian sequence. Broad moods or *gunas* influence the ways and the ages of men. *Tamo guna* is the mood of passivity, more static. *Rajo guna* is the mood of activity, more dynamic. *Sattva guna* is the mood of equilibrium and harmony. *'Sat'* in Sanskrit means 'truth.' Hippies trekking to Katmandu were looking for the pass to the third dimension, trying to read Hegel in fine *Devanagari* script. A hard thing to do through the smoke of hashish.

Even our economic theories reflect our perception of the law of contradiction and of its regulating function. Adam Smith, the father of capitalism, likewise aspires to find equilibrium between supply and demand. He seeks some sort of synthesis between private interest and common good as he describes the play of the operating system of the *gunas*. Hence these famous lines: "When the entrepreneur intends only his own gain, he is led by an invisible hand to promote an end which was not a part of his intention ... By pursuing his own interest, he frequently promotes that of society more effectively than when he really intends to promote it."

Modern psychological theories develop from the perception of the law of contradiction in our own psyche. Adler studied the will to power of the Channel of Action. Freud, heir to the misogynist tradition, misread in his investigation of the libido the structure of the Channel of Desire. Jung perceived the mechanism of harmony on the Channel of Evolution and its connection with the inspiration coming from the universal unconscious, the mind of the Virata.

The rising of the Kundalini takes us beyond the three *gunas*. The number three is itself interesting: the 'Third' Reich of Adolf Hitler, the 'Third Wave' of Alvin Toffler, the 'Third Way' of Tony Blair and of the European social democrats. But before reaching three, let us count one and two. I will recapitulate what we already said about it.

WHOSE 'THIRD REICH'?

In the history of the German people, the first empire was the Holy Roman Empire of the German Nations, which was terminated by Napoleon at the beginning of the nineteenth century. The second empire was the Empire of the Prussian *Hohenzollern* dynasty, which ended at the end of World War I. And the third empire, meant to be the higher order lasting one thousand years, was the one of Adolf Hitler. It looks like these schemes are dangerous toys to play with.

One-two-three sounds deceptively simple. However, there is a catch. There is three and Three. The banal three, the little synthesis, is merely the new thesis, the new step one of the next phase in the rolling sequence of contradictions. It is a step in the sequence, forwards or backwards, but nothing more. The big Three, the achievement of harmony, that fuels the ideologies and inspires the masses, is never to be reached in any sort of permanent way. This is why synthesis is ever elusive and the Anglo-Saxon press understandably derided the ride of Prime Minister Tony Blair to the Third Way as a cheap opportunistic political philosophy which borrows from left and right to keep not the balance, but the power.

The Big Three was the longed for breakthrough into a new dimension of consciousness never quite to be reached, the metamorphosis that would never materialize. Instructors of mankind urged us to become spiritual beings but never told us exactly how. Not surprisingly, the realists mocked the utopian seekers for their never-ending quest towards nowhere. We now understand why it is so. The Third Way of *Sattwa guna* on the central *Sushumna nadi* is part of a closed circuit where energy flows laterally left and right unless and until the rising of the Kundalini opens its inner most thread, leading to and beyond the seventh center of the Sahasrara on the top of the brain.

The story of millenarism tells us that this is deep, deep stuff. The Third Way has been predicted in the ancient scriptures, sought by alchemists, Crusaders, the Templars and Holy Roman German Emperors. It has been achieved, it is said, by some Zen masters and missed by just about everybody else. It also inspired deeply militant ideologies. Those who found themselves in the path of this collective mirage did not laugh at it. Many saw it as their destiny to lead the last struggle. It was supposed to be the New Jerusalem for Godefroy de Bouillon who brutally conquered and sacked the earthly Jerusalem. It inspired the dark mysticism of the Nazis in the theories of Goebels, Rosenberg and Himmler. It probably equally inspires the fundamentalist orthodox Jews and fundamentalist Muslims who would gladly eliminate each other in the name of this higher order. It was supposed to be the culmination of the class conflict, the communist Stateless State for the toiling masses of the Soviet Union. As I visit the corpses of all the white elephant disasters of the communist economy, which litter and pollute the territory of the Aral Sea Basin, I wonder who will still see some sense in the eschatological scheme. But the fact is that we always took the small three for the big one. We acted without guidelines, before knowing the operating procedure of the Virata. Something was missing.

Without the opening of the *Sahasrara* and the activation of its powers in the brain, the third dimension is constantly eroded and threatened. With this opening, the great transformation takes place: man enters the Fourth State *(Turya)*. The Fourth State is beyond the three modes *(trigunatmika)*; it is the real destination. *Turya* is also described as the state beyond sleep, dream and waking conditions. Guru Nanak prophesizes: "You will attain sunya which is also the fourth state, *Turya Avastha. Sunya* is the great stillness within and without and pervades the three regions. It is in the state of *Turya t*hat a human being is identified with God." The treatise of *Hatha yoga pradipika* tells us: "Sahaja and turya, all these are synonymous." And: "When the mind is quiescent, this state is known as Turya. There, Time (death) is not."

THE POWER OF THE SPIRIT TO ALL

In Thy wind - in Thy light - How insignificant is everything else, how small are we — and how happy in that which alone is great.

— Dag Hammarskjoeld, Markings

Join me in a fairytale, one you can experience for yourself. A fairytale which will bring magic into your life, and in which you will be the magician, except the magic will be real and you will never be the same again. You will be so thankful that finally what was missing has been found and you will be amazed that the peace you feel will be a peace that passes all understanding. The happiness you experience will be of a quality that leaves an expression of pure bliss on your face so that others will just want to be near you. Give it a try. The tale is your own destiny. Greet it. Get it. You won't regret it.

We must know how to read old mythologies to better understand the present state of affairs. For instance, through tales and legends, we find that mankind has been waiting for this moment of transformation. Actually, we can follow the fine print of eschatological expectations both in the Indian and Judeo Christian traditions. *'Eschatos'* means the last, that is, the last days.

For the people of the Bible there will be an end to history, an end to hopping through sufferings and meaninglessness. The culmination of our Christian collective fulfillment manifests through a religious turning point, the Apocalypse. John sees the end of history as we know it, and his vision of this mega crisis tells us that it opens for the survivors the era of the Golden Age. History does not end in Indian thought. There is no definite culmination as such; it is described as cyclical but it also rides through a critical turning point. *Kali Yuga,* the cycle of darkness, reaching its peak, turns into *Sattya Yuga,* the golden cycle. Again it happens through a religious event, a catharsis, and the radix *'Sat'* again suggests that the turning point has something to do with the capacity of the human consciousness to reach the truth. In the final chapter of this book we return to this theme and the meaning of Judgment Day.

By now the sense of Adam's destiny reveals itself. As we enter the Third Age of Revelation, the Kundalini, the Holy Spirit is awakened within us, for all who desire it, and thence the transformation into the promised stage of the higher consciousness. As this process can happen at the collective level, its impact can transcend our contradictions.

We reviewed in Part Three how we are trapped within the *gunas* and how the freezing of the heart is due to malfunctions of the right hemisphere of our brains. The stress on the liver is linked to the overactivity of the left hemisphere of the brain, and in this condition, the central channel of our evolution is closed, and the awareness of Self is clouded and numbed. Redemption time occurs when the Kundalini pierces the fontanel bone at the top of the brain; it does so at the very point that triggers the dynamic of integration and balancing of the two hemispheres.

This breakthrough is a concrete happening. It takes place at a given point in the life of the psyche and when it happens to a sufficient number of individuals, transformation works on society as a whole. The click, the trigger, is hidden in our nervous system.

Something must happen to change the way we know, before we can change the way we act. Individual transformation precedes the transformation of the community, of the corporation, of the city; collective transformation precedes the transformation of the *Yuga*, of the historical cycle.

Let us understand Shri Mataji's demonstrated ability to empower the seekers of Self-realization in a global context. The opening of the Third Way, the big historical synthesis, corresponds to the moment when Self-realization is available for all - and not only for the spiritually gifted elite. Spiritual democracy or democratic spirituality mean that access to the power of the spirit is opened to all, and that no Pharisee can any longer block the access door.

It is the advent of a democratic spirituality - without high priests or political commissars - which will in turn lead to the enlightened management of human collectives: states, cities and corporations. As society consequently matures we might further witness the advent of a spiritual democracy. The two worlds that Plato wanted to reconcile in the philosopher-king will be reconciled in the enlightened citizen. We can hope that no savvy clergy will again confiscate this revolution because the process of transformation does not depend on dogma controlled by someone else; it takes place through a psychosomatic happening within one's brain. We will also have to remain wary of clever foxes and spiritual charlatans, the false prophets of the Apocalypse, who will pursue their attempts to control the hopes and faith of the masses for self-serving purposes.

But there is ground for sensible optimism too. With the discovery of vibratory consciousness, everybody can find out who is who. A person with the right attitude on the central path emits positive vibrations registered as cool breeze in the palm of the hands. Somebody equipped with the will to control, cheat and take power in the garb of religion, for instance, emits negative vibrations registered as heat or pain in the fingers of the twice born. Their vibrations expose false prophets. Conclusion: it is not easy to cheat a collective of twice born. This is why we can claim we see the dawning of the big historical synthesis and not the path of ideologies, empires and charlatans. Other gurus, sects or cults are missing the point because, even if they come close to the solution in a theoretical sense, they do not have the power to awaken the Kundalini. But someone does have that power – and this is the fundamental truth, which struck me like a thunderbolt when I met Shri Mataji in Hurst Green.

The radiant evidence of Gurdjieff's 'I Am' state; the enlightened *satori* or illumination of Zen Buddhism; the nectar *(amrit)* of liberation *(sammadhi);* the joy *(ananda)* or even the ecstasy described by the mystical explorer; the second birth of the Spirit prophesized by Jesus Christ: all these are promised states of consciousness which seekers and philosophers have tried to approach. This quest became a social phenomenon in the second half of the twentieth century. We went looking for the new cognitive instrument and some of us, in despair, took to virtual spirituality and accepted a fake guru who slept with our girl friend or promised to make us fly, so we lost our way. We took opium, angel dust or Ecstasy, chemical shortcuts to the centers of pleasure in the limbic area of the brain and we kept on missing the entrance door. Christ said, "I am the Door." Did he speak in vain? His was the door to reality on the sixth center, leading to the brain. Christian preachers, busy with temporal power, were only too happy to marginalize the Gnostics, the few who knew, and to burble verbose metaphors which concealed their ignorance of the building, the door and the pathway. Beyond thought and emotion, beyond the Third Way that reconciles them, beyond the narrow gate of Christ, there is a new dimension, the Fourth State *(Turya)*.

Alternatives to this breakthrough are not encouraging. Societies, corporations, communities reflect in their processes the shortcomings of our own personalities. This includes our deficient understanding and lack of insight into the operating system of God, the Virata.

Shri Mataji observes: "On the firm foundation of absolute truth only can one have complete confidence and an absolutely peaceful, non violent stand in the face of the relative world of uncertainty, contradiction and confusion."

Damages caused by unruly egos are incalculable. Damages caused by conditionings are deep rooted. We repeat costly mistakes, pursue wasteful turf battles, we perpetuate the same forms of imbalances. Of course it is an invariable fact that those who benefit from the status quo will tend to ridicule or oppose the possibility of change. But change is stubborn; we never bathe twice in the same river and the sheer number of those who suffer from the contradictions of modern life build a strong incentive for the more powerful momentum of change announced by the Joachite prophecy.

16. BIPOLARITY INDUCED ATTITUDES

Only that country is peaceful
Which has one ruler, not many.
I have not seen any happiness
In a kingdom where two are in authority;
Nor can one with divided personality be ever happy.

– Kabir

Tamo guna and *Rajo guna* are expressed by innumerable forms of bipolarity: they are moon and sun, night and day, woman and man, feeling and thought. They are Adam and Eve looking at the tree. But the cold can become warm, the hot can cool down; day succeeds night, Yin flows into Yang and vice versa. The opposites dance, interweave, balancing in a fleeting unity. Adam and Eve start seeking. This play of contraries can be observed in natural and social processes alike. It explains some of the dynamics of our collectivities, be they cities, organizations or corporations. Understanding bipolarity has always been the object of human curiosity. We see it in the stone image of the androgynous *Shiva* of the temple of Elephanta, constructed in the eighth century A.D. on an island near the present day metropolis of Mumbai. His right side is male, his left side female, expressing the fact that the integration between himself and his wife is total. The thread of the law of contradictions runs through the texts of Chinese wisdom such as the *Tao Te Ching*, the *Kuang Tzu*, and the *I Ching*.

MICRO LEVEL POLARITY

At the micro level, the *gunas* influence the full range of cultural features and behavior styles. Again, the *Bhagavad Gita* contains a full description of the corresponding personalities and characters and we need not quote it here. These remarks introduce us to a simplified presentation of bipolarity at the micro level of our psychosomatic set up. Indications are merely illustrative. The list could cover pages. These patterns concern all human beings, no matter the background, no matter the differences, races or cultures. For we all function according to the same inner operating system *(yantra)*. What makes the difference between our respective personalities and characters is the pattern of energy movements between the poles of the system at the level of each chakra.

PERSONALITY PREFERENCES

I've probably by now sorely tried the reader who is uneasy with theoretical frameworks and concepts: we walked a shortcut through millennia of mythologies and spiritual history to follow man's quest for lasting satisfaction. We projected an overview of the manner in which the operating system of the three *gunas* was handled in the history of ideas. We embraced in this search for meaning both Eastern mythology and Western philosophy. We have presented Self-realization as the chief hypothesis leading to an evolutionary breakthrough. We hinted at the profound relevance of Self-

RIGHT SIDE	**LEFT SIDE**
Sympathetic Nervous System	**Sympathetic Nervous System**
LEFT HEMISPHERE BRAIN	RIGHT HEMISPHERE BRAIN
EGO	SUPEREGO
LIVER	HEART
THOUGHT	EMOTION
ACTION	DESIRE
GIVING	ABSORBING
METHODICAL	SENSITIVE
FORWARD LOOKING	NOSTALGIC

mastery for walking, through the screen of ego and superego, to the other side of the human existential state of contradiction. If men are from Mars and women from Venus, then to prosper on earth we need to recognize how both poles of the polarity interact within each of us.

In these last pages, I would like to try to show how this line of enquiry will make a difference in the way people interact and do business in the outside world. For whether we are a householder, a student, or a businesswoman, we all are reacting to the *gunas*.

Let us give examples from the world of business. Today there is a new interest in the understanding of these patterns as global players try to understand the behavior, assumptions and likely reactions of partners from another culture. We can give examples relevant to modern management practices. The observation of negotiating teams from different cultures reveals different approaches to making a deal. Approaches concern, for instance, the deference shown to the team leader, the speed of negotiation, the importance given to consultation among all those concerned before taking a position, the importance given to building relationships before talking about the substance, the way disagreement is expressed or the importance given to a legal contract. The way staff in different cultures treat their CEO is another cultural issue. We register differences in the manipulation of status symbols, in the use of first names, and in subtle domination patterns such as the boss's habit of influencing a discussion by giving his or her opinion first. Cultural upbringing will produce a variety of leadership styles, ranging from authoritarian to democratic and casual.

One manager likes to have his door closed and the phone line diverted so that he can concentrate properly. Another walks the floor, preferring to have people around her, talking over ideas informally with colleagues before writing anything down. Another relies on charts, facts and figures in order to present his case, while still another prefers to focus in a concise manner on priority issues, strategic guidance and recommendations. What has this to do with the *gunas*?

The line of enquiry of this book postulates that the *gunas* influence personality types. The influence of personality on management is today recognized in management theory. Let us start from the four scales measured by the Myers Briggs Type Indicator (MBTI). Katherine Briggs and her daughter Isabel Myers, based on the work of Jung, developed the MBTI. Jung, in his analysis of archetypes, was sensitive to the theory of the *gunas* and he argued that seemingly random behaviors can be explained in terms of patterns that are influenced by personality preferences. People are born with certain preferences, which strongly influence their behavior. These include their behavior as family members, lovers and professionals. These preferences relate to the way their brains function and they stay with them for the rest of their lives, although the preferences by adopted behaviors (like the skins of an onion) by adopted behaviors as they grow up through family upbringing, school and careers. People do then develop skills in areas where they do not have a preference, but the process can be difficult and it will take time and energy.

The MBTI has been employed for many years as an analytical tool by a variety of users: in small businesses and large corporations, service industries and manufacturing concerns, consulting and training firms and by entrepreneurs and governments. The MBTI provides a tested reference on personality structure by looking at eight personality preferences that everybody uses at different times. These eight preferences are organized into four bi-polar scales. The four preferences (e.g., extravert vs. introvert) combine into a personality type. Again the MBTI is not a mechanistically rigid model; because of the self-regulating movements between the contraries, personality patterns may evolve. The pairs are presented here in the MBTI usual format, that is, the right-side *guna* is on the left of the page and the left side *guna* is on the right.

RELATED TO PINGALA NADI	RELATED TO IDA NADI
EXTRAVERSION	INTROVERSION
SENSATION	INTUITION
THINKING	FEELING
JUDGING	PERCEIVING

Scale 1. (Extraversion-Introversion) refers to the way a person is energized.

E: preference for drawing energy support from the outside: contacts, activities or things. I: preference for drawing the energy from the inner world: ideas, emotions, and impressions.

Scale 2. (Sensation-Intuition) deals with perception and the way people use their attention. S: focus on sense oriented matters and facts. I: inclination towards instant recognition and sense of anticipation.

Scale 3. (Thinking-Feeling) indicates preferences in the decision making process.

T: Analytical and logical approach, preference for organization and structure. F: strong on instinct and preference for decisions taken on personal, value oriented criteria.

Scale 4. (Judging-Perceiving) indicates lifestyle orientations and relationships to the outside world. J: preference for a planned life, regulated schedule, controls over the environment. P: favors going with the flow, adapting and adjusting to circumstances in an open and flexible manner.

MBTI tests help people in their private and public life in various ways. They can understand themselves and their behavior, strengthen their impact in work situations, and increase the effectiveness of their communication. They can learn to understand others and to make a constructive use of different personality types. They can use multiple approaches to problem solving, improve teamwork, management styles and conflict resolution. The analysis of types helps in career counseling and in maximizing the potential for the organization's human resources.

During MBTI training, preferences are identified through a series of questionnaires whose results are projected on to graphs. For instance, taking only the scale Extraversion-Introversion, the results of the questionnaire will position the preferences of the subject along the following lines.

PINGALA NADI   **IDA NADI**

Figure A

E_____x_____I

Figure B

E_____x_____I

Figure C

E_____x_____I

In Figure A, the subject is clearly extraverted; in Figure B clearly introverted. In Figure C the subject has a slight preference for extraversion but he also uses extensively the potential of introverted concentration. He is more complete and versatile, in a sense, because he can tap the potential of the two preferences, and mobilize the energy of the right and left sympathetic nervous system. Hence a concentration of X near the center visually expresses a Sattvic temperament whose characteristics point towards a rich, balanced and gifted personality with a strong potential for evolution. Clearly, an X in the center would mark the middle way, the central path advocated by the ancient Chinese masters. In contrast, individuals too identified with one preference may swing to the other occasionally but this movement will be expressed through a reactive, at times unbalanced, personality.

The MBTI interests the corporate world of organizations and business because it has the potential: a) to increase employee self-understanding and inter personal skills; b) to improve the efficiency and impact of collaborators, staff and business operators. Furthermore, an improved understanding may challenge the status quo of acquired behaviors and rules. Old assumptions and the traditional way of doing things may be enriched through innovation.

However, this is where the usefulness of the MBTI and critical analysis ends. MBTI points out significant patterns of a personality. This is certainly helpful but on the whole this analytical method is not meant to be an agent of inner transformation. Management training invites people to disengage from the pace of normal activities and to take time for personal observation and evaluation. But back into the everyday rat race, the potential for personal growth does not actualize itself, or if it does, it is only through self-conscious efforts and usually with limited results.

If a subject sets himself the goal of implementing a new behavior or translating insights into practical working methods, results of this self training are usually well below expectations. Planning for change does not carry the empowering or enabling effect of going beyond the law of polarity, from where the traits of temperament and character emerge. Furthermore, such attempts at redefining roles may in the end turn out to be perceived as artificial manipulation. An egoistic boss who understands the need to motivate his collaborators or improve interpersonal relationships with colleagues will try to improve the score. He will try to act as a caring person and in so doing, he will frustrate the most observant by an approach perceived by them as hypocritical. This boss cannot genuinely express a heartfelt sense of caring without a deeper change in his chakras. Thus breeding cynicism among his colleagues, the attempt at being nice backfires. The result could be worse than the ill it was meant to cure.

People have yet to discover that it is through the work of the awakened Kundalini on our chakras that personality change can occur spontaneously. It is work done from the inside. Only then can we avoid the risks of artificiality and manipulation.

THE ARCHETYPE OF MACRO LEVEL POLARITY

I told you we would try to get a glimpse at a fresco. Let us now move back to the big picture, littered with the failed attempts of history to reach the higher synthesis. Examples of macro level polarities proposed here again relate to the *gunas*, the broad orientations which shaped the advent of modern societies. We will not repeat what was said on the perception of the bipolarity archetype in the world cultures but simply summarize here some of its aspects.

STEP TWO: THE ANTITHESIS	STEP ONE: THE THESIS
ADAM, THE MAN	EVE, THE WOMAN
SUN CHANNEL	MOON CHANNEL
RAJO GUNA	TAMO GUNA
IINTELLECTUAL COEFFICIENT	EMOTIONAL COEFFICIENT
YANG	YIN
FUTURE	PAST

OR...AT THE MACRO LEVEL

FREE WILL	PREDESTINATION
INDIVIDUAL ASSERTION	COMMUNITY TOGETHERNESS
ECONOMY	SOCIETY
LIBERALISM (Hobbes)	DEMOCRACY (Rousseau)
CAPITALISM (A. Smith)	SOCIALISM (Marx, Engels)
PRIVATE SECTOR	PUBLIC INTEREST
SHAREHOLDER VALUES	STAKE HOLDER VALUES

Whether at the macro or at the micro level, the law of polarity implies constant interaction. On the physical level, the system is self-regulating. If an individual uses too much the energy of the right sympathetic nervous system it is not the right side organs which will register the damage but those controlling the left side. For instance, an overactive, cerebral or aggressive person may be prone to heart attacks. In contrast, a person who is very conditioned or absorbed in emotional attachments is draining too much energy from the left sympathetic nervous system and in extreme cases, may be exposed to strokes affecting the brain. Similarly, at the psychological level, the law of polarity is constantly at work. People driven by hard work or the thirst for power on the sun channel need emotional compensations on the left side. Periods of puritanical sexual repression tend to be followed by moments of self-indulgence and sexual licentiousness.

One, two, three, as we said, is the rhythm of evolution and change. But passing beyond one and two can prove deceptive. Every attempt at reaching a third stage of higher stability leads to yet another set of contradictions. Some scientists, Jungian psychologists or followers of the German school of history acknowledge that the search for Gestalt shapes, carved out of significant correlation, was a legitimate form of enquiry into reality. The French philosopher, Bertrand de Jouvenel, observed that man could be tamed by images. W. Heisenberg, the atomic physicist, was wondering: "Are the shapes not more like abstract expressions of natural laws?" Jung, who considered archetypes to be the abstract expressions of psychic laws, echoed this question.

The Trinitarian scheme of action-reaction-synthesis is printed in our collective unconscious. It is in this context that the millennial theory of the *gunas* is interesting because these broad moods are said to influence critical aspects of human cultures and behaviors. It is one of the most powerful archetypes in the universal history of ideas. Is this science? Perhaps not exactly. But it works, because we can see that nature, our brain and history work that way.

Once contradictions are recognized, rational models tend to claim a synthetic capacity such as the Social Contract of Jean Jacques Rousseau, which is the foundation of modern democracy. This basic charter of modern democracy combines the interest of the individual and of society as do, in different ways, the economic theories of Adam Smith or Lord Keynes. The quest for balance is a constant feature of our conceptual constructions. China, still grounded in the Confucian heritage, which strives for righteousness and order, has become a powerhouse of the world economy. Is it still threatened by an excess of contradictions between its rich coastal areas and the poorer Northwestern region? The response to this question has to do with knowing how to play the *gunas*. The heritage of Taoist and Marxist thought in China shows that the Chinese are aware of such dialectics. The history of their continent is a long struggle between balance and disorder.

"Hot heads and cold hearts never solved anything," goes the saying. This is because they are not integrated. A recent attempt at reconciling contradictions can be found in Anthony Gidden's book, *The Third Way*. It is an effort at reconciling socialism and capitalism through an integrated political program covering each of the major sectors of society in the changing context of globalization. The synthetic dimensions may, and indeed did appeal to politicians such as Romano Prodi, Tony Blair, Gerhard Schroeder or even Bill Clinton. But to a reader who lacks understanding of the spiritual and psychosomatic foundations of the laws of dialectic, Mr. Gidden's proposal will easily look like nonsense. It may be seen as a magisterial ideology to dress up the opportunism of 'new labor' politicians' readiness to hedge any bet and duck every hard choice. Mr. Gidden himself probably does not know that the third way is the path of the *Sushumna* within his own spinal chord. Perhaps the London School of Economics should introduce a course on the subject.

The real question of evolution is: does the third way lead anywhere? And the answer may be yes and no. Both Lenin and Mao Tse Tung tried and failed. Both William Blake and Kahlil Gibran tried and succeeded. The real answer is not to strive to achieve the elusive third stage at the psychological or political level, but rather, to find access through the *Sushumna nadi* to the Fourth State at the spiritual level.

THE MODUS OPERANDI

To summarize the argument on *gunas* and polarity presented thus far, we could try to establish an illustrative list of patterns of response to polarity, without reading too much into it. Let us not fail to specify that because of the law of polarity itself, the scales are not immutable opposites, but poles of dynamic tension.

Bipolarity in the psychological, social or political world has inspired many a theory and generated various attitudes, each in turn conditioning a group of responses or sets of behaviors. To schematize the response to bipolarity we can propose the three following types:

One Polarity Response: The temptation here is to eliminate the difference. The tension or dilemma between the poles is negated and solved by emphasizing one element of the pair to the detriment of the other. Psychologically, we find here characters who are either pushing their own views on others *(Pingala nadi)* or those who willingly accept conditionings and rules *(Ida nadi)*. One-polarity political or corporate systems are intolerant and tend to eliminate differences. One Polarity Response can lead to aggression, domination and conflicts. It fosters conformist and gregarious behavior. At the political level, One Polarity Response is totalitarian.

Dichotomy Response: The dilemma between the poles is acknowledged but considered as radically unsolvable. We find here pessimistic individuals with split identities and confused objectives and a sense of alienation, as there is no reconciliation in sight. Corporate systems shun comprehensive models, focus on the short term and brace themselves for conflicts. Politically, this response leads to a horse trading style, to secure immediate gains, and dealing without vision or long term strategy.

Synthetic Response: The contradiction between the poles can be overcome by managing the dynamics, by the actualization of a process of negotiation or by strategic thinking to chart the path ahead. Individuals have a fast learning curve and are adjustable. Social and corporate systems tend to assimilate, compromise and accommodate differences. Political systems are dynamic and ready to adjust to changes. Alas, often it may turn out that the Synthetic

Response ends up into a one-polarity assertion because the space of the central channel has not been reached.

If we read the pairs horizontally, we recognize that the dynamics of interaction and contradiction are the canvases which support the world of phenomena. Some pairs are simple, like hot and cold or day and night. It is the third movement resulting from their interaction that is harder to predict. Between day and night, are we at dawn or at dusk? Will our thoughts and feelings forever alternate without much connection? How far are we genetically or culturally conditioned and how far can we steer our destiny from the power of our own free will? How can we combine wealth creation through the channel of ego-centered pursuits with its eventual distribution on the left side in meeting social concerns? We must recognize that the poles indicate moods and preferences but to cast them into a definite pattern is to ignore the dynamics of polarity and to miss the point. Each entity contains features from both scales, as can be seen, for instance, in corresponding aesthetic sensitivities. Chopin and Beethoven play the emotions of the moon channel, while Bach and Bartok cast in their notes the clarity of the sun channel, but there is light and shadow, order and passion in the work of all these composers.

If we read the pairs vertically, we see the morphology or Gestalt of a psychological paradigm, much as described in the *Gita* or in the work of the historian Oswald Spengler.

On the *Pingala nadi*, we see the assertion of action and conquest, the masculine world of the hard driving, future oriented, individual ego which finally led to predatory economics. This corresponds overall to the expansive dynamics of Western civilization in the last centuries and successive expressions of the strong identification of the West with action. Heroes of this model are conquerors: Alexander, Julius Caesar, Charles XII of Sweden or Napoleon. From the Portuguese navigators to the American industrial baron, the culture of the West claims: I do therefore I am.

On the *Ida nadi*, a culture will emphasize collective goals and common destiny. It strives to emphasize communal values and collective wellbeing. Some traditional cultural models of antiquity refer to it. Asia values introspection and the search for inner personal fulfillment and social order, as expressed in Buddhism or Confucianism. The major powers of Asia such as India and China did not engage in colonial ventures outside their traditional boundaries. India was devoted to the aim of self-realization and China was invested in the Confucian quest for order and harmony. Political models emphasized the preservation of the community and social values. Typically, the Japanese corporate style values togetherness, workforce cohesion and loyalty to the firm. Africa, similarly on the left channel, values the notion of belonging to a totemic group, a clan or a tribe. The feminine world, which rules feelings and emotions, emphasizes the virtue of compassion and sharing.

Of course, both sides are necessary. More precisely, each side is a condition for the proper functioning of its opposite. We register in the collective superego, which comprises the memory or stored conditionings from the past, the accumulated codes for the survival of the species. Without access to this code encrypted in the left side, without feelers from the heart, the right-sided operator can become an unguided missile, an oppressor, a Tamerlane or a Hitler. On the other hand, without the energizing dynamism of the sun channel, there is neither progress nor growth. The left-sided operator stagnates in apathy and fatalism or can even be swallowed in the hazy darkness of addictions or witchcraft.

This is why, to prevent such extremes, Yin has to flow into Yang and vice versa. The pairs are never rigid but interactive and constantly evolving. They repel and attract each other. They generate their respective opposites. For instance, we positioned socialism on the left but we could also describe communism on the right side, as having evolved into a rigid system of right-sided totalitarian oppression. Capitalism in turn, originally on the right side because of its inherent dynamism, could be portrayed as leading to the ultimate state of left-sided self-indulgence. In its promotion of consumer bingeing and libertarian or loose life styles, it celebrates our abandonment into the multiplicity of our desires projected on the material world.

This leads to an important point. There are two types of interactions between the poles, destructive and constructive. Swings between left and right, lateral movements of Yin and Yang energies from one extreme to another can be destructive. They express reactive processes which, in their automaticity, overpower the subject or control the destiny of a nation. The constructive interaction occurs when the two energies are complementing each other and achieving balance, leading the way to a richer synthesis.

17. THE SHEER JOY OF FREEDOM

For truly, on getting the essence (rasa) of existence, one becomes blissful. For who indeed would breathe, who would live, if there were not this bliss in space! For truly, this essence causes bliss. For truly, when one finds fearlessness as a foundation in that which is invisible, bodiless, undefined, without base, then he has reached fearlessness.

— Taittirya Upanishad

The nature of Spirit may be understood by a glance at its direct opposite - Matter. As the essence of Matter is Gravity, so, on the other hand, we may affirm that the substance, the essence of Spirit is Freedom.

— G.W.F. Hegel, The Philosophy of History

THE MAGIC TRIANGLE

In order to reach the innermost depth of our being, to taste the ocean of its joy, we have to dive deep. Attachment and involvement in our daily life keeps us floating on the surface. We are tossed about by events, challenges and problems that confront us every day. How does *homo spiritualis* handle this relationship with daily surroundings that can be so fraught with adversity?

We can find a response in the synergy between Antar yoga and Karma yoga brought about by the Sahaja system as taught by Shri Mataji. It manifests a capacity to face the outside dimension of life, equipped with spiritual powers that are awakened by the practice of meditation. This creates 'win-win' opportunities. I have tried to show this mechanism with a drawing, shown in figure 3.

The triangle represents the field of our existence, the battlefield (Kurukshetra) of our daily life. This is the field where we desire and act, where we perform and want to win at the game of life.

Pole A of the Triangle represents a twice born, having gone through the experience of Kundalini awakening, yet still facing the regular challenges of the normal daily life of a householder. He still is in the process of discovering or testing his spiritual powers and finding out how to apply them in his surroundings.

Pole B of the Triangle represents the option, opened to *homo spiritualis* by Self-realization, to activate Antar yoga through meditation. When the subject has mastered the art of meditation, the Kundalini takes the consciousness into the state of thoughtless awareness *(Nirvichara sammadhi)*. B is thoughtless awareness; it is the inner dimension. This movement, however, is a process that may take some time, depending on the condition of the liver. A bad liver generates mental agitation.

Pole C represents the solid dimension of our everyday surroundings, with its rich variety of challenges. It contains the shifting shapes of our outside dimension. Our lives, the world over, are not that different. Regular people face difficulties or ordeals that are largely similar, whatever the

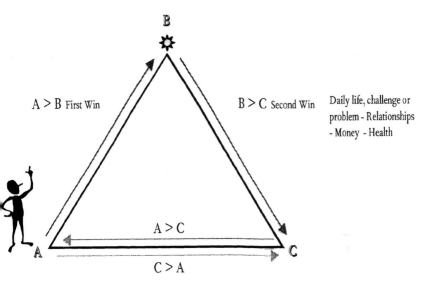

Figure 3. The Magic Triangle

country or culture. We face difficulties in our relationships: family, love affairs, friendships, and clan. We may be under stress in positioning ourselves within society: within profession, group assimilation and peer recognition. Many of us are facing financial constraints. Moreover, later in life, we increasingly face difficulties in the area of health. Indeed, the person for whom all these areas of life are free of problems would be very lucky indeed. But most of us, even after realization, still confront such challenges. How do we fare and how does spirituality help in daily life? Where is the magic?

The trend A>C represents the fact that now I face a specific difficulty. Something is going wrong; I cannot ignore it and I must find a solution to the problem. This compulsion absorbs my attention, no matter where the problem lies, be it with relationships, money, job or health.

The trend C>A expresses the effect that the outside world has on me. In fact, as far as my state of being is concerned, I become reactive and the problem is having an impact on my consciousness. Let us assume the problem is serious and I cannot solve it at once. I cannot, for example, pay back my debts, or perhaps my boss is unfair to me, or my job is at risk. The succession of action and reaction in my ego and superego is troubling my equilibrium as I try to sort out the problem. I am upset, and the disturbing circumstances in my outside world rob me of a condition of satisfaction in my inner world. I am in a losing position, for on top of the outside problem, I now face an inner one: my peace of mind is disturbed and my consciousness is unhappy. The movements A>C and C>A are the stuff of everyday struggle for *homo sapiens*.

The trend A>B expresses the new consciousness response of *homo spiritualis* when faced with exactly the same range of challenges. This is where the magic starts. The subject diverts his attention from the problem, and wherever he is, he goes into meditation. Through entering thoughtless awareness, the subject regains his inner composure and peace of mind. This is the first win. Although the outside problem still exists, the problem no longer exerts a disturbing impact on his consciousness. Thoughtless awareness pushes the disturbance out of his mind, and the subject is cool and unstressed.

The trend B>C is a little hard to explain, for this is where the full magic unfolds. As my consciousness reaches B, I get connected to the inner powers of the spirit. These powers are acting on my outside environment, instead of the outside environment acting on me. Information on my problem is passed to the primordial computer of the Virata.

The connection through the Sahasrara is wiring me into the greater power of the *Paramchaitanya,* the force of God that controls all the causalities of history. This, in turn, acts on the outside according to its own logic. It often happens that suddenly, the problem is solved, without my doing anything about it. One finds a new source of income to pay one's debts, or a difficult boss is suddenly transferred elsewhere. B>C is not automatic, nor does it conform always to expectations. Sometimes it works, sometimes it does not and in any case, it works only after the consciousness has reached B. One cannot achieve the second win without the first one.

OVERCOMING THE SIX ENEMIES OF THE SOUL

The time is always right to do what is right.

— Martin Luther King

The discussion that follows represents a radical change from the way we are conditioned to think and be, and as such, I hope that it is something the reader can come to understand and appreciate. It can help to shift one's focus, and to understand that there is a better way to be and to see this in relation to the qualities of the chakras. One needs to understand the process of the Kundalini passing through the chakras, and in doing so, automatically improving the specific qualities within them. This will make us wish to be connected and to improve from within in a totally natural process that just requires some silence and letting it happen once realization has taken place.

The realized state is characterized, in principle, by the enjoyment of pure inner freedom, without any psychological bondage. Of course, it may take some time to develop this condition, even after realization, for old conditionings linger on and must dissolve gradually. Introspection is the necessary mechanism for freeing oneself from these chains and it cuts the ties that keep us from growing inwardly. It is interesting to discover that every chakra can be under the attack of a specific defect, behavior or addiction, but that the awakening of the chakra's power by the Kundalini progressively eliminates these defects.

Lust is caused by a malfunction of the first center (Mooladhara chakra). By lust, we mean here an addictive and compulsive interest in sex. Sex has jumped into the eyes and the brain of the modern Christian, despite a prophetic warning of Christ against "adulterous eyes." Eroticism is supposed to be an art form, but pornography becomes obsessive, a fact sadly confirmed by the history of many sex offenders arrested on criminal charges. People think about sex and can hardly any longer enjoy having it, as a spontaneous parasympathetic activity. Lust rarely releases its captives; it ensnares the attention of the young and not so young alike, and when people follow its impulse, their behavior can lead to the destruction of relationships and families. Betrayed spouses, broken hearts and damaged relationships litter its path. But the restoring of the integrity of the Mooladhara chakra is possible through Sahaja meditation practices. A restored Mooladhara implies the return of innocence; it greatly facilitates a mature and fulfilled sexuality and thence the re-emergence of stable families.

"Anger," Horace advises, "is momentary madness, so control your passion or it will control you." Anger represents a malfunction of the second center (Swadishtan chakra) and can take a variety of forms. This chakra is the power store of the energy of action, but if it overheats this energy can express itself in angry behavior. Anger breeds conflict and stress, bursts out into patterns of aggression, calls for violence, and pits man against man, and corporations and collective groupings against each other. The cycle triggered by anger is endless: turf battles, devious plots and power challenges all aggressively fuel angry responses in a never-ending cycle of destructive competition. Another form of addiction attacking the Swadishtan chakra is the phenomena known today as 'workaholism', a compulsive involvement in one's own activity whereby inner peace is lost. Improvement in the Swadishtan chakra turns its energy into constructive purposes, creativity and dynamism. It becomes the engine of progress. People with a well-functioning Swadishtan are imaginative in their designs, talented and competent in their undertakings and are definite assets in the organizations or corporations employing them. While they efficiently deliver the goods, they keep their inner distance and personal freedom, and are not captives but masters of the field of action.

Greed relates to a contraction or constriction of the third center (Manipur or Nabhi chakra) and because of this, the energy of the being is diverted from inner growth into acquiring external possessions - 'to have' rather than 'to be' in the realm of one's identity. Greed projects a fixation on ownership and an addiction to material accumulation. Sound economics represents a regulation and channeling of desire, but greed produces uncontrolled desire and by its very nature tends towards excess. It encourages the hubris of the ego. For instance, the speculative attacks of short-term investors on Asian currencies are an incidence of greed gone global, a feature of the 1990s. If a society does not control greed it will gradually undermine its foundations because it destroys the collective values which are indispensable for its long-term survival. Greed takes away from the many to give even more wealth to the few; it consumes natural resources in an unsustainable manner; it encourages corruption and organized crime. In this respect, an important feature of a healthy third center is a spontaneous adherence to an inner ethical code. The manifestation of the qualities of the Nabhi include an innate feeling of wellbeing and satisfaction, a condition that makes greed superfluous and irrelevant. The third center grants balance to the personality and this factor of equilibrium, between the movements of the lateral channels, provides the basis for the capacity to adapt and evolve.

Attachment strangles the opening of the fourth center (Anahata chakra). It is a conditioning which curtails the power of the heart to love in a generous and giving way. Attachment is a lower form of love, and a selfish one: it takes instead of giving and is a manifestation of excess. Attached love binds emotions in such a manner that the phenomenon of addiction, is this time vested in specific personal relationships: mother, sister, son, friend etc. Attachment is the killer of freedom, mixing, as it does, love with distorting feelings such as cravings and emotional dependency. It is both cause and consequence of a lack of inner security. Social manifestation of attachments can take many forms: favoritism, nepotism, or, as seen more frequently in many organizations, the practice of selecting collaborators based on personal loyalty rather than competence.

Jealousy blocks the passage through the fifth center (Vishuddhi) and it can be understood as an addiction of the ego, which is absorbed in the attainment of its own achievements. Consequently the success of another person will be resented, and jealousy prevents the establishment of common purpose and teamwork. It is thus destructive to the smooth functioning of any human collectivity. To the jealous mind, someone else's gain is its own loss. This feeling is a killer of friendship and togetherness as it pours the greenish poison of envy, where instead there should be fun and merrymaking. A person with a healthy Vishuddhi chakra is sensitive to the needs of the whole, to the interests of the collectivity and to the organization of which he or she is part. They keep their focus on the 'big picture' and are good at charting out a strategic course. Such a person will invariably improve the effectiveness of the workplace through interpersonal skills. Their concern for others is not faked and colleagues recognize the qualities of a genuine team builder.

In the words of George Eliot, a vain man would be "Like a cock who thought the sun had risen to hear him crow." In *Le Bourgeois Gentilhomme*, Molière recognizes, with his usual humor, the underlying shortcut between vanity and idiocy.

Vanity obstructs the opening of the Third Eye, the sixth center (Agnya). Like Narcissus absorbed in his own image, the vain character is addicted to himself. He places appearance above substance, and the narcissist often may inflict his strange malfunction on the surroundings in the form of pride. The movement corresponds to the flight from the real identity, the Self, towards an outside construction of the ego, a virtual identity carved out of successive layers of conditionings and misidentifications. Vanity has taken many entertaining forms through the ages: for example, the ludicrous wigs of Louis XIV or the pompous uniforms of Mussolini. On the economic plane, the vanity of today's consumers primes the pump of the entrepreneurs and they cash in on it, developing totally unnecessary goods in an artificial world of brands and fashions. The inattentive consumer gradually builds up his identity in what he has, and not in what he is. This is not a very reliable proposition, and in both social life and in the workplace, vanity translates into a lack of discrimination, poor judgment and wrong decisions. When the Agnya clears, the brain of the subject is no longer blinded or misled by the projections of ego or the residue of conditionings, and is capable of settling into a deeper self-identity: a source of personal strength, confidence and resilience.

All of these vices, then, are the enemies of our self-mastery, unseen 'twisters' riding the dark horses of our thoughts and desires. They often like riding together. Addiction, in its multiple forms, naturally tending towards the extremes, screams for more: more sex (lust), more violence (anger) more money (greed), more attention (attachment) or more self glorification (vanity). More of everything for 'I, me, and mine' and less for everybody else. It cannot work. This is why ancestral wisdom was translated into religious or moral precepts to avoid these all too common forms of psychic addictions. But preaching is not enough.

Technically speaking, the malfunctions of the psychosomatic and spiritual centers correspond to lateral pulls, constrictions and distortions caused by the swings of energy from the lateral channels of *Ida* and *Pingala*. If the chakras could spin and release their energies unhindered, they would unfold the powers of the initiation path that is hinted at Mozart's opera, *The Magic Flute*. Actually the flute, the preferred instrument of Lord Krishna, is a fit analogy. The air must flow through its seven holes to create the music, just as our Kundalini must pass through the seven centers that house our subtler energies in order to unfold the full potential of our Being.

The happening of Self-realization creates a new flow of energy in the *Sushumna*, which counters and balances various negative influences. It thereby makes the potential of the chakras dynamic, as the ascending force of the Kundalini lines up the chakras through, as it were, an inner thread. The qualities of the chakras are activated through the parasympathetic nervous system, that is, in a spontaneous manner, beyond 'ontogenesis training' or other forms of manipulations. The entire personality gains in strength and coherence, and furthermore, in one form or another, awakened chakras express themselves in altruistic behavior.

The stabilization of the chakras along the *Sushumna* manifest, at the social level, sensitivity and compassion as well as the capacity to provide credible and sustained leadership. They build up the features of a personality structure that is wholesome and magnetic. The world today faces a lack of leadership across a broad spectrum of human affairs, at a time when we need more enlightened responses to the challenges of an emerging global society. A fully functional inner instrument manifests a leadership grounded in the qualities of the Self, a leadership that is proactive and inspired, that perceives the longer term and the common good of the whole. A leadership that is made strong by vision, sustained by ethics and manifested through transparent and clear-cut decision making.

SEVEN HOUSES FOR A NEW CITY

Ecology comes from the Greek, *oikos logos*, the principle that rules the house while economy comes from, *oikos nomos*, the regulation that applies to the house. In both cases the house of man is a collective entity abiding by a set of norms. The old polis of ancient Greece is long gone and so are many of the dreams of establishing a congenial community living in equality and freedom. But as Boethius said, to change oneself is to change the world. The house of Man in the Third Age will abide by new rules and each one of us can participate in the construction of this global house, home to a new society, through our own inner transformation. At the center of our togetherness we must secure open access to the seven magic houses of spirituality whose powers work for the individual and the collectivity alike. The raising of the Kundalini can be thought of as a sort of package deal where we are blessed by an amazing number of breakthroughs. It unfolds the tremendous potential stored in our seven inner chambers, the houses of inner energy.

Quite clearly, the implications of the awakening of our inner potential unfold for all aspects of our life, such as our wellbeing, our home and relationships. But for the sake of paradox, I would like to illustrate some of these specific implications for our jobs. The long hours spent on our professional and business commitments often seem to constitute a part of our life that is remote from spirituality, and on the whole, the business world is slow to recognize that ethics and spirituality could be good for business. I hope the reader will not mind if we emphasize some implications of this yoga breakthrough for something as mundane as business practices. I agree it sounds a bit trivial to establish such connections, when the subject of spiritual transformation is really our relationship with God. Yet, as we all toil in the furnaces of the modern factory described by William Blake, should we not wish that the business environment itself could be transformed and lend support to the improvement of our societies?

Let us review, by way of illustration, some implications of fully operational chakras, at both personal and corporate levels. The purpose is to suggest to the corporate world that we need more enlightened and ethical business practices if the present cycle of aggression, waste and corruption, that only too often prevails in our economies, is to be abolished.

The First Center (Mooladhara Chakra)

The House of Earth plays host to the principles that provide the roots of any individual, collectivity or institution. Through this center we are grounded and find stability. Our being finds its place within reality, through innocence, spontaneity, wisdom and humility. The combination of these qualities brings about what people call good luck, that is, an auspicious or fortunate course of action. As the saying goes, "Luck is the way God travels incognito." From the King to the beggar, we all need good luck, and this is why Shri Ganesha, the elephant-headed God who controls this chakra, is one of the most popular Deities in India.

A sound Mooladhara offers the blessings of spontaneity, innocence and wisdom; it is at the core of trust in the couple, in successful relationships and in a happy sex life. The strength of the union of man and woman provides for stable families, where children can grow and blossom. In a nutshell, the health of society depends on it.

Through our grounding within reality, we maintain a healthy relationship with nature, balancing the satisfaction of our needs with the availability of natural resources. In a context of growing scarcity of resources, our economies would adjust to environmental preservation, at the local and global levels. The linkage with cultural and social roots would become part of a company's strategy, with a view to fostering continuity between cultural backgrounds and economic behavior. Such principles are already at work in small-scale enterprises as well as in the informal sector of the economy where strong family and cultural links embedded in business strategies can increase the effectiveness and profitability of family-size companies.

The Second Center (Swadishtan Chakra)

The House of Fire is the powerhouse for action, creativity and innovation. Its qualities bless those who seek fulfillment through action with discipline, productivity, and efficiency. This chakra is also responsible for art, music and aesthetics, as it provides the inspiration for all manner of artistic achievement. It is the source of elegance, beauty and scientific discovery. It is the provider of intellect and analytical skills. The Swadishtan gives energy and discipline, and the importance of this center for society is paramount, being the center that inspires performance orientation and the delivery of results.

A well-functioning Swadishtan supplies energy for physical and mental activity; it helps the student to concentrate, the scientist to analyze, the architect to draw a building and the psychologist to understand a patient. It rules over our cognitive processes and informs our sense of invention and discovery.

But we will only point here at one salient feature. The lack of creativity, in an individual or on a collective scale, marks the exhaustion of this center and the resultant decline of a corporation, or indeed, it can herald the decline of an entire civilization. To avoid this risk, societies should promote innovation. This does not only mean innovation from a technological perspective but culturally and professionally. Trained, motivated and competent staff who can develop their creativity and enjoy their work will achieve maximum results. Innovation must become a part of an organization's internal policies, as a creative tool to increase employee satisfaction and productivity. Accepting changes, fostering new ideas and products, opening paths for staff development are some of the expressions of a corporate creative process.

The Third Center (Manipura or Nabhi Chakra):

As the British, the Dutch, the Portuguese and all sea-faring people know, water brings wealth through fishing, trade and the opening of communication lines, but we are trying here to make a subtler point. Although considered as a free commodity until recently, water is the ultimate creator of wealth. But we have managed to turn clean water into a scarce and increasingly expensive resource. The House of Water contains the secret of wealth creation and the successful operation of this chakra brings both material and spiritual wealth. The first conquest of the Manipura or Nabhi is the achievement of a satisfied and peaceful frame of mind that spontaneously grasps the balance in everything. The advantage of a good Nabhi shows in the spontaneous regulation of the energies of the two lateral *nadis*. This helps to avoid the pitfalls of stress that may be the consequence of an overactive Swadishtan. The opening of the Nabhi promotes a strong sense of harmony, of compromise and of what is feasible, and it gifts the subject with an intuitive mind, well suited for peacemaking, negotiations and strategic thinking.

At the economic level, we must understand how to generate an abundance of goods, services and options. Wealth creation needs to abide by a set of rules that are sustained at the collective level. If wealth is merely seen as the spoils of war in the competitive struggles for domination and control - a fairly prevalent perception in history - it cannot be maintained in the long term. Hence wealth creation must be guided and sustained by a set of values (dharma). Companies would integrate moral values into their corporate vision to include: a) a code of conduct at the individual level (to extirpate corruption and fraud - whose cost to business is staggering) and b) a collective ethical code of conduct, covering humanitarian and social concerns (to optimize wealth distribution). Social responsibility will grow at a different pace in different companies but with the adherence to an ethical vision, the role of business in fostering a better distribution of wealth will create strong demands in the internal and international markets to fuel balanced but robust economic growth. Stable, widespread and sustained wealth creation is feasible.

Awareness of the ethical paradigm will grow and expand to a point where public authorities will reconsider policy formulation, taking into account moral issues. Policy tools will be developed to take into account higher ideals. These ideals will preserve corporate profitability but will further secure the cohesion of business and society and the compatibility between short-term profit and longer-term wealth sustainability. Compliance and conformity with social requirements will bring about a more optimal market, where the goods and services offered will better correspond to the real needs of consumers, who will be empowered to clearly formulate their demands. Economic operators will feel compelled to build moral imperatives into their criteria for developing a holistic corporate strategy. The losers will be those left behind, unable to adapt.

The Fourth Center (Anahata Chakra)

Everyone breathes the same air and is sustained by one and the same energy. The fourth center is the chakra of the heart, which pumps and gives out the universal energy of love, the ultimate and divine energy that feeds our race. For those of us who are lucky enough to feel love, giving or receiving, we know that it is at the core of our most enjoyable moments. The opening of the heart chakra squeezes out of our system fear, anxieties and worries. We escape the mental and psychic tortures that we so often inflict upon ourselves by rehearsing in our heads possible worst case scenarios. Confidence is a key ingredient of our wellbeing. Love brings forth the comfort of shared perceptions, of self-respect and dignity.

The activation of love, as an energy that may improve and reward social processes, will have a far-reaching impact for our psychic wellbeing, our homes and our cities. Violence and aggression will lose their appeal. Internally, people will learn how to share their experiences and emotions. Working will mean sharing, team building, and will be much more fun. Employees will feel secure, self confident and loyal to the company. Targeted social security policies, such as healthcare and pension schemes, will rely on cooperative attitudes among insurance companies, workers, business and government.

An ethical company will inspire a new feeling of devotion in its employees, and altruistic attitudes will develop internally, for their welfare, and externally, towards the customers, the local community, and society in general.

The focus will shift from short-term shareholder values, which try to please the financial markets with cost containment and other strategies that are biased towards shareholder values, and PERs (price-earnings ratios). Instead, demand creation will not rely so strongly on psychological manipulation in favor of brands, ephemeral fashions, or on the power of advertising, but on empowering a broad-based demand from customers through improvement of their purchasing power. After all, there are five billion lower-income human beings out there who are still waiting to strengthen demand in the real global economy, if only appropriate policies can lift them from their various degrees of poverty. Altruism will breed prosperity. If it is true that, as President Franklin D. Roosevelt said, "Poverty anywhere is a threat to prosperity everywhere," it should also become true, in the global economy, that prosperity anywhere should reduce poverty everywhere. The much-vilified President Mahatir of Malaysia had a point when he said that the global economy should not merely open a vaster hunting ground for transnational corporations and financial speculators. The real global economy will be the one that will be able to create income for these billions of new customers and to integrate them as consumers in a sustainable new world market.

The Fifth Center (Vishuddhi Chakra)

The Ether carries magnetic waves and communication. The power of the House of Ether brings us the full magnitude of an enlarged vision. The witness stage brings both acuity of judgment and clarity of perception. It creates a strong defensive barrier against the onslaught of thought waves, suggestions, conditionings and manipulations that confuse so many of us. This expanded vision transcends the location of the individual thinker, *(Standortsbewusstsein)*, and enables us to develop collective consciousness. This multiplies the epistemological capacities of man in the Third Age. The opening of this chakra favors self-esteem and dignity, transcending the feelings of guilt that are often pushed on us by our environment.

Improvement of communication skills is an acknowledged necessity in our global world. To start with, the information revolution is expanding the scope of this center of communication with respect to connectivity and play. Playing is an under-rated but all-important notion because it implies the faculty to act with the protective inner distance of detachment from everyday problems. That inner distance improves sight; it enhances problem solving, the identification of critical paths and the projection of a coherent vision. More importantly, it is only through the notion of play that work can become truly stress free. Obstacles, deadlines and challenges remain but they lose their power to worry or upset.

Managers who can cultivate some sense of detachment are better negotiators than their more forceful colleagues who are captured by the power of their own arguments and are consequently incapable of seeing a contentious issue from different angles. At the same time, those in charge must re-establish fading ties with the bottom level. Interactions must allow management to stay closer to the production line, while at the same time, holding the corporate vision for the company. Through opened communication channels, improvement processes within the enterprise can be an ongoing and democratic exercise. Ideas are sought from all organizational levels. Within a group or a collectivity, the willingness to share, to listen and to express, will reinforce the sense of belonging, will forge a common purpose and a more cohesive will to achieve this purpose together. Collective consciousness leads to better communication.

The Sixth Center (Agnya Chakra)

Beyond the five material elements linked to the previous centers, the sixth chakra is the gate to intrinsic spiritual qualities, and its property is to illuminate a deeper and more spiritual understanding of existence and its daily challenges. Christ is the Guardian of the House of Light that is in our forehead. Everything that looks tentative or dubious, in the shadows of the usual mental confusion, is endowed with new clarity once the light of the Third Eye is turned on. On a spiritual plane, this chakra's opening is conducive to the enlightenment and inspiration that flows from the universal unconscious, bringing about a powerful harmony of intellectual and emotional coefficients.

The Agnya manifests two principal qualities. Firstly, as the working of the previous chakra introduces to the psyche a sense of collective consciousness and togetherness, the Agnya chakra, as a logical consequence, develops a spontaneous sense of compassion and forgiveness. The 'other person' is no longer perceived as alien, foreign or hostile but someone to be assisted or helped as part and parcel of a global improvement project. Mistakes from colleagues are not seized upon as opportunities for humiliation or punishment, but considered as occurrences on a learning curve that the manager wants to accelerate. The achievements of his staff are sought by the manager as a desirable indicator of the efforts he has undertaken to enhance staff productivity. This attitude in a leader inspires employees' commitment and trust.

On the other hand, this chakra develops a definite assertion of one's own being and values, that has nothing to do with ego or arrogance, but reflects instead a quiet recognition of one's own inner being. The resulting self-confidence in one's own identity and values expresses itself in courage and in the willingness to do what is right in the face of risks. A risk can take the form of a real or perceived threat to oneself, or to one's reputation or career. Such a decision maker will have sharper judgment and a strong preference for substance over appearance, and will be ready, if necessary, to challenge the status quo. A manager with a clear Agnya will more easily be able to resist solutions that may be popular or politically astute, but which are in fact detrimental to the real interests of the company.

The Agnya sets up new standards of excellence which, going beyond such considerations as the quantity of labor employed, or the possession of managerial skills, imply the capacity for tuning into the principles of life, and the understanding of psychic and collective phenomena. Indeed, broader vision rests on the grasp of deeper correlations and interactions that may be invisible to the average person, but whose impact is important. Economic operators will become aware of people's needs and expectations as well as emerging trends.

The Seventh Center (Sahasrara Chakra)

Whereupon, opening the center of their skulls, he entered. The door by which he entered is called the door of bliss.

   — Aitareya Upanishad

On the seventh day, the Lord rested and saw that everything that had been made was good. "This is the center of our bond with the Divine," says Shri Mataji. It grants the enlightened consciousness and contains one thousand powers that may flow into us. But to access the Sahasrara, it is necessary to reduce and correct the ego. To this effect, it is useful to develop the state of the witness *(sakshi swarup)*, for only in the witness state can we really see the moves and twists and plots of our own ego. "Ego is your own enemy created by you" Shri Mataji says, "and the power of the Sahasrara can be activated only by the highest power of love and not by the lower will to power that haunts lower level human beings." It is with "a passionate compassion" she goes on, "that the powers of Sahasrara can be used for mankind's benevolence." This again echoes the wisdom of the ages. Kabir was a poet of the Absolute and he writes: "Banish your egotism, drive it far away; then will even-mindedness be born; only then can you realize that within all abides the self-same Lord; only then can you realize oneness."

'*Ni*', in Sanskrit, is a prefix indicating a negation: 'neither this, nor that' The seventh center is neither this, nor that. It is what it is, in the splendor of itself, when everything said and done, fails to reach or express it. The House of Ni negates all shortcomings and limitations and opens the gates of the blissful state longed for by the best-informed seekers of mankind's long quest for total fulfillment. It is the mystical chamber of the union between the Atman and the Kundalini, which bridges the gap between the Child and his God. It integrates the other six centers and yet is much more than the sum of their parts. Perhaps the best way to characterize the Sahasrara is to describe it as the holistic center of synergy and integration, the global chakra. Until the end of the Second Age, it had largely been hidden from our knowledge and beyond the reach of the human race. So it may be hazardous to venture any comments on the impact of the opening of this center on collective human processes.

It is at the opening of this last, global center, that *homo sapiens* becomes instantly *homo spiritualis,* a universal being. The categories of perceptions are vastly expanded. He or she enjoys collective consciousness, the faculty to know through direct perception the condition of another person's system, *nadis* and chakras. We enjoy vibratory awareness, the faculty to know the exact coefficient of any living being: plant, animal or human. Seeing is believing but feeling is God's own truth.

The key word here is integration. Of course, this dimension is more vast than the context of our professional world, but as it permeates everything, it can, of course, transform the workplace for the better. This capacity to feel at one with the whole can open a new dimension to corporate cohesion. Values and common purpose will flow spontaneously among realized individuals who will share a new, common, interior language. The consensus on ultimate values will bring together citizens and administrators, shareholders and stakeholders, managers and employees. The fusion of goals and wills will transform the enterprise into an efficient engine for wealth creation, ecological improvement and social change. For if it is true that the sixth center releases our visionary potential, it is at the seventh center that the vision becomes collective. A company cannot have a vision - only its managers and employees can. A shared vision, grounded in the understanding of reality, is a by-product of Self-realization.

BEYOND REACTIVITY

We walk in our shoes, rarely touching the earth with our naked feet. Yet sometimes we have the urge to take our shoes off and feel, with delight, the dew on the grass refreshing our toes or the fullness of the sand on the beach warming our feet. Would it not be nice if we could do the same with our brain, take off its 'shoes,' that is, its projections and concepts, and just see, just know. Often our thoughts work as tainted or distorting lenses. Why is it so?

A man sits on a bench beside Lake Geneva. His mind goes into overdrive as he sees a pretty woman walking by. He thinks that her skirt is too short, her hair too long. He sees that she wears an expensive watch and she reminds him of a Piz Buin poster that he saw in the pharmacy. She looks like she could be going out with a rich Arab tourist waiting for her in front of the Hilton, in a red Ferrari. It's not fair. These guys are so rich just because they have some gas under the ground. This fellow sees and thinks all kinds of things but is he capable of just seeing without thinking?

We react more through reflex actions than through reflected responses. Thought comes at lighting speed, following the message from the eye to the brain and then electric circuitry sends back a thought or a feeling before 'I' has a chance to notice. We thus go on in our lives, endlessly seeing, hearing, touching, smelling and reacting to the senses with thoughts and feelings. The senses are the horses of our chariots but it is they, the horses, who lead the chariot, not 'I' the charioteer. Other charioteers do not even notice that the chariot merely goes where the horses want to go.

Interestingly, when Lord Krishna speaks in the *Bhagavad Gita*, it is in the role of a charioteer to his warrior disciple Arjuna, on the battlefield of the *Kurukshetra*. The British colonizers discredited Hinduism as being merely backward superstitions, and even today, whereas Buddhism is very much in fashion with American and European intellectuals, Hinduism is largely ignored. Given that all the essential premises of Buddhism are already contained in Hinduism, including how and why it is helpful to be able to control the senses, it is a shame that so few Westerners are interested in what it has to say. In the Hindu pantheon, Lord Vishnu has been identified as the 'Manager' of evolution, on the *Sushumna*, the central channel. He is, in the words of Blaise Pascal, "The God of Abraham, of Isaac and of Jacob", that is, the one who at appointed times intervenes directly in the course of history. Krishna is worshipped by Hindus as a manifestation (Avatar) of Vishnu and is praised with one thousand Sanskrit names. One of them is *Sahishnu*, the One who bears the duality of heat and cold. Another of his names is *Lokadaksha*, the One who watches the play of the worlds. Bringing the two meanings together, we read a precise script: the capacity to evolve on the central channel has something to do with the capacity to master bipolarity through the witness stage.

Our normal condition is a bit like a rider looking at a landscape on a galloping horse through a smoke screen. The galloping horse is the brain which races from one thought to another, from one feeling to the next. The fumes of ego in our thoughts, and those of our superego in our emotions constitute the smokescreen. The smoke we produce is the fruit of our reactivity, which prevents us seeing clearly the landscape through which we pursue our journey. We react with the ego: perhaps with a sense of hurt pride or the desire to be 'center stage.' We react too, with the superego: fear of loneliness, or of not being loved, attachments, sexual attraction etc. If the horse could somehow slow down and the smokescreen clear out, then the 'I' could just see the landscape as it is and understand what is happening there. We could then see both the friend on the hill and the enemy in the woods. Without the impulses from ego and superego we would just see things as they are, a perception so direct and simple that it escapes us. As we said before: in *homo sapiens* mode, we live in virtual reality.

In the universal mythology, Shri Krishna represents the divine charioteer, the Self, who drives the horses of the five senses. "Don't react, just see," is the message of Shri Mataji that echoes the teachings of Shri Krishna. But how to achieve a state of freedom from reactivity? It is easier said than done, but we instinctively understand that he who keeps his head cool will have a definite advantage in any situation involving stress and pressure.

For instance, let us go back to the example of the gentleman sitting on the bench looking at the passing girl. The ego may wish to send to the awareness such messages as the desire to push oneself forward, to conquer or seduce the girl, or to make judgmental remarks on her appearance; the superego on the other hand, may send the following messages: fear of being rejected, insecurity, loneliness, sexual attraction. Messages will combine: for instance, the will to seduce goes well with sexual attraction. This is already a mind hard at work, just at the sight of a pretty girl passing by. Energy has been wasted and control of the attention lost. In *homo spiritualis*, the waves of energy from the Kundalini activate the soothing impact of the parasympathetic nervous system and gradually increase the space between two thoughts (or feelings). The space of silence thus created *(vilamba)* spontaneously balances the two bipolar energy channels. In that condition the reactivity is minimum and the subject will just see. When we just see, we absorb direct knowledge, crystal clear information.

Let us take the case of a difficult boardroom meeting, where members of the board discuss a hostile take over bid from a competitive firm. Perceptions matter. If the CEO is processing the situation through the reactive *homo sapiens* mode, his vision may be blurred and his ego whispers, "How dare they do this to me?" Superego answers, " I am finished, the means at their disposal are too formidable, we cannot resist." But if he is closer to the central channel he will avoid the confusion and pain linked with reactivity and simply be a keen observer of the situation.

Or, even better, as *homo spiritualis* having entered the Fourth State, he will sit on the throne of the witness stage and uncover with his detached view all the intricacies of the situation, uncover the hidden plots, e.g. how Mr. Black is pushing for his own private deal and how Mr. White is in fact trying to save the company. Then, with full clarity, he will see the way out, providing that there is one. The crystal clarity of mind provides *episteme*, absolute information, and decision makers with such an access will have a huge advantage over their competitors, in all areas from strategic thinking to day-to-day problem solving.

BEHAVIORS IN THE FOURTH STATE

The state of consciousness in man which witnesses everything is called Turya.

— Shri Ramdas (1608-1682)

In order to excel in the world of action we need more than just technical competence, we need the qualities necessary for leadership, and our effectiveness in this respect is intimately linked to our psychosomatic set-up. Before Self-realization, temperaments already close to the third, *Sattvic* dimension exhibit some of the qualities that will characterize *homo spiritualis*. But the Third Way only too often turns into yet another first step, the prelude for a new set of contradictions. This is because the inner channel within the spine, which opens and releases the Kundalini into the seven centers of energy, is not yet opened, and thus the manifestation of this channel *(Sushumna)* is still partial and limited. Of course a *Sattvic* subject (one who is Self-realized and has the *Sushumna* opened) is, as a rule, more dynamic, more harmonious, satisfied and sensitive to his or her environment. But it is really the ascent of the Kundalini which activates the qualities of the chakras, and liberates the potential of the brain from the smokescreen of the left and right sympathetic nervous systems. We can indicate four sets of trends in qualities that are set in motion by the happening of Self-realization. The gradual assertion of these trends unfolds in corresponding areas of competence in the day-to-day behavior of *homo spiritualis*.

Again we have somehow to reduce the discourse to a few limited applications of this transformation, in an attempt to illustrate how such improvements relate to and benefit the non-spiritual dimension of our lives, notably in professional interactions such as management effectiveness.

1. From Self-confidence to Integrity

The cleansing of the *Ida nadi* brings about a quiet confidence in the Self, a feeling of wellbeing which comes from a sense of comfort about one's own identity. The self-respect associated with this recognition carries an innate ethical sensitivity. The subject becomes inclined automatically to adopt ethical behavior. He will feel gratified by his adherence to a clean code of moral conduct in his private and public life. His integrity will establish him as a person with a high degree of personal credibility and trustworthiness, backed by standards of honesty, probity, loyalty and freedom from external influence, which are naturally adhered to. This key competency will be demonstrated in the work place by a range of appropriate behaviors. Such a person will:

- show self confidence without arrogance and manage in a deliberate and predictable way;
- stand by decisions which are in the organization's best interest even if they are, at the time, unpopular;
- accept responsibility for decisions made, including those which subsequently reveal shortcomings or mistakes;

- treat others with compassion, fairness and respect;
- act without consideration for personal gain, and demonstrate the ability to resist undue pressure in decision making.

2. From Creativity to Vision

As the *Pingala nadi* is activated through Karma yoga, the opportunities for action and growth are identified. The subject has hunches and insights that open new paths and innovations, which anticipate forthcoming conditions and trends. Such is the case in matters pertaining to his or her private life as well in a professional capacity. In management this translates into the ability to develop a comprehensive understanding of a subject, to project a holistic vision and to be able to chart a strategic course through the various identified options. The sharpened analytical skills, strong grasp of the current environment and the capacity to anticipate the needs of the future will result in an above average rate of success. Such a manager will:

- identify and develop strategies while adjusting, as necessary, to changing options and circumstances;
- cope well with uncertainties and overcome obstacles in converting vision into action and results;
- mobilize corporate energies and motivate colleagues with a view to inspiring future possibilities and clearly defined goals;
- find innovative solutions to challenge deadlocked situations and a stagnating status quo.

3. From Balance to Stability

With the opening of the third channel, the *Sushumna nadi*, the action of the left and right sympathetic nervous systems will combine more smoothly. This improved condition will manifest coherence and depth, which entails a capacity not to react, to balance thoughts and feelings, IQ and EQ. This expresses itself in strong common sense and sound judgment, which inspires confidence from colleagues and clients. The person is discrete and subtle in discrimination. But this balance is dynamic, for it carries the potential for evolution and change; the subject will tune more easily to 'Third Way' solutions, which overcome the perceived contradictions and push progress further. The person will remain calm and self controlled in stressful situations and would:

- be conscientious about meeting commitments, delivering results and showing persistence in facing difficulties;
- show openness, flexibility, willingness to learn, the capacity to listen and to see, while at the same time taking interest in alternative suggestions or in new ways of doing things;
- see each side of the coin and quickly grasp the point of view of other people;
- settle conflicts and identify paths for reaching consensus.

4. From Empathy to Collective Consciousness

As the Kundalini integrates the autonomous and central nervous systems, the benefits of Self-realization will be experienced at the physical, mental, emotional and spiritual levels in day-to-day life. With the opening of the seventh center, *homo spiritualis* develops the new awareness of the Fourth State. He enters into a new web of relationships with the cosmos, the nature, all living beings and himself. Through vibratory awareness he develops a collective consciousness for the 'We': the common good of the community and the needs and aspirations of others. Cohesion of the community, togetherness and a sense of a common purpose are enhanced by the action of *homo spiritualis* in a leadership role. For instance he will:

- support colleagues, bring out the best in them and translate their potential and aspirations into corporate results, thereby inspiring commitment in others;

- work collaboratively and encourage productive team spirit;

- delegate authority and give autonomy to others in important areas of work;

- value and reward the performance and achievements of colleagues;

- create a climate of genuine trust and create a sense of belonging and common purpose, thereby increasing corporate productivity.

Of course these qualities are sometimes found already in some of today's managers, but it is the extent of their combination and integration within a single individual that is less common. A word of warning must be offered here on various current methods for relating to self-improvement or personality development. They usually rely on structured courses and voluntary efforts. But no ontogenous training, relying on voluntary processes can favor or advance this holistic profile of a spiritually enlightened professional active in society. For voluntary processes rely by definition on the imperfect mode of the sympathetic nervous system, and trying to achieve the integration of these competencies through conscious efforts will produce forced behavior, fake feelings and artificial results. It is like a politician saying to the electorate that he cares, while everyone knows that what he really cares about is himself and his career. *Homo spiritualis* manifests these competencies through the spontaneous working of the parasympathetic nervous system, whose subtler potential contained in the seven chakras has been triggered by the awakening of the Kundalini in the sacrum bone.

We must emphasize here the notion of trend. Self-realization does not necessarily transform people overnight, but it does open the path to perfectibility and brings within reach a range of transformations that would not otherwise be possible. But we must remain realistic. Some people get their initial realization and then lose the realized state thereafter because they do not meditate and do not manage to keep open the *Sushumna nadi*. Also, realized people with specific conditionings or obstacles stored in their chakras may take more time to develop their full potential. Suffice to say that the trends are beneficial in many ways.

In a nutshell, we can say that Self-realization will benefit anyone active in society, for it transforms the core of his or her being, rather than merely adjusting or fixing some segmented aspects of the personality where the need for improvement is most pressing. It is like accessing the code that will reveal the passwords of access to every chakra, and thus, grant access to the programs and data stored therein. It is securing the key that can open all doors.

As a matter of logic, just as we cannot transform society without transforming man - and this was the challenge facing all the revolutions of the past - so we cannot transform man without transforming his core being - and this was the challenge that faced all the great religions. But as the hypothesis proposed in this book submits that this core transformation is indeed feasible, we must realize the consequences. Although intensely private and personal, the inner moment of Self-realization triggers dynamic and extravert consequences. Impact flows, so to speak, from inside to out and affects all dimensions of life.

A person endowed with Sahaja yoga will gain a better grasp of inner reality that will enhance the degree of his or her self-control. Then also an understanding of other types of people will improve social interactions. Finally, as Self-realization unfolds its potential, the subject will become more interested in his or her own growth, at the physical, psychic and spiritual levels. Those who are intellectually more gifted will benefit from their increased understanding of the Virata, the primordial operating system. Those who are spiritually more gifted will explore their options as they enter into the more collective consciousness of vibratory awareness. *Homo spiritualis* will manage relationships with the environment in a compassionate, creative and mature way. This is bound therefore to bring new dimensions to our operational styles and social interactions. Enlightened Self-realization opens the conditions for a politician or a corporate leader to tune into the right wavelength for optimal decision-making.

I once heard Shri Mataji say: "To lead does not mean solving problems, it means giving problems to solve." By this she meant that people can evolve and develop through the process of learning to handle and solve problems for themselves. Others claim: "To rule means to share a vision." Or:"To govern is to administer pressures." Whatever our definitions of leadership, from mundane to mystical, it is undisputed that the exercise of power (imperium) depends on the individual style of leadership (potestas) of those who discharge it. This is why, in the sixteenth and seventeenth centuries, the Catholic militant order of the Jesuits, to stem the wave of the Reformation, concentrated on giving spiritual advice and education to the young Princes of Europe's ruling dynasties. But today's ruling houses are the economic enterprises, and their sets of beliefs place them beyond such forms of manipulation. Although some sects, in a Jesuitical way, have already penetrated business in an effort to influence top management, it will soon be found that they do not deliver the goods. It seems that corporate culture should rather evolve through a bottom-up process, as more and more collaborators share new sets of values.

There is an encouraging trend among recent business management theories towards the valorization of human assets to maximize a corporation's effectiveness and productivity. In the USA, a country with a more vibrant multicultural history, new paradigms may be adopted more easily than in Europe where parochial attitudes are still only too often the rule. This goes together with a more ethical and comprehensive understanding of the role of a global CEO. Newsweek quoted J.E. Garten, Dean of the Yale school of Management: "The era of the swashbuckling CEO who enriches shareholders by treating workers as commodity, who views his company as a bundle of assets to be sold off or put together, is gone. The future is for more genuinely global companies - profitable to be sure - that assume many more social responsibilities."

Again, I feel I owe an apology to the reader for my focus in this chapter on management issues that seem to narrow the perspective and betray the greatness of a spiritual process that is so much more broad and deep. Self-realization has been manifested to enhance the lives of all of us, whatever our race, beliefs, gender, status or skills. I am keenly aware that I have not done justice to the sheer magnitude of this fantastic potential. But the traders, merchants and their financial acolytes have dominated the end of the Second Age and I wanted to say that they too could be transformed. Whether we go to the Davos Forum among CEOs or to its opposite, the Porto Allegre Forum among political activists, we can get our transformation, provided we desire it and are sincere. Of course, more people may be sensitive to this spiritual breakthrough among those who are humble, but why not end on an optimistic note? In due time, one may imagine that the corporate world, as corporate behavior becomes enlightened, can activate on the collective level its formidable power for bringing about the 'Third Way' to social change. We thus see the possible opening of a dimension where people in charge can make an enormous, and perhaps decisive, contribution in developing a sustainable economic system for a global, more equitable and humanistic society.

LOVE STORY

Even the smallest wave is no different from the sea; so the Self is not distinct from God. If one attains this blissful state of the vision of one's identity with God, it is the highest form of devotion. This vision is the quintessence of knowledge and yoga.

— Shri Jnaneshwar, The Jnasneshwari

It was generally considered, at the turn of the next century, that the next divine Incarnation was about to come on earth and would be female, the advent of divine wisdom, or Theo-Sophia, and that the present age would be the age of making known all that which has been kept secret from the beginning.

— Lady Caithness, The Mysteries of the Ages (1887)

It has the very great advantage of being a fact and not a fiction.

— Socrates

Let us end where we started as we embarked on the exploratory path of our self-discovery channel. Following the spiritual footprints of history, past and future, as contained in countless myths, traditions and teachings, we deciphered the passage to the other side of man's existential limits. The Third Advent of the feminine power of spirituality, vested in each and every one of us as the residual force known as Kundalini, opens the Third Age. Neither incredulity, skepticism nor derision can change the facts and hundreds of thousands of people are now getting their Self-realization, and feel it on their central nervous systems. If we share in the spirit of honesty, the experience of this silences argument. It can be verified and communicated and the process is irreversible. The moment of Self-realization gives, in a series of responses, the knowledge that seeking minds had have sought during the last several millennia.

I am well aware that mankind prefers to revere spiritual masters after they are long gone, but frankly there is no hiding from the critical role played by Shri Mataji Nirmala Devi. In telling us: "You just need to know who you really are," she revealed this phenomenal process of spontaneous union (Sahaja yoga). For the last thirty years, Shri Mataji, now 80 years old, has herself raised the Kundalini of hundreds of thousands of people, an unprecedented event in the history of spirituality. People in all walks of life, belonging to every conceivable social status, religion and race, verify the beneficial impacts of her teachings across the five continents.

In April 2002 in Istanbul, hundreds of Muslims attained Self-realization during a public programme given by Shri Mataji. A baffled journalist asked her: "Are you a saint, a prophet or what?" She laughed: "Don't worry about me. Worry about yourself." It is a fact; followers worship her as an Avatar. The issue of worship of a living individual can be an obstacle for many, I know, but this expression of love and respect is in this instance based on the gifts that were offered. The gift is never greater than the giver and when the gift is the awakening of the Kundalini, the giver is very generous indeed.

I would like to return to a beautiful reality that manifests with the opening of the Sahasrara. If the essence of the seventh chakra is integration, one of the blessings of the enthroning of the Kundalini in the royal chakra is the blessed feeling of being connected. Feeling integrated with the whole, and connected with nature, realized souls and all living beings is a fantastic new dimension of life in the Third Age. Access to such states of union allows us to enjoy the all-pervading energy of Love that created this universe in the first place. Of course, as new practitioners of meditation, we may not live all the time in this condition of connectivity but the capacity to join it is already a tremendous improvement that erases the temptations of arbitrary and egoistic actions, as well as the fear of loneliness and boredom.

There is need here for yet another book, a book of miracles, to recall how episodes of this connectivity have embellished the lives of thousands of ordinary people. They have expanded the reach of their Sahasrara through Sahaja meditation but I shall just illustrate my point with two very small incidents that occurred in relationship with Shri Mataji.

I was eating in a Greek restaurant with Till, a German friend who is a Sahaja yogi. He was recalling how he was participating, with some hundred people or so, in a Sahaja festival in England celebrating the birth of Lord Krishna. He was perhaps in the tenth row of the audience, sitting like everybody else, on the ground. Mother (Shri Mataji) was sitting, facing them, enjoying a musical performance. He was meditating with closed eyes and praying intensely. At some point he felt a sense of adoration for Shri Krishna and he asked whether he has some personal relationship with Him. He spontaneously opened his eyes, and at that very second, Shri Mataji was looking straight at him with a beautiful and radiant smile. This event was so small and yet overwhelming, an instance of connectivity that Till will never forget.

I may also offer a humble memory that illustrates the playful and poetic nature of such occurrences. It was in the spring of 1987, on a train between Lausanne and Berne. Shri Mataji was sitting nonchalantly in front of me wearing a green and yellow sari. The train sped by a field, green and sprinkled with yellow spring flowers of the emerging Spring. I said, "Mother, look at the fields, they are exactly the colors of your sari." Of course, it was true. Half an hour later, through the window, the same landscape, but with the brown of the forest in the background for the leaves were not yet out. Shri Mataji said, "See there is also the color of my jacket, you had not noticed that!" "No, Mother, I had not noticed." Mother's jacket was indeed of the same shade of brown. I love being so poetically outsmarted. Swiss first class wagons are comfortable and silent, the trains glide and purr cozily along.

Gradually we become the right man or the right woman, in the right place, at the right time. Planes wait for you at the airport. Flowers in your garden, sprinkled with water in which you have channeled the vibrations, have an extraordinary fragrance and events work out to respond to your needs or prayers. Difficulties are sorted out. Ordinary people develop healing powers. For many of us, to pray and indeed to get an answer is a strangely new and wonderful experience, which at times is quite intimidating but always full of love and joy.

The raising of the Kundalini manifests a spontaneous power of tuning in. She grants integration and redemption, the Holy Ghost within. We indeed have walked through the secret passage to the other side of the screen of our existence. The potential unfolds, the mechanism is found, the divide is crossed between man and God. Because, in the last analysis, the oldest love story is between Him and us. Lao Tzu spoke of 'The Way', Confucius of 'The Path', Shri Krishna, of yoga, Christ, of the second birth. When we can go more fully into the state of thoughtless awareness, or *Nirvichara sammadhi*, after some deepening practice of Sahaja meditation, we realize that the state of Being is accessible. The opening of the last chakra opens to us the bliss of pure freedom, without limitation of any kind. When we love, we know, and by manifesting the Kundalini, He gave us, through His compassion, the way of knowing. The oldest love story in this world is between God and His creation. We read in the *Svetasvatara Upanishad (6.15)*:

"Only by knowing Him does one pass over death.
There is no other path for going there.
He who is the Maker of all, the All Knower, Self-sourced
Intelligent, the Author of time, Possessor of qualities, Omniscient,
Is the Ruler of primary matter and of the Spirit,
The Lord of qualities, the Cause of reincarnation and of liberation,
Of continuance and of bondage.
Consisting of That, Immortal, existing as the Lord,
Intelligent, Omnipresent, the Guardian of this world,
Is He who constantly rules this world.
There is no other Cause found for the ruling."

These then are the rules of the game. There is only one God and He has many forms and manifestations. After all, if He is God, He can do what He pleases: have a Son, have children of the Spirit, share His perfection in His movement of compassion, generosity and love. At times, the Manifestations of the Most High, the Avatars, visit history. Shri Mataji invites His children in the human race to understand the play, to break the access code and to join in the collective consciousness of the Third Age.

18. WHAT ABOUT JUDGMENT DAY?

Watch therefore, for you do not know on what day your Lord is coming.
— Matthew 24.42

And the rain-washed naked throng came before them,
Trembling to receive their judgment.
For their sins were many, and they had defiled the earth,
Yea, they had destroyed the creatures of land and sea,
Poisoned the ground, fouled the air,
And buried alive the Mother who had given them birth.
— The Essene Book of Revelation

Peace I bring to thee, my children, the sevenfold peace of the earthly Mother and the heavenly Father. Peace I bring to thy body, guided by the angel of power; peace I bring to thy heart guided by the angel of love; peace I bring to thy mind guided by the angel of wisdom. Through the Angels of power, love and wisdom, thou shalt travel the seven paths of the infinite garden, and thy body, thy heart and thy mind shall join in Oneness, in the sacred flight to the heavenly sea of peace.

Yea I tell you truly, the paths are seven through the infinite garden, and each must be traversed by the body, the heart and the mind as one.
— The Essene Book of Jesus

Muslim pilgrims for the Hadj in Mecca pray that they may be spared on the day of the Last Judgment. Modern Christians, on the whole, are more forgetful. This chapter illustrates that the unconscious expectation of the Last Judgment, lurking in the Muslim and Christian 'collective unconscious,' may after all contain the promise of brighter days ahead. The sense that history is going somewhere, to some appointed destination does not belong to religion only. Philosophers expressed this idea in their own terms. The relationship between ancient scriptures and contemporary events depicts emerging shapes that will influence the development of our societies.

A Dutch poem goes: "God does not pay weekly, but he pays at the end". Judgment Day has been a lingering, yet powerful concept in the unconscious of Muslims and Christians alike, as a number of stern admonitions refer to it in the *Bible* and the *Koran*. But these texts are often parabolic or poetic and it has been hard to figure out from them what is really likely to happen. For instance, the Christians and Muslims expect human beings to be raised from the dead and paintings on the topic represented skeletons and corpses creeping out of their graves. But for someone who takes reincarnation into the scheme of things, everyone is raised from the dead in the sense that a dead person reincarnates in a new body. The Last Judgment would then indicate merely that all beings having lived before, would then be reincarnated in the human race at a given time to face the judgment, a hypothesis corroborated by the billions of people alive today that represent an all-time population record.

Likewise, the timing need not be understood too literally. As written in the *Gospel of Peter* - to the Lord, one day is like a thousand years. Judgment Day could refer to a process covering an extended period of our human time.

Admittedly, this period is described in a consistent manner through various prophecies. It is characterized by moral decay, great tribulations and hardships, conflicts, natural catastrophes and cataclysms of great magnitude. In a sense, one could recognize some of these features in the contemporary state of affairs, but what might this process be? Today some authors are producing bestsellers, riding in on Judgment Day anticipations but their success is unlikely to do the rest of us any good. The question is: "What is in it for me?"

The two quotes above, from the scrolls of the Essene, project the two aspects of Judgment Day. The first quote suggests that our race needs to pay a price for the mistakes committed. This is the frightening dimension of the karmic law at work and the most familiar aspect of the prophecy. I have tried to show in this book how many forms of destruction are already at work; more may be on its way. A catharsis? We simply do not know. But reading the Bible anew, one is struck by the consistency of the references to the Last Judgment. The Age of the Son is reaching its end with rumbles of war in the Middle East and in Kashmir, the two areas of the planet that have been associated with His manifestation in the Gospels and Apocrypha writings. It seems sometimes as if peace in Jerusalem must somehow be achieved for the advent of the Third Age.

MUSLIM PROPHECIES IN THE WAKE OF 9/11

In the *Koran*, there are many references to Judgment Day; some evoke a catharsis, others imply a process of introspection and Self-knowledge:

"On that day mankind will come in broken bands to be shown their labors. Whoever has done an atom's weight of good shall see it, and whoever has done an atom's weight of evil shall see it also." The Earthquake 99:8

"Would that you knew what the Day of Judgment is! Oh, would that you knew what the Day of Judgment is! It is the day when every soul will stand alone and Allah will reign supreme." The Cataclysm 82: 19

"On that day (of Resurrection) man shall be informed of all that he has done and all that he has failed to do. He shall become his own witness." The Resurrection 75:15

"They underrate the might of Allah. But on the day of resurrection he will hold the entire earth in His grasp and fold up the heaven in His right hand." Sad 39:66

"Every soul shall be paid according to its deeds, for Allah knows of all their actions." Sad 39:68 [40]

Television audiences in the west scramble to come to terms with the notion of Jihad. They look with disbelief at grimacing shopkeepers, running in the streets of Karachi in support of fundamentalist terrorists, or at veiled women in Somalia or Indonesia burning the American flag. Saddam Hussein and Bin Laden, like Hitler before them, have tried to carry the mantle of self-appointed doomsday makers. Where do such fantasies come from?

It may be worthwhile here to review the expectations of Islam from a historical perspective. Islam is a great and noble religion, which is defiled by

[40] *The Koran*, Penguin Books, N.J. Dawood, p. 16,55,284.

fundamentalism of the Inquisition. Islam is not a monolithic religion and contains about some 72 main currents, branches or sects. Before giving birth to Bin Laden's crazy claims, the rigid Sunni Wahabites had been seen as promoting expansionist warfare and misogynist repression. Like the Roman pope and his Crusaders, the Caliph killed in the name of God; but Wahabism does not reveal the full measure of Islam. According to many eminent Muslim scholars, it represents only a dogmatic and limited understanding of the *Koran* and its main achievement may have been the familiar manipulation of religion for the purpose of political supremacy. The mystical depth of Islam is more vested in the Sufis and its historical consciousness in the lineage of the imams. We will refer here to the Shiite tradition.

The *Mahdi*, (the name of the last of the twelve imams, the first being Ali, son-in-law of Mohammed) according to Islam, and in particular its Shiite branch, is the Savior to come at the time of the Last Judgment to save the world. It is interesting to recall that *Mahdi*, in Sanskrit, is the contraction of *Ma Adi* (Primordial Mother) in the same way that the returning Savior according to Buddha, *Maitreya*, is a contraction of *Ma Treya* (Mother threefold, *trimorphic protonnoia* or *trigunatmika*).

The function of the *Mahdi* is similar to those attributed to the *Kalki* of the Hindus, the *Maitreya* of the Buddhists or the Christ King of the Christians. The return of the *Mahdi* constitutes the most frequent prediction of the imams. *Al-Kultani* and *al-Nu'mani* consecrated an entire chapter and *Ibn Babunye* passed down in thirteen chapters the predictions of the Prophet, Fatima and of the eleven imams on the subject of the Twelfth imam.

The obscure presence of *Mahdi* dominates totally the religious conscience of imamism during the period from the disappearance of Ali until the return of the awaited Savior. But here and there, throughout the prophetic texts, there are hints of an esoteric knowledge. "At the moment of birth a light pierced the top of the child's head (a possible reference to the opening of the seventh chakra) and reached into the depths of the sky. This child is the *Mahdi*, He who will fill the earth with equality and justice just as it is now filled with oppression and injustice." [41]

The universal precursory Sign of the return of *Mahdi*, "He who Guides," consists of the general invasion of the earth by Evil and the victory of the forces of Evil over those of Good. This dire condition demands the manifestation of an ultimate and final Savior. Without such a manifestation, the entirety of humanity would be engulfed by darkness.

Here we find extracts from the eulogies of *Ali Abi Talib* describing various components of the sign announcing the return of *Mahdi*. The Sign consists of the following traits: the people will neglect prayer, squander the divinity which is conferred on them, legalize untruths, practice usury, accept bribes, construct huge edifices, sell religion to win this lower world, employ idiots, consult with women, break family ties, obey passion and consider insignificant the letting of blood. Magnanimity will be considered as weakness and injustice as glory, princes will be debauched and ministers will be oppressors, intellectuals will be traitors and the readers of the *Koran* vicious. False witness will be brought openly and immorality proclaimed in loud voices. A word of promise will be slander, sin and exaggeration.

[41] Amir Moizzi, *Guide Divine*, Paris, 1/E.P.H.E., Paris en Sorbonne.

"The sacred Books will be ornate, the mosques disguised, the minarets extended. Criminals will be praised, the lines of combat narrowed, hearts in disaccord and pacts broken. Women, greedy for the riches of this lower world, will involve themselves in the business of their husbands; the vicious voices of man will be loud and will be listened to. The most ignoble of the people will become leaders, the debauched will be believed for fear of the Evil they will cause, the liar will be considered as truthful and the traitor as trustworthy... They will resort to singers and musical instruments ... and women will horse ride, they will resemble men and the men will resemble women. The people will prefer the activities of this lower-world to those of the Higher-World and will cover up with lambskin the hearts of wolves."[42]

The *Qa'im (Mahdi)* comes to re-establish the lost sense of sanctity. Firstly He will re-establish Islam to its original purity and integrity.[43] The imam is described also as energy giving. The imam says: "As to the way of benefiting from my presence (literally - "to benefit of me") during my disappearance, it is similar to the profit we gain from the sun while it is hidden from sight by the clouds."[44]

According to Majid Golpur, a scholar who reviewed the relationship between ancient Muslim writings and new revelations, some language seems to refer to new cognitive powers that may be associated with the rise of the Kundalini. All the faithful joining the ranks of *Mahdi* will be gifted with special miraculous powers, in particular those of super sensitive communication with the imam. "At the time of the Advent of our *Qa'im*," says Ja'far, "God, may He be exalted and glorified, will develop the hearing and sight of our faithful in such a manner that, without there being a messenger between the *Qa'im* and themselves, He will speak with them and they will hear and see Him without Him having left the place where He is."[45]

This text probably refers to the dawn of collective consciousness, whose property is the connectivity described in previous chapters. More specifically, we can recognize a mention of the vibratory consciousness of the chakras, which correspond to specific locations in the hands. "For decisions which they have difficulty in taking, they will receive instructions and direction from the imam who will write on the palms of their hands, they need only look and then execute the orders."[46]

The following language could possibly indicate a succession of imams or the collectivity of realized souls, through the reference to the wind. But, without the subtler spiritual experience, it can also easily feed the delusion of self-appointed elect fanatics. God speaks: "O Mohammad. These are My friends, My pure elect, and My proof after you for mankind. They are your legatees and your priests and the best of My creatures after you. By My Glory and My Majesty I will manifest through them. My religion and I will raise through them My Word; by the last of them (*Mahdi*) I will make the earth

[42]*al-Kulayni*, UsGl K K. al-Hujjan, Bab MS JS a fi l-ithna' ashar, 11/468-485; al-Nu'Mani, K al-Ghayba,bab., p. 201, 281.

Ibn-Babuye, Kamal al-Din, Bab-5 24 - 38, p. 256, 385, see also Id, Hal, Bab 12; Nahj al-Balagha, p. 295, 424, 25,458,1158,1180, 1222.

Kamal, bab 47, n° 1,11/525-28

[43] al-Nu 'mani, op cit pages 333-59 "The Qa 'im

[44] bab 45, n° 4, 11/485. Ibn- Babunye

[45] Al-Kulyni, al-Rawda, 11149

[46] Al-Nu 'mdni, op. cit, bob 214

pure of My enemies. I will establish him from the sunrise to the sunset throughout the entire earth; I will confer to his power the wind and will lower for him the stubborn clouds. I will help him with My Army and aid him with My Angels until he raises My Name and the creatures acknowledge My uniqueness, and then I will prolong his reign and I will ensure the succession of My Friends over the time until the Day of Resurrection." 47

In this way the awaited Imam *(al-Muntaẓar) Mad-hdi, Qa'im,* will prepare the earth for the Last Judgment and the Resurrection. The battle of *Qa'im* will mark the ultimate victory of the 'believers' against their 'enemies' and the universal and final establishment of the 'religion' of the imams. The community of the faithful is a familiar theme of all eschatology.

It is interesting to note that these texts imply a profound criticism of Islam as some parts of the Arab world seem to know it. The returned *Mahdi* will do as did the Prophet, destroying that which was before, just as the Prophet destroyed the rituals of the period of ignorance, and He will establish once again Islam. Our *Qa'im* will repair the Mosque and will reconstruct His Mecca. The *Qa'im* will bring a new Order, a new Book, a new Legislation and a new Tradition. 48

Of course the primary ambiguity of these prophecies is that they may refer to more spiritual and ethical realities or be understood as a militant call for a violent upheaval. But there are texts indicating that these prophecies do not invite the fight of Islam against other religions but rather, the fight of all religions for their inner renewal. *Mahdi* will equally re-establish the other religions, also abandoned and disfigured, in their original Truth and Purity.

Indeed: "The *Mahdi* will extract the *Torah* and the other Divine Books from their caverns and will judge amongst the faithful of the *Torah* according to the *Torah,* amongst the faithful of the Evangiles according to the Evangiles, amongst the faithful of *al-Zabur (The Book of David)* according to the *al-Zabur* and amongst the faithful of the *Koran* according to the *Koran.*" 49

It is the universal initiation by the imam of all men into the secrets of existence and of their own religions, and this is without doubt the meaning which must be understood by the term *Mahdi* given by the fifth imam al-Bagir: *Mahdi* (the Guide) is named as such because it is he who will guide (*Yahdi*) us in the secret teachings." 50

If so, the prediction of the *Mahdi* does not announce the victory of zealot warriors who will wipe out non-believers, understood to be other races or religions. Rather, the prophecies talk of the power of love, not the might of hate. They would then refer to the fight against ignorance, no doubt the most formidable of all battles. But if Allah is indeed the Merciful and the Compassionate, such is the most likely meaning of the predictions of the imams. The real jihad is an internal fight for our own purification, so that our full spiritual potential might finally manifest. Consequently, even in the stern Muslim prophecies we can read the hopeful and promising light of mankind's renewal. This may or may not combine with events of massive destruction that can still manifest. But let us focus on the hopeful dimension of this momentous period.

47 Ibn Babunye, 'Ilal, bab 7, pages 6-7, Kamal, bab 23, n°4,1/256, 'Uyan, I/bob 26, n° 22, page 263

48 al-Numani - bab 13 page 336, bab 14, pages 36 ad 378

49 Ibn-Babuyne, bab 129, 1/161; Ibn-Ayyash, Mugtad-Ab, 18159.

50 al~Nu'mani , op, cit, p. 342.

BRIDGING THE GREAT DIVIDE

Human reason has this peculiar fate that in one species of its knowledge it is burdened by questions which, as prescribed by the very nature of reason itself, it is not able to ignore, but which, transcending all its powers, it is also not able to answer.

— Immanuel Kant, The Critique of Pure Reason

It is most important that you should be born; you ought to come into this world otherwise you cannot realize the Self and the purpose of this world has been missed.

— C.J. Jung, The Psychology of Kundalini Yoga Lecture 2, 19.10.32

The apex of history at the end of the Second Age is about the movement from illusion to reality. About shifting the focus from 'having' to 'being'. A move prepared by countless centuries of progress. To be or not to be is not the question. It is the answer.

The hypothesis of Self-realization states that our consciousness can touch the deeper dimension of our being, the Spirit, which is divine in its essence. It is a part, or spark, of the Primordial Soul known as *Paramatma*. Bridging the divide between the finite human consciousness and the infinity of the Spirit within us means bridging the divide between man and God. It means solving the oldest problem of philosophy, which is how to reconcile the universal (pure Being, Virata) with the accidental and often strange ways of men. Aristotle had proposed that it is impossible to be and not to be at the same time but Shakespeare was not the only one to wonder about the slightly schizophrenic nature of man. Augustine walked, most agitatedly, between the City of Man and the City of God while two souls inhabit the Faust of Goethe. Paul Valery observes that man is too particular and the soul too general; Sartre told us in *Being and Nothingness*: "Many men, in fact, know that the goal of their pursuit is being ... But to the extent that this attempt still shares the spirit of seriousness... they are condemned to despair; for they discover at the same time that all human activities are equivalent ... and that all are in principle doomed to failure. Thus it amounts to the same whether one gets drunk alone or is a leader of nations." Man is absurdly condemned to desire what he cannot reach. Satisfaction is denied in a very fundamental sense.

In his *Phenomenology of Spirit*, Hegel submitted that human reason could overcome the contradictions of man's unhappy consciousness. Both Kierkegaard and Sartre reacted scornfully against this pretence and they dismissed it as a cheap intellectual trick. They saw correctly that the condition of man is basically absurd, for reason alone cannot trigger the happening of *'satori.'* They thought that the possibility for the individual consciousness to become one with the universal consciousness would fade away and be denied by post Hegelian thought.

Thus Western ontology reached a state of entropy. It got caught in the cosmic-microcosmic dilemma and any further elaboration seemed to add to the confusion. Claiming to reach the Virata would be just adding an unwanted chapter to the book of the priesthood's blind faith or to the treatise of the philosophers' bad faith. After colliding with the limit set by the cosmic-microcosmic contradiction, modern philosophy took a U-turn. Marxism built a materialist mausoleum on the Hegelian pedestal. Later, Ayer and Wittgenstein drove away into the realm of linguistics. Atheists had, somewhat pompously, proclaimed that God is dead; they had first abandoned the path of metaphysical enquiry and did not yearn any longer for the solitary and ungraspable splendor of the One. But the past masters whisper with a smile in their eyes: "What was not born cannot die."

Psychologists fared better and progressed where philosophers failed. Eminent psychiatrists have approached the 'God revealed' or Virata in the First Age as the collective or Universal Unconscious. C.J. Jung thought that it was from this Unconscious that humanity had taken its gods and its demons, the great intuitions of philosophers and savants, and "all those superlatively powerful thoughts without which Man ceases to be Man." A view shared by no less a personage than Albert Einstein who said that the theory of relativity dawned upon him as he was playing with soap bubbles in his garden.

In the First Age, the Universal Unconscious, stored in the brain of the Virata, sends the primordial images and intuitions which form the basis of our conceptual systems, social ethics and creative inspiration. Adam becomes aware. In other words, the creativity of human beings is a function of an unconscious connection with the Virata. Frequently messages from the Virata reveal themselves in ideas, intuitions or dreams, or through the agency of suggestive events.

Guided by the Son, the Shepherd of the Second Age, Adam, taking with him Eve and mankind, is a seeker progressing on this pilgrimage towards selfhood that links us up to the revelation of God. God inspires man: He sent the Pieta to Michelangelo and the Mona Lisa to Leonardo. But, as Erich Fromm remarks, we, the modern people, lose very quickly this imperceptible thread of *Ariadne*, repressing the inner voice and losing the sense of discrimination between good and evil, between true and false. With materialism, subtlety is gradually fading away. Our society seems to have lost access to the cosmic and contact with the Virata, which is omniscient attention, omnipresent bliss, the knowledge of the Knower and embodiment of truth.

At the opening of the Third Age, broadly corresponding to the third Christian millennium, the pilgrim Adam reaches his destination. With the unfolding of Kundalini, he receives the fruit from the tree of knowledge. We can start imagining what this new world will look like. Those who can receive the energy or message (*Paramchaitanya*) directly from the Virata are those who excel. Hence connection matters. The twice born are capable, connected, compassionate and wise.

What do we know about the force, the Energy of God? In the age of globalization, we can search references in various cultures. Symbols tell the same story: the mystical rose in Dante's vision of Paradise and the thousand petal lotus crowning the Buddha represents the same mystic flower, the seat of the higher power. Tongues of fire appear on top of the heads of the Disciples of Christ in the representation of the night of Pentecost by El Greco, and customarily too on the head of the Buddha. How is that we get a similar description of 'tongues of fire' both in Burma and in Spain? What did our ancestors know about Pentecost? What is the jet of energy streaming out of the Buddha's head in almost all his statues made according to the sacred tradition of Thailand? Is it what Christians call the tongues of flame of the Holy Ghost? How come the Muslims pray with their hands open, as did the ancient Christian Gnostics of Byzantium and Ukraine? Is it to feel the force, a specific energy or power? Is it to feel the manifestation of the Holy Breath, (*nous* or *pneuma* in ancient Greek)? Is it the same wind of Pentecost, which is also emitted by other energetically charged stones such as Celtic menhirs or sacred mountains? This Pentecostal wind, Shri Mataji contends, was emitted from the Buddha, from the Virgin Mary, from the body of the resurrected Christ and from the experience of Self-realization.

This is the 'Breath of Life' or the 'Water of Life' expressing the residual force of the Primordial Being. It flows from the Kaaba, the holy stone in Mecca, and from specific sacred spots in nature such as *Uluru* (Ayers Rock), which, indeed, is sacred to native Australians. Retrospectively we understand better the nature of aboriginal cults or popular beliefs, which, in the past, worshipped sacred sites or venerated the saints. Such people and places emitted the force. Alas, to the educated and knowledgeable rationalist, the notion of the cosmic force is a fiction belonging to the Star Wars trilogy of George Lucas.

The second quote from the Essenene scrolls refers to the integration of energies though the inner opening of the seven chakras. It relates also to aspects of the prophecy of John in *The Book of Revelation (the Apocalypse)*. After the tribulations of the last days, the New Jerusalem is revealed and in its midst, we find the Tree of Life, whose fruits will heal the nations, and the river of the water of life. The New Jerusalem looks like an allegory of a new society that benefits from the knowledge of the Tree of Life: of the inner instrument, and of the water of life: of the vibrations. In other words it describes the other, hopeful and promising dimension of Judgment Day. It is the rite of passage to the higher consciousness. We judge ourselves, either in making the choice to progress on the path of consciousness, or in deciding not to do so. The field of the last struggle is our brain where we have to rise above the reactivity of ego and superego to develop enlightened awareness and the behavior of a realized soul. Think about it. It makes sense.

FROM HEGEL TO THE WHITE HORSE

It may be said of Universal History, that it is the exhibition of Spirit in the process of working out the knowledge of that which it is potentially...

The History of the world is none other than the progress of the consciousness of Freedom.

History in general is therefore the development of Spirit in Time, as Nature is the development of the Idea in Space.

But what Spirit is it has always been essentially; distinctions are only the development of this essential nature. The life of the ever-present spirit is a circle of progressive embodiments

- G.W.F Hegel, The Philosophy of History

I have submitted, in the light of Shri Mataji's teachings, that the moment of breakthrough at the level of the individual consciousness also opens up the possibility of a colossal breakthrough for the evolution of human societies. Germaine de Staël, a leading voice of the early Romantic Movement, wrote as the nineteenth century opened: "While studying history, it seems one becomes convinced that all main events lead towards the same the universal civilization." In the nineteenth century, the German scholars endeavored to grasp the true purpose of history. Nevertheless, the knowledge of psychology and of our psychosomatic instrument was not available at that time. It was not possible then to recognize the features of the culmination of history, the secular substitute for the more frightening religious Judgment Day. Rather, philosophers following Feuerbach, Schopenhauer, Herder and Hegel saw the fulfillment of history in some sort of political grand scheme. Without the experience of Self-realization indeed, the expected breakthrough could not take place and the knowledge of the Spirit was not accessible. Thenceforth, politics manipulated spirituality. But the experiences of countless numbers of people over recent decades suggest that it would be possible for a large number of people to experience the cognitive breakthrough of Self-realization, thus leading to a democratization of spirituality.

In Hegel's phenomenology, the evolution of life and consciousness on earth follows a well-charted, yet circuitous plot: to bring about the ever-growing actualization of consciousness. He calls it *Weltgeist* or World Spirit. As an acknowledged Lutheran, Hegel most probably believed in the Holy Ghost, the spirit of a personal God, as the force that activates progress. Nevertheless, as the Holy Ghost has been so elusive, the reading of its will has been fraught with dangers. "Such are all great historical men - whose own particular aims involve those larger issues which are the will of the World Spirit," said Hegel. He observed that Alexander the Great died young, Caesar was murdered, and Napoleon was exiled to Saint Helena. Conquerors, by their nature, tend to be oblivious to the spiritual dimension of the grand scheme and, aspiring to become the instrument of destiny, go too far on the *Pingala nadi*. Genghis Khan himself once conveniently saw himself as expressing the wrath of God. Probably, so do the Al Qaeda martyrs. The misunderstanding of the *Weltgeist* remains a lurking temptation for present day fundamentalists seeking to legitimize violence.

It is most likely from their writings that both Schopenhauer and Hegel were influenced by Indian thought. In Indian cosmology, it is the Primordial Power, the Adi Shakti, that leads evolution. Hegelian history is the unfolding of the Spirit's Desire. Through millennia, history represents successive steps in the fulfillment of the Spirit's Desire to manifest itself. The destination of history, as Teilhard de Chardin would repeat after Hegel, is mankind's spiritual fulfillment.

Obviously, modern rationalists would scoff at such propositions, but spiritual experimentation has progressed with giant strides over the last few decades, and hundreds of thousands of people today get the response directly, by the experience of Self-realization on their central nervous system. Will a rational man deny the value of repeated and replicable experiments? Self-realization was depicted in the past as a metaphysical illumination that no one could explain. Recent evidence gathered from thousands of ordinary people suggests instead that it is carried through psychosomatic processes in our body and not because of a paranormal state, arbitrary beliefs or the ingestion of chemical drugs.

Reading for sense in history may sound hopelessly ambitious but it is in line with an ancient Western tradition. Since the *Apocalypse of Saint John* and later Gnostic prophecies such as the writings of Joachim di Fiore and the book of John the Templar, the promise of a culmination of history has been lingering in the subconscious of occidental political philosophy. The eschatology, the coming of the last days, would manifest through the last struggle against evil and the coming of redemption. The advent of the Golden Age was expected to be the result of the victory of good over evil but this dream did not come true for believers during the Christian Middle Ages who were fervently awaiting it. In modern times, such dreams turned into nightmares. They bred the communist and fascist ideologies of the twentieth century, which promised a millennial regime, such as the Third Phase of the communist society of Marx, Engels and Lenin, or the Third Reich of Adolf Hitler.

When we place the expectations of the Day of Judgment in the right perspective, that is, related to the potential of our inner psychosomatic instrument, the real scheme is infinitely more reassuring than the interpretations of conquistadors who pretended to implement it. Contrary to the frightened expectations of the Christian Middle Ages, these last days need not be the culmination of doom but the opening of a brighter future.

Self-realization implies the opening of new doors of perception, to speak in the words of the English visionary, William Blake. This happening awakens a more global consciousness within us and it connects us to the Virata. In the body of a realized being, the autonomous nervous system and the central nervous system thus get enlightened and register the information. The arena of the last struggle is our brain where we have to rise above the reactivity of ego and superego to develop the enlightened awareness and behavior of a realized soul.

Our scout on this journey, Joachim di Fiori, tells us about the present time: "The third status will come toward the end of the world, no longer under the veil of the letter, but in the full freedom of the Spirit when ... those who will teach many about justice will be like the splendor of the firmament and like the stars forever ... In that status the Holy Spirit will seem to call out in the scripture. 'The Father and the Son have worked until now; and I am at work'."[51]

The traditions which prophesized the great transformation of man and society hinted at the potential of our perfectibility. These prophecies were known as eschatology, announcing the 'last days,' that is the last days of *homo sapiens* as we know him, with all his pretences, ignorance and worthy strivings.

The collective consciousness of code seekers, who, together, turn the keys in the lock, is the precondition to establish a prosperous, just and harmonious society. I shall revert here to the eleventh century and the vision of the knight John of Jerusalem that was previously quoted in Chapter Four. He speaks of redemption, collective consciousness, en masse Self-realization, international relations firmly based on solidarity and ecological restoration. In the year 1119, he possibly hints at the events of the 11th September 2001, a day of infamy, that may however carries a promise of transformation:

"When the millennium that comes after this millennium ends, men will have finally opened their eyes. They will no longer be imprisoned in their head and in their cities, but will be able to see from one end of the earth to another

---

[51] Joachim of Fiori, *Expositio in Apocalypsim,* quoted in Prophecies on the Adi Shakti, Life Eternal Trust, Cabella (2002) p. 16.

and understand each other. They will know that what makes one suffer hurts another. Men will form one huge body of which each one will be a tiny part. Together they will form the heart of this body. There will be a common language spoken by everybody and thus, finally, a glorious humanity will come into existence ... there will be roads that connect one end of the earth and the sky to the other; the woods will once more be dense, the desert will be once more irrigated and the water will once again be pure. The earth will be like a garden: man will take care of every living thing and he will clean everything he has dirtied. He will understand that the whole of Earth is his home and he will think with wisdom of the morrow. Man will know everything on earth and his own body. Diseases will be cured before they are manifested and everybody will cure themselves and each other. Man will have understood that he has to help himself to stay upright; and after the days of reticence and avarice, man will open his heart and his purse to the poor; he will define himself curator of the human species and so, finally a new era will begin. When man has learnt to give and share, the bitter days of solitude will be at an end. He will once more believe in the spirit, and the barbarians will be unheard of ... but all this will happen after the wars and the fires, all this will arise from the ashes of the burnt towers of Babel."[52]

I have already made some numerical reference to the date 9.11. It is interesting to note that stanza 9.11 of the *Bhagavad Gita* reads: " But the fools of the world know me not when they see me in my own human body. They know not my spirit supreme, the infinite God of all this."[53] Insensitivity of the modern mind to divinity and its manifestation could thus be inferred as yet another characteristic of the time of Judgment.

The vision of the Apostle John in Patmos announces the return of the Christ King in an allegory of the last fight and the ultimate redemption. "Then I saw heaven open and behold a white horse. He who sat upon it is called Faithful and True and in righteousness he judges and makes war." *The Apocalypse* and the *Kalki Purana* are the two major pieces of eschatological writings in world literature. Interestingly enough, it is the same white horse, which appears dramatically in both writings, carrying a Savior.

This white horse, Shri Mataji tells us, is a symbol for the brain. As we enter the enlightened consciousness, beyond the ongoing confusion, we gain self-mastery, as a rider masters his horse. The whiteness of the horse indicates the completion of the process of purification from ego and superego. The white horse of the apocalypse is the purified brain, washed clean by the gentle care of the Kundalini. In that condition, our attention – the galloping horse - is connected with the source of energy and it works. As was said, in the Muslim world, the coming of the 12th *Mahdi* will fulfill this prophecy of salvation.

Shri Mataji's elaboration on such ancient teachings actualizes the role of the bridging energy hidden in man, the Kundalini. We have seen that it is a subtle force stored at the base of the spine. This energy is of a feminine nature, which may surprise traditional theologians. When she advances along the central channel of the Sushumna within the spine, she awakens the Tree

[52] John of Jerusalem, *Secret Register of Prophecies*, op cit, p. 13.

[53] *The Bhagavad Gita*, Juan Mascaro, Penguin Books, op.cit.

of Life, the many branches and ramifications of our central nervous system. The essential element of Sahaja Yoga's contribution is that it makes it happen. It is the new Eve that makes the new Adam a reality.

When Kundalini crosses on her path the various psychosomatic centers (chakras), she delivers the fruits of the tree, thereby activating the quality of these centers and triggering new evolutionary possibilities. As she cleanses the chakras, she dissolves the negative impact of past mistakes and sins. She dresses the child in the new, white linen, the dress of the riders that John saw in his vision. In this way, the Mother washes and prepares the child so that it may stand Judgment. We are then equipped to see, and to correct ourselves.

Who judges whom? Through the powers of meditation and introspection, everybody becomes witness to his or her own deeds.

When this residual energy of pure desire meets the Spirit in the seventh center, enlightenment occurs; the vibrations flow, which is the water of life that John saw flowing in the midst of the New Jerusalem, the symbol of the community of realized souls. We have completed the phase of our cosmic journey that started in the Book of Genesis. The Divine within us starts recognizing itself, through the awareness of the twice born. The attention *(chitta)* and joy *(ananda)* fuse to recognize the truth *(sat)* of one's Being. This play of recognition was at the roots of God's original act of creation.

As I reach the end of this book, I am quite humbled by the realization that I have hardly done justice to my subject. I take some comfort in the words of Shri Mataji who said of Sahaja Yoga in a public programme in Caxton Hall, London:

" It is a very wide subject. After all it is eternal and you cannot explain eternity in such a short time."

The intensity of this reality cannot be denied. In the cycle of creation and destruction, whatever goes against the truth in the end destroys itself, because it lacks the sustenance of reality, in the same way that clouds eventually clear but the sky remains. When the code seekers become the code breakers, they break the bonds of illusion that trap us in the *gunas*, reactivity and contradictions. From now on, it is back to where we came from. Man's unfinished business is attended to and as the prophecies have told us: the worst may be at hand but the best is yet to come.

APPENDIX

The future will be hard to decipher without some deeper understanding of the past. This is particularly true in the fields of knowledge dealing with the essence of man such as religion or philosophy. Religion deals with the most fundamental beliefs of man. It influences his knowledge system and his emotional response to his environment. As we end this book, we revisit a few arguments. Parts One and Two of this Appendix look at patterns of institutions in the Second Age and suggest that initially admirable institutions do not survive unscathed as they fall into the hands of less than admirable people. Corruption of the original ideal is always a possibility even though generous visions and worthy efforts often bring the institutions a long way. We take two influential institutions as cases in point: the Catholic Church, and modern democracy: two 'institutions' that did not turn out the way they were intended to. Thus it is worth reiterating that our priority ought now to be for a personal transformation, leading to a genuine revival of ethics, humanism and institutions that reflect these qualities.

The purpose of this investigation is neither to condone nor to condemn. Past mistakes have a great meaning, if only we can learn from them. So this book has been about trying to find out whether we can go forward to the very core of ancient teachings and get out of the current labyrinth by absorbing new discoveries.

APPENDIX ONE   A SHADOW ON THE SECOND AGE

The more we love our friends, the less we flatter them. It is by excusing nothing that pure love shows itself.

– Molière

I was born in a Catholic family. I studied Greek and Latin and spent my college years in the school of one of the oldest Catholic abbeys in Europe. I had many friends, relatives and teachers there who were priests and some of them were very good people indeed. I saw the Church from quite close up and this chapter is about how I see it now. I do not want to hurt anybody but I really feel that we should not give up wanting to get it right. This culture was my heritage and I feel we need to restore its purity, to do justice to ideals that once were sincere and worthy. How does a mother feel whose child has been abused by a priest in a Catholic school? Anyone who cares about Christ should be concerned about this.

The story of the Apostolic, Roman Catholic Church is unique, in that this is the only known institution on the planet that endured for the entirety of the Second Age. Its relationship with the Second Age is intimate. It claims indeed to represent the Ruler of the Second Age, God the Son, as the pope is said to be the Vicar of Christ on earth, until Christ's promised return. Such endurance is indeed an amazing feat, the more so that the Church did not start on the solid rock it eventually claimed for itself with regard to the official versions of the gospels. Over the centuries, the Church, both in its capacity as a temporal power and as a spiritual teacher, seemed to have lost something. The great Goethe uses Mephistopheles' irreverence to make the point:

"Die Kirche hat en guten Magen
Hat ganze Länder aufgefressen
Und doch noch nie sich übergessen;
Die Kirch'allein, meine liebe Frauen,
Kann ungerechtes Gut verdauen."

"The Church has a good stomach; it digested entire countries and never had any indigestion; only the Church, my dear lady can digest ill begotten wealth."

"Mein Liebchen, wer darf sagen:
Ich glaub'an Gott?
Magst Priester oder weise fragen,
Und ihre Antwort scheint nur Spott
Über den Frager zu sein."

"My darling, who can say: I believe in God?
Try to ask the priest or the wise man
and their answer seems only to mock at the questioner."[54]

---

[54] Goethe Faust Collection, Bilingue Aubier Montaigne, Paris, H Lichtenberger p. 93, 114.

A TALENTED BUREAUCRAT TAKES OVER

It was probably not meant to happen in this *Kali Yuga*, the age of darkness corresponding to the First and Second Age of Joachim. It was a time for searching but not for finding. To reconstruct what happened in the first years of Christianity, one needs to refer to the totality of material available by not ignoring scriptures that were banned or cast aside by the official interpretation of the Church. The picture is then more blurred and evokes an early fight for control of the new religion. After his resurrection, Jesus did not stay to guide the young Christian community that faced early persecutions. In the ensuing confusion, alliances formed. We need to go back to the character of Saul of Tarsus, later know as the Apostle Paul. Paul needed Peter and he was smart enough to hide behind him. He had not himself received the gift of the Holy Spirit at Pentecost and this was his main problem. The experience of the blessed consciousness granted by the Holy Spirit to the real Apostles and cherished by the true early Christians Gnostics was not within the grasp of Paul and of his followers. He compensated for his shortcomings in four ways.

Firstly, as a capable evangelist and organizer, Paul built up the communities of believers. He forged the early community as the nucleus of an underground force in the Roman Empire. In the battle to exit the catacombs and grab temporal power, the end justified the means. This struggle created a dynamic ideology that unfortunately evolved later into a sectarian, militant and aggressive Christian culture.

Secondly, he replaced spiritual substance with intellectual interpretation. He asserted his missionary zeal through his epistolary writings and prolific preaching, a process that was going to be duly exploited by his successors in the Church. His mental constructions are at the origin of the increasingly empty jargon of Christian theology that was to put modern churchgoers to sleep and discourage those spiritual seekers who were endowed with some level of enquiring intelligence.

Thirdly, Paul provided an early legitimacy for para-psychological manifestations, similar to his own epileptic hallucination, to pretend that the contact was maintained with the source of legitimacy flowing from the Holy Spirit. Psychic disturbances as a sign of connection with the Divine came to influence some forms of western spirituality and it can be found at the roots of damaging Pentecostal practices or in aspects of certain New Age cults.

Fourthly, Paul was a busybody without much of a private life. His apostolic zeal was the reverse expression of a libido that he would not channel in a healthy sexuality. Paul did not like women much and his misogyny fed the fundamental Christian contradiction between sex and spirituality, the tension between carnal and spiritual pursuits that we discussed earlier.

Hence the worm inserted himself into the fruit and while the Catholic Church made some magnificent contributions to the development of western culture and art, on a more subtle level the legacy is mixed. An autocratic clergy was to remain typically characteristic of the Catholic top-down governance. It showed that, at the practical level, Christianity took its guidelines from Peter and Paul and not from Christ. Through the feuds between the Churches of Antioch and Jerusalem and the early Councils, the Gnostics, who were closer to the living message, gradually lost ground.

When the Emperor Constantine published the memorable edict of toleration in 313A.D., the Church came close to power in Italy, a power it would relinquish only in the nineteenth century when facing the armies of Piedmont and Garibaldi. The Holy See was thus the oldest European power until it was brought down by Italian patriotism. And what is this Church?

THE CALCIFICATION OF WESTERN SPIRITUALITY

Saint John the Evangelist had a powerful vision in Patmos that he recounted in the text of the *Apocalypse*. Who is the harlot dressed in scarlet, sitting on Rome's seven hills who cavorts with the kings of the earth and is intoxicated with the blood of the saints? According to the reformists such as Martin Luther, Calvin or Zwingli, John had seen the medieval Church of the pope, the heir of Peter and the creation of Paul.

Out of the Garden, Adam races fast, leaving Eve far behind. The true intoxication of the church was for power and the conquest of Western power by the Church was swift and ruthless.

First Act: the period of persecution against the early Christians, which would continue until the end of the third century, forged a strong resolve in many believers. By Tertullian´s time (c160–c200 A.D.) the ranks of the Christian Church had swollen to an estimated 200,000 members. At the same time, the Church leaders sharpened the lines of doctrine, hardening the structures of ecclesiastical authority and denounced the false teachings of the heretics. Christianity calcified in formulae and rituals while the focus on spiritual experience as the basis of the faith subsided. The ancient manuscripts discovered in 1945 in Nag Hammadi in Egypt, shed new light on the teachings of the Gnostics and the experimental dimension of earlier beliefs and practices that were gradually ostracized. The conquest of the Roman Empire by the Church started when Emperor Constantine converted to Christianity after his victory over his rival Maxence. Within 50 years of Constantine's time, Christians would number over 30 million and account for about half the Empire's population. Over the centuries, the Catholic Church maintained its grip on the Western part of the empire, leaving the east to the Orthodox Church that was more tolerant of mystical practices. When the Church survived the fall of the Roman Empire, it eventually converted the barbarous tribes, which had brought Rome down, thus demonstrating its own political versatility.

Second Act: the Church's domination of the Christian world during the Middle Ages was consolidated by the use of both military and ideological weapons against political rivals. German Emperors opposing the hegemonic pretence of the pope on Christian countries were excommunicated. The German Emperor Frederic II von Hohenstaufen opposed the Roman pope and his armies surrounded Rome, but to no avail. The pope relied on preachers to get the masses on his side and the conflict between Guelfs and Ghiblelines raged and divided the Florence of Dante and most of Europe. In the end the Emperors lost.

Third Act: again, in the sixteenth century, German Princes following Martin Luther opposed the Church. With the Hussies of Bohemia and the Calvinists from Hungary, they claimed the right to enquiry and to freedom of belief. However, under the Habsburg dynasty, the Church brought under its control the former rival, the Germanic imperial power. The Holy Roman German Empire, a prime carrier of the early millenarist vision, became a tool of the Vatican. The empire did the bidding of the pope and the full might of the Emperor Ferdinand now repressed the seekers of that time, the Protestants. The Thirty Years War in Germany and central Europe was a ruthless carnage: blood, rage, devastation, rape and fire. The soldiers of Tilly and Wallenstein criss-crossed Germany and chased the armies of the Protestant Captain von Mansfelf and those of the Nordic kings, Christian VI of Denmark and Gustav Adolf of Sweden. Thanks mostly to the military skills of the latter, the Catholic armies did not succeed. The Treaty of Westphalia concluded the war in 1648. The Church had been stopped but at a price. Germany had been ransacked.

Fourth Act: in modern times, having lost its influence in Europe, the Church of the popes moved to the Third World to mobilize a new following. This apostolic dimension is a central piece of the wider survival scheme of the institution. Indeed Catholics, like Muslims, use demography and number of adherents as a political weapon. In the age of democracy, numbers count more than ever. Let us note here that the Vatican uses its particular status as a state in the context of the United Nations to counter progress in family planning and reproductive health worldwide. Many argue that the prevention of birth control that contributes to over population in developing countries leads also to poverty and facilitates the spreading of the HIV pandemic. It is typically misogynistic in its assumption that women cannot make procreation choices.

THE NO EXIT DOGMA

There are excellent reasons why the Catholic Church harbored and entertained the original confusion pertaining to the distorted interpretation of original sin that was explained at the beginning of the book. Over the millennia, the following factors influenced the understanding of our spiritual genetic coding.

Firstly, to the authoritarian keepers of dogmas, the most dangerous sin was to foster free-willed inquiry. The very survival of the Church relied on obedience to, and unquestioning faith in a dogma whose obscurity called for the priests to decipher its provisions. Dividing man and woman, inquiry and faith, the City of God and the City of man, the church developed a paradigm that was to establish its role as a necessary intermediary. The exploitation of the original confusion in the account of the *Book of Genesis* legitimized such manipulations. As it is, they served the Church well; obedience was divine, while to question was satanic. Spiritual reality was not to be known or experienced, it would be handed down from the mouth of the priest who would thus justify his public legitimacy, and in due time and with good logic, claim for himself a fat share of prestige, wealth and power.

The oppressive regime that characterizes the theocratic Islamic Republic of Iran left by Ayatollah Khomeini may seem foreign to us. However, in past history, in our countries too, the priests were the sole custodians of truth and salvation. The Church has proved consistent in its aversion to the seeking minds of the past or the scientific minds of modern times. We forget that as long as it controlled the secular power up to the sixteenth century, the totalitarian clerical hierarchy inhibited medical progress, sending doctors, healers and pharmacists to the burning pyres.

Then again, the guilt associated with the dogma that man is born in sin facilitated the role of the Church as the needed redeemer. Fear of the doom of the pending Judgment Day begets obedience. In the Middle Ages, the Church was selling indulgences to the believers, that is, certificates that the sinner would, after all, go to heaven. Modern American televangelists broadcasting to the wealthy retiree communities in Florida and elsewhere are cashing in on the same combination of primeval fears and ignorance. Ignorance was helpful, and it was duly maintained.

Finally, it was important for the Church to maintain its celibate clergy and to keep them away from women. It wanted to ensure their emotional dependency; a condition for unquestioning obedience, which a relationship with a wife would have weakened. Here again, the story of Eve came in handy and beyond the demonizing of spiritual seeking, the exploitation of the original confusion introduced avowed misogyny. As a woman in Eden, Eve brought man into deep existential trouble because, in so many ways she represents the troubling power of desire. Over the period of enforced celibacy, the clergy were afraid of their own sexual impulses, and for them, women as sex temptresses were the enemy and had to be subdued. Priests believe in a male dominated cosmology and believe that the sexes are not equal.

The dividing paradigm put into place by the theologians not only reviled women, it was to doom the very progress of Christian spirituality, taking appearance for substance, the oyster shell for the pearl. Examples abound in the liturgy. The tenets of the Catholic faith are contained in the sacraments, which interestingly enough, represent the emptied rituals and symbols of a deeper meaning of spiritual reality that has been lost. Let us illustrate this.

For instance, in the sacrament of the Eucharist, one is supposed to eat the body and drink the blood of Christ while eating bread and drinking wine. This bizarre rite is central to Catholic practices. Non-Christians wondered what sort of sectarian brainwashing can distillate such cannibalistic certainties in the mind of intelligent men and women? As it is, the Eucharist is a commemoration of the Last Supper where Jesus took bread, and distributed it to His disciples, saying: "Take, eat, this is My body." Why? As Shri Mataji once explained it, Christ was a Divine being vibrating with inner spiritual powers and He had the capacity to transmit His vibrations of this higher energy into the bread. The Apostles felt this and they entered a higher awareness, as the powers of Christ passed into them through the bread and the grape juice that He had touched. It was Divine energy, not hocus-pocus in Greek and Latin. Any priest touching a piece of bread or drinking fermented wine cannot, unfortunately, achieve the same result or impact.

Similarly, the sacrament of the baptism consists of pouring water on to the head of a baby so as to wash away the consequences of original sin. It also makes sure that it becomes a Catholic and that it will in due time, pay its taxes to the church. This ceremony is the commemoration of the baptism of Christ by John the Baptist in the River Jordan. But John the Baptist was no ordinary being and he too had the power to pass subtler spiritual energies into matter, in this case into the waters of the Jordan. He poured it on to the Head of Christ. The ceremony symbolizes the water of life or vibrations, flowing into the seventh chakra. The top of the head is the seat of higher consciousness. This is testified by the presence of the tongues of flame of the Holy Spirit on the heads of the Apostles, during the night of Pentecost. But the sacrament of confirmation to recall the Holy Spirit in young Catholics is again a powerless ritual without any effective power to manifest the energy of the Holy Spirit.

Shri Mataji, speaking about God, once observed that. "He is all common sense. He is the source of all understanding. He is the source of all feelings." If religion ceases making sense it is because of our limited interpretations.

HUNTING DOWN THOSE WHO DISSENT

Stuck in this absurd emptiness, the Catholic dogma would stubbornly defend the status quo of spiritual ignorance and encourage the persecution of those who would move forwards on the path of Self-discovery. Only in the nineteenth century was the freedom of belief enshrined in most European constitutions. This contrasts poorly with such tolerant religions as Hinduism or Buddhism.

Modern writings have documented the long list of religiously motivated abuses that darken our history. The persecutions against the Jews, the Gypsies and others throughout Europe during the Middle Ages were encouraged. The massacre of the Hussite in Bohemia and the repression of Calvinism in Hungary illustrate persecution throughout the vast Habsburg Empire. In France, we register the destruction of the Order of the Temple by the pope and the King of France, the Dominican Inquisition and the crusade against the Cathars in the south. During the night of Saint Barthelemy, the Protestants in Paris were massacred in their sleep under the orders of King Charles IX. The Revocation of the Edict of Nantes by Louis XIV led to a mass migration of Protestants out of France. The persecution of any dissenting faith, in short, was common practice.

France provided much of the landscape for this repression and, unfortunately, the legacy of intolerance stuck with the French even when they dropped Catholicism. Indeed, in the eighteenth century, the French rationalists turned their back on the Catholic Church and spirituality as a result of the Church's inept teachings. Notably the sect of the freemasons that permeates the French bureaucratic elite carried this secular movement of rationalism into modern times to an intolerant level of secular dogmatism. They remain in some weird way under the spell of original sin and negate the quest for spirituality. This points to France as a country where new ideas are no longer likely to emerge, a fact that is sadly exemplified by the contemporary witch-hunt against alternative thinking originating from both the Catholic and rationalist traditions. With such a background of conformists, it is a huge paradox that the French consider themselves libertarians.

It is worth dwelling on France, for its history illustrates the limitation of an Adam absorbed in thought only. The French reticence to explore spirituality goes back to Descartes' creed: "Je pense donc je suis," "I think therefore I am." This naive faith in the mental side of our psyche, Adam without Eve, represents only a partial understanding of our cognitive potential and does not allow for expanding it. This one-legged approach again represses the feminine power of emotions and feelings, quite in line

COVERING UP BEHAVIOR DEVIATIONS

Of course one gladly recognizes that Catholicism, throughout history, has fostered some great achievements; the *Summa Theologica* of Aquinas, the Roman Abbeys and the great Gothic cathedrals, the Sistine Chapel and countless works of art that constitute an impressive cultural legacy. Catholicism has also encouraged morality, reminded people of their God and praised Him through the centuries with elevating sacred music. The Catholic faith, despite its rulers, kept the flame of devotion burning for generations of simple hearted believers that sought in their God and in Mother Mary their comfort and rest. Much credit goes to all those, through the ages, who sincerely committed themselves to make Catholicism work despite its contradictions. It may seem one-sided to emphasize its dark side without mentioning the drawbacks of other religions or cultures that are also quite considerable. As a matter of fact, in the Second Age, most religions and theories were brought to the extreme and thus missed the point. The more extreme forms of negative influences that surfaced in the past, such as fascism or racism, have been recognized evils, and they have already been dismissed by history. Similarly, contemporary forms of violent Muslim fundamentalism are easily recognized as unacceptable. But the level of damage done by the Catholic Church to our civilization is not well understood and it is more sustained and subtler than many scholars yet acknowledge. This is why some focus on the subject is called for.

Many have stated that hypocrisy characterizes the relationship between Catholicism and morality. While the Church had influence, it constantly covered up its own abuses, such as, typically, sexual abuses of young people by priests in positions of authority. In fact, the official ban on the marriage of priests pushed scores of them into deviant practices. Of course the notion of deviation implies a right path of sexual behavior from which one might deviate, something that is politically incorrect for today's intelligentsia which legitimizes a variety of excesses. The notion of proper sexual behavior is a challenge to contemporary relativism. Nevertheless, the existence of a path of moral rectitude was not questioned in the traditions of spirituality.

All religions claim in essence that God is a loving Being and that we as spiritual beings will try to emulate His qualities through moral righteousness, compassion and benevolence. It is because this message is so widely accepted in various cultures that the religious establishment, priests, monks, lamas and mullahs at one time enjoyed the respect of the masses. How does the Church hold up against these standards? The response of the *Pontifex Maximus* was to proclaim his infallibility.

Technology helps in modern times and especially with television, where appearance counts for more than reality and show carries more weight than substance. The record of the present papacy, to many progressive Catholics, reads like a grim account of stagnation. Pope John Paul II consistently blocked any progress to adjust Catholic theology to the human reality of this century and he nominated a cohort of reactionary prelates, and, largely as a result of these misguided policies, he emptied the Western churches and the seminaries. But he shines on television through the careful orchestration of mega events: his countless trips, mammoth masses, pilgrimages, earth-kissing stopovers in politically sensitive locations, youth festivals and rock concerts, all designed to dissimulate the contemporary decay of the Church and project an apparent image of dynamism. For a fleeting moment, the Church, immortalized by the media, counts its millions of adherents and looks like it is going somewhere. The show hides the lack of substance and is carried to extremes. The aged pope, sick and trembling with Parkinson's disease is paraded around and his sufferings, we are told, recall those of Christ on the cross. But as the Popemobile was driving down the streets of The Hague, Dutch youngsters stood by silently with a large banner that read: "Pope, step down! We want to see Christ."

The pope steers and operates his ministry at the level of the media. His contrite recognition of the Church's past sins, notably towards the Jews, during the celebration of the Advent 2000, was a successful coup. The American newspapers gave him rave reviews and little did they remember that confession is another tested trick of the clergy: confess the sins of yesterday while planning those for tomorrow.

The papal release of the third Fatima secret is another shot at media manipulation for the sake of a wider dissimulation. Authoritative sources revealed that the third secret of Fatima, that caused so much dread to the Church, was as follows: At the end of time, it is Mother Mary that would bring an end to a degraded Church. The intense and well-publicized devotion of this pope to Mary might express the hope of preventing this outcome. After the failed attempt on the pope's life by Ali Agca, the Church rationalized that these gunshots in Saint Peter's Square were indeed what had been prophesied by the Virgin appearing to children in Fatima, Portugal. The pope had avoided the fatal outcome thanks to his devotion to Mary. Why did they wait over ten years after the assassination attempt to tell us?

Activities of the Church have traditionally been cloaked in secrecy. Pope John XXIII had realized this to be incompatible with the contemporary thrust for open information and he opened up the Church to a new dimension of transparency through the Second Vatican Council. But the systematic and sometimes ferocious dismantling of the heritage of the Council by the traditionalists, who followed him, Paul VI and John Paul II, suggests how bold - yet futile - his attempt had been.

The Jesuits who had been the storm troopers of the pope since they countered the Reformation in the sixteenth century had become more social minded and enlightened. They had taken the side of the poor, notably in Latin America where they spread the tenets of liberation theology. This did not amuse the hierarchy who always line up with the interests of the ruling classes, and thence the Jesuits lost ground, and influence within the Church instead moved to the profit of a secret sect, born out of Franco's fascist regime during the Spanish civil war: the Opus Dei. John Paul II recently, to the astonishment of many, declared its founder a saint.

Exploitation is another behavioral trait of the Church. Walking in the pleasant streets of the Aventino, one of the loveliest hills of Rome, it is common to come across flocks of young nuns from Kerala, India, who, for a brief moment, escape from the convents where they serve as domestics to the ageing Europe nuns and priests. The snapshot aptly shows why the drive for evangelization is vital to the Church, because despite its television peaks and set-pieces, it has in fact, lost the brains and hearts of the western nations and must now turn to Third World converts to ensure its long-term survival. The Church in the Third World was always part of the colonial set up but it survived decolonization mainly because it positioned itself as a provider of prized education through countless colleges, high schools and universities. These schools target the elite and represent a lucrative business. But if the forms of exploitations are reinvented, the reality of the Church exploiting the people is almost as old as the Church itself.

Most of all, the Church exploits its own members. It is symbolic that a Catholic priest, at the moment of ordination, must take the vows of obedience, chastity and poverty. These vows deliver him helplessly to the domination and abuses of the institution to which he devotes his life. The three vows mean in fact: a) servility to the hierarchy; b) an unnatural life of repressed sexuality that will keep him out of emotional balance to maintain the fervor of a zealot; c) his own wealth, family inheritance or possessions will be turned over to the Church.

Part of the obfuscatory scheme of the Church is its bizarre relationship with alcohol. Let us recall the Caanan wedding. Christ attended a wedding and provided unexpected help for the hosts who had run out of drinks for the guests; he changed the water into grape juice. In ancient Hebrew, the word for grape-juice and wine is the same. How could a spiritual leader that fosters higher awareness endorse a fermented drug that goes against spirituality? Growth in spirituality means growth in consciousness, a condition that is related to our psychosomatic wellbeing. I have enjoyed in my time the occasional glass of Romanée Conti, but the bottom line is that alcohol is a toxic substance: it generates addiction and, thus, it goes against spirituality that postulates the freedom of the consciousness. Jesus would have agreed with the Prophet Mohammed on this account. Indeed the Prophet banned alcohol.

Yet, medieval monks produced fine liquors and very early on, the Church endorsed alcohol, perhaps in conformity with its undercurrent assumption that higher awareness would be a challenge of its domination over the enfeebled western mind. In the early Middle Ages, throughout France, Italy and Germany, abbeys and convents specialized in the manufacture of various blessed drinks, such as Benedictine. It is only with the blessings of the Church that alcohol in its various forms became a mainstream drinking habit. Only Islam and Hinduism resisted this trend.

THE DRIFT INTO CRIMINALITY

Problems too have their purpose.

    – Saint Francis of Sales

How could they get away with it for so long? It is Catholic theory, which provides this answer. The *"Confiteor"*, is the old Latin prayer by which the Catholics declare their faith, and what they believe in. The creed of this traditional prayer spells out the objects of the Catholic faith. These do not only include the Father, the Son and the Holy Ghost but also *"et unam sanctam catholicam"* and *"apostolicam ecclesiam"* that is, the one, saintly, Catholic and Apostolic Church.

In other words, the Church is not just a medium to carry or spread the message of Christ; its institutional existence is declared a very object of faith by itself and in itself. Thus, preserving its existence becomes an end in itself, irrespective of what it does. The means has become the end and that end, i.e. the survival of the Church, justifies all means. This was aptly expressed by the smug confidence of Roman cardinals when questioned about the endless scandals which rocked the Church in the 1980s: an institution that survived for two thousand years is not going to be brought down by a few revelations of its misdeeds. The device of the Jesuits *"perinde ac cadaver"*, an uncritical service of the Church until death, meant also the death of critical intelligence.

Library shelves are filled with books, ancient and new, which detail the turpitude of the Church. Dissimulation became an art. This culture is sadly demonstrated by the response of prelates in the USA to the emergency created by sex abuses committed by priests in Catholic institutions. Shifting the priests convicted of such abuses from one parish to another was not protecting the children of the next parish.

The crimes of the Church are often dismissed as a thing of the past. While the historical record of the Church, from the Middle Ages to modern times, is replete with episodes, which are repulsive to a modern conscience or completely incompatible with contemporary standards of human rights, the astonishing fact is that the criminal record of the Church is still adding new chapters. Despite sporadic denunciations, these episodes escape the hand of the law. The Church's continuous impunity is largely explained by the pretence of holiness that hides the dark side and by the extraterritoriality of the Vatican as a State independent from the Italian legislation.

This chapter will refrain from providing an overview of the many recent books that report on various contemporary criminal activities where an involvement of the Church is alleged: association with the Mafia; shoddy financial dealings; contract murders; attacks on the liberation theologians in Latin America (fostered by Opus Dei and the hierarchy); the collapse of morality within the Vatican itself. The sexual abuse of children and other crimes cannot be indicative of an institution that represents Christ. The magnitude of the sex-related scandals affecting the clergy, from Spain to the USA, is shaking the very foundations of the Vatican.

Theology has become the theoretical foundation for impunity. A main question arises when pondering on the strange course taken by the Church. How is it that so many of its members, who had taken to priesthood, could reconcile themselves with a pattern of activities so clearly incompatible with sainthood? How could they reconcile themselves, on the theoretical level, with these activities? There is an answer for this too. Suffering is an essential part of spiritual ascent and thus, if you want to ascend, you will suffer. What else should happen to sinners anyway?

But among many who still practice the faith, the realization is dawning that a time of renewal and purification is on its way. The call for a thorough reform of the Church is getting louder. Many, of course, are those who had followed the Catholic faith in a sincere movement of worship. It is also for their sake that the Church must cleanse its act. Out of this evil, some good may yet come.

One of the Latin names of the holy Virgin Mary is *"Honor et Gloria nostra:"* "Our Honor and our Glory." But what have we done to the honor of Her Son and the purity of Her lofty banner? Those who are true to the devotion that flew to Her over the centuries would wish to reform these institutions and to overcome the obstacles that blocked the path of spirituality. They would leave the path that led Christian countries into gross materialism, so that, as children of God, worshippers of Mary, they may claim the right to know who they really are.

APPENDIX TWO   WHO IS DEMOCRACY'S MASTER?

All things derive their essential character from their function and their capacity; and it follows that if they are no longer fit to discharge their function, we ought not to say that they are still the same things, but only that, by an ambiguity, they still have the same names.

— Aristotle, the Politics

This critical review of the history of the clergy in the west is not new. Perhaps a criticism of democracy is less common and we shall offer one. Modern democracy was born in the generous but slightly utopian vision of Jean Jacques Rousseau. It is, most of us firmly believe, the best system we have and we love it. But, as is said in Latin *"Qui bene amat, bene castigat"*: "Who loves well chastises well." We should love democracy enough to identify its shortcomings, with a view to improve it. To do this, we must marvel at the surreptitiousness with which we manage to turn our best institutions upside down. Thoreau noted: "Thus, under the name of order and civil government, we are all made at last to pay homage to and support our own meanness. After the first blush of sin comes its indifference; and from immoral it becomes, as it were, unmoral, and not quite unnecessary to that life which we have made."[55]

THE BRAVE, EVER NEW WORLD

What makes us tick? What gets us going? Desire matters but desires are the source of sufferings, said Prince Siddhartha, for most people do not understand their own desires. Andre Gide promises, "Where my desire goes, there I shall go." What we desire makes a difference in life because, more often than we think, we will get there. In the beginning was Desire, not Action. Buddha, the sage from the East, got it right. Goethe's Faust, the typical herald of the modern Western seeker, made a German suggestion that in the beginning was Action: "Am Anfang war die Tat." But guys acting around me do so without really knowing what they desire or how to go about achieving it. 'Actionoholics' agitate in all spheres of life. What are they busy about? Have they met their deep desires? Wisdom would have that actions follow desires, to give them body and shapes, to create the world we would wish for ourselves and for those we love.

It is 1988, on an island in the sun. I am taking a break from my job in New York and trying to rediscover in the surrounding splendor of nature the charge of energy that seems spent as I push myself to the limits in my Manhattan based job. Sand in my hair, deep blue sky and a generous sun, how lovely is the feeling of the water droplets, which slowly die on my skin. It is a good day to pick up the trail of this enquiry between pebbles and shells on the shores of Nantucket, a beautiful island off the coast of Massachusetts, which oozes discrete wealth. The rich and leisurely relax in preciously restored houses and the boys of Boston's top schools, suitably tanned, ride the waves

---

[55] Henry David Thoreau Walden, *Civil Disobedience*, Penguin Classics, New York, (1986), p. 394.

and chase the girls. A dream of the great American Democracy - 'oligarchy' - is a forgotten word - a showpiece of the affluent Reagan-Bush era with a Kennedy touch of social sophistication.

At the end of the Second Age, market economy democracy triumphs worldwide over its old rival, Marxist socialism. I walk the beaches of Nantucket and watch the glittering fleet of private yachts and the surfers at sport; should we not give the highest marks to a system of society which allows for so much leisure and entertainment? So now, where will our desire take us, where is the next ice-cream parlor, the next trip, the next desire?

If Germans believed in action, the French, on the other side of the Rhine, were of the opinion that in the beginning was thought. The children of Descartes trusted too much in their own mental constructs but thoughts can be shades on the walls of our brains' inner caves; they can be mere opinion *(doxa)*, as Plato had warned us, never leading to true knowledge *(episteme)*. We saw how the eighteenth century French philosophers, Voltaire, Diderot, d'Alembert, anxious to get rid of Catholic clerical obscurantism, rediscovered reason. Thoughts would be properly trimmed and aligned to present the orderly beauty of a French garden. Ironically, reason became the new faith of the French and, as Burke could see clearly, this unconditional faith in thoughts only too often turned the French into political extremists. After all, Pol Pot, the leader of the Red Khmers, was not educated in England. His concept of emptying the urban population into the countryside denotes the French preference for intellectual symmetry. Ideas can be dangerous. As France celebrated the 200th anniversary of the storming of the Bastille, the goddess Freedom had been celebrated by the blood of Chinese students spilled on Tiananmen Square: is bloodshed part of the ritual baptism of democracy? The scale of the killing in the French Revolution, 17,000 executions in one year or so, including Marie Antoinette, a gracious Queen, was considerable for the time.

Not everything was wrong in the preceding monarchic system. In the royal gardens of the Versailles palace, mere blue ribbons stretched between the trees kept the commoners at bay. There may have been some merits in a system where ribbons and not riot gear are perceived as effective crowd control devices. Yet, the *'Ancient Regime'* had to fall, like a rotten fruit. The unchallenged power of the French monarchy by 'Divine right' had bred too many worms. Poor Louis XVI was not responsible for the mess; he loved hunting, clocks, his wife and his subjects, and possibly he was sweetly dumb. Better than his brother, the Count of Artois, who turned from playboy into an arch bigot like his ancestor Louis XIV. Louis XVI did not deserve to be beheaded, nor did Tsar Nicholas II deserve to be shot along with his whole family, but they had to pay for centuries of inequality and oppression. Karma with a vengeance, as usual, but then again, Kings and Tsars had outlived their usefulness.

What happened after the baptism of democracy? Where were people heading? Desires, thought, action - will we ever get this merry-go-round right? Politics suffer from this confusion. After the Jacobean Republic of Saint-Just and Robespierre came Napoleon and his empire. An improvement, perhaps, but hardly democracy. Again, Napoleon had it all sorted out in his head. The map of Europe would reflect the geometry of his thoughts, but at dusk, on the plains of Waterloo, it is Blucher and his Prussians who appeared, not Grouchy and the French reserve army. Fate struck again and sent the great political Geometrician to the Island of Saint Helena. Military analysts reckon that the emperor could easily have won the decisive battle, and had this happened, this book would most likely have been written in French.

Marxists are also the children of Jean Jacques Rousseau but they quickly lost their way. After Lenin came Stalin, definitely not an improvement, as Boukharine and millions of others soon found out. In an atheist world, the temptation to reconstruct God was irresistible. Stalin, a former seminarist, found himself ideally suited for the role. The companions of Lenin were compelled to validate the fabricated charges against them during the infamous show trials and to confess their crimes before being executed. It is not always freedom that smiles in the cradle of democracy.

What was the desire of the people who brought these changes to their world? What was the revolutionaries' wish in the first place? They thought they wanted freedom; or was it power they really sought? The meaning of the very word democracy is power to the people, not freedom. The trouble is that the people did not get much training in learning how to handle power. It seems that the relationship between democracy and freedom depends upon the tension between power and people. Must freedom in a democracy mean a free-for-all grab at power? If so, we are precisely in these deeper troubles that Rousseau, Jefferson and other godfathers of modern democracy wanted to prevent.

The pendulum swung: from absolute monarchy to relative democracy. From relative simplicity in the way we run things, to obscure complexity. One man, one sword, and one crown: "Long live the King!" Our ancestors knew who ruled. However, who is the real ruler when the people rule? Nobody? Everybody? Or somebody. This body may act with such familiarity that its existence is unnoticed. Its shape is ill defined and, more ominously, its desire and purposes are not understood. Is this hypothetical ruler of democracy now inheriting the earth?

IS THE STATE FADING AWAY?

The welfare state is meant to be the peacemaker, the holder of the balance of power and the provider of distributive justice. Little do we recall that these attributes have a long mythological prehistory that can be deciphered with the help of symbols. What is the most widespread symbol of the State? People are used to seeing the American bald eagle opening its wings on the seal of the President of the United States, but before landing there, this eagle had a long flight. In the Aryan tradition, the great eagle Garuda is the vehicle of the God Vishnu, who intervenes in history as and when required to swiftly distribute justice. In their different names, the three aspects of God, as Existence (Shiva), as Operator (Vishnu), and as Creator (Brahma) correspond to the three *gunas* or channels. The second aspect matters for this discussion. As the force that sustains the evolutionary process, Vishnu holds the balance between the *gunas* and thus is also the God of Justice.

In fact, the sixth incarnation of Vishnu, Lord Rama, represents the righteous King, the perfect being *(Purushottaama)* to lead the Aryan race *(Aryaputra)*. He lived about 8000 years B.C. and so powerful is his fame and might that the tales of his exploits are still alive to this day in India, Thailand, Cambodia and Bali. His first lieutenant, the swift Hanuman, inspired the tale of the white monkey deep into China. Of Hanuman, Shri Mataji says, "He is the messenger of God known elsewhere as Hermes, Mercury or Gabriel."

The Eagle God, Garuda, is the archetype that became the universal symbol for the might of the State. As Garuda carries Vishnu, the State should carry God's benevolence and justice. That eagle led the Roman legions, took its flight from Rome to Byzantium and adorned the imperial crests of the Habsburg, Hohenzollern and Romanov dynasties as an unconscious reminder that power should be righteous. The eagle is the symbolic link between Vishnu's principle of justice and the modern state.

But gods and heroes faded away and the pretension of empires to represent the authority of God became increasingly futile. Contemporary western states lost perception of their connection with the Virata. Too many present day Muslim states claim this connection, through that blood and violence which was first expressed in the slaughter of the family of the Prophet by those who coveted the might of the Caliphate. Indeed the meaning of the sacred eagle is lost and the State became the prized trophy for power seekers.

In the past, the state was the power. Machiavelli, enlightened writer of the Italian Renaissance, was weary of the conflicts between the pope and the Emperor. He felt that too much of religion intruding into politics was not a good thing, and projected in The Prince the image of the modern secular ruler. The princes would build territorial domains around their dynasty, asserting dominion through space and time without seeking mystical justifications. Gradually a framework of rules appeared. The notion of the State first appeared in the writings of the fifteenth century French writer Jean Bodin, but the State, as we know it, is really an invention of the nineteenth century. It is worth noting that, from the very beginning, one of the constitutional prerogatives of the Prince, and latterly of the State, was to control money. This no longer is the case as we saw in Chapter 6.

The 18th Brumaire of Napoleon Bonaparte is the date of his first attempt at seizing power in Paris. In his writing on the subject, Marx made an analysis of the State that we can summarize as follows. As it controls society's means of production, the capitalist bourgeoisie generate an institutional superstructure, the State, whose task is to mediate and deflect the class struggle between bourgeoisie and proletariat. Although a creation of the bourgeoisie, the State can thus be called upon to take measures which apparently go against the immediate interests of the bourgeoisie, or which seem to serve the interests of the working class. Nevertheless, this is only, in the last analysis, to ensure the longer-term survival and hegemonic position of the bourgeoisie. The set of regulatory frameworks set in place by the State generally aim at reaching some balance in distributing the fruits of economic growth among the various stakeholders of the civil society. Sure enough, the happy bourgeoisie continues to eat the lion's share of the pie, but, as there is something for everybody, social peace and cohesion is preserved, a key factor for the smooth functioning of capitalism.

Of course, the State carried out its own excesses. From the Prussian rigidity of Otto von Bismarck to its twentieth century, extreme exhaled through Nazi and fascist megalomania and the Stalinist totalitarian regime. History dealt with such aberrations. But the State's more benign and benevolent Keynesian or social-democratic version had to heed the interest of the national collectivity as a whole. As such it became the guardian of democracy. A certain vision of the future of a united Europe was going to expand its scope at the regional level but the successful outcome of this project is today in doubt.

It seems indeed that the last line of defense for democracy's set of checks and balances, that is the regulatory framework maintained by the state, is no longer deemed useful for the CEO captains of a world bourgeoisie who are no longer threatened by Marxist militancy. Therefore the time may have come to marginalize the role of governments in the economic sphere. The same veil of opprobrium is cast on the regulatory framework of inter-governmental agencies such as the United Nations or the European Union. However, the term bourgeoisie, with its connotation of quiet respectability, is not really appropriate for today's hot money grabbers, xenophobic populists and right wing mobs.

For Marx, the State was a front, an alibi. In the ultimate phase of the communist society there was to be no State. Not because it would have become sacked by its bourgeois masters - no doubt the way Marx would have interpreted the 1995 global market - but because society would be run by self-managed associations of citizens. True to the Marxist analysis, reality shows an uncanny collusion between the State and business interests. Krupp supported Nazism, and IG Farbenindustrien, a giant German trans-national conglomerate, used the slave labor of the SS to run the concentration camps.

More mildly, when business indirectly or directly controls communications and the media, it is in the best position to grab control of the government of democratic countries. The story of Italy's prosecution of corruption scandals is edifying. Since the judiciary power closed in on the relationship between the Mafia, business and politics, the pool of Milanese magistrates found itself under fire from Mr. Berlusconi, the media tycoon turned Prime Minister.

The forces of money in the 1990s made the rules, moved capital around and commanded workers across the globe, speculated against currencies, delocalized production sites as they pleased, invested for immediate profit in and out of traditional or emerging markets and provoked recessions. Financial and economic mega-systems are the prime movers of economic policies. They privatize, they restructure, they sack. They also launder the astronomical profits of organized criminality from Columbia, China, Italy or Russia. Servants of the State, discredited by years of complacency, and sometimes, outright corruption, were utterly confused as they tried to face the challenge. States comply, or prosperity will pass them by. As the world became a global village, the dark side of the force sacked the village elders.

In present day democracies, political leaders fight hard for re-election, only to find that they are powerless against seemingly invisible foes. Finances, trading, information, propelled by the new technologies have exploded into a new imperial constellation of economic power. Its planetary battleships are the multinational corporations. The Death Star is global electronic finance and its Imperial troopers are the yuppies. Darth Vader wears its mask and the Emperor is Mr. D.

It is most unlikely that the grand chamberlains in Mr. D's private council would collectively plot their way towards world domination, as would the Mafia's top institution, the sinister *"cupola"*. Probably they are well-meaning people when they gather at the Davos Forum to sing the praises of globalization. I do not think that they want to give a new meaning to Armageddon fantasies. However, the accumulated impact of the impulse they give to society is perceived as dangerous.

MISSING THE TURN

It is 1994, on a grey sky somewhere in Europe. Mikhail Gorbachov, the King Lear of the Second Russian Revolution is long gone, having taken in his stride the Nobel Prize and the sack. Microsoft is getting into the software market in China while Coca-Cola and Pepsi fight for India. The IMF and the World Bank preach the gospel of the market place to economies in transition and to developing countries. The GATT turns into the World Trade Organization. Free Market Democracy asserts itself, a golden calf for the believers on Capitol Hill, a golden bull for the resourceful in Wall Street and in the City of London.

Of course we, in the First World, write the rules of the game in our favor. We love the freedom of the market when it is good for us, not when it is good for them. The Organization for Economic Cooperation and Development (OECD) estimates that protectionist support to agriculture in the form of subsidies among its members, most of them industrialized developed countries, amounts to about US $1 billion dollars per day. Experts say subsidized farm exports from the rich countries compete unfairly with the production of poor countries.

The appeal of the market economy is glorified by contrasting the obvious economic backwardness of the countries that had followed the Marxist model and the political wasteland in those Muslim places dedicated to religious integration. It is terrible but it is all happening out there, among the aliens. We are fine, we are democrats and we know what democracy is. The western democracies know best. Why recall the warnings of Socrates or Montesquieu.

We should have held a huge party, filled the swimming pool with champagne and jumped in, adorned with our tuxedos, celebrating with the new Republican right in America: the right to be extremely right. So why are we instead so stressed and confused, why this feeling of hangover without even having had the party? At the time of the long sought after victory over communism, suddenly the old continent seems out of breath, ruled by dwarfs, losing at the same time its traditions and its vision. The then leader of the free world, Bill Clinton, felt quite free to play the sort of games that cannot easily be described to children, with a White House intern.

Indeed, the 'vision thing', as President Bush-the-father used to say, is some sort of slogan for politicians to posture over. Of course, we do not believe our leaders and we mostly enjoy them when they feature in the puppet show, however, we still buy their show. *'Sua Emittenza'* Mr. Berlusconi got 57% of the Italian voters to save his quasi-monopolistic ownership of TV networks. Political self-marketing is a grand art but it comes down to dealership instead of leadership.

When the Berlin Wall fell we missed an historic opportunity. I watched it on TV, from my home in New Rochelle, New York and saw how East and West Germans stood together on the wall at Checkpoint Charlie and sang Beethoven's Hymn to Joy. For a while, time entered a magic realm and every dream could be dreamt. It was a turning point and if our statesmen had had the courage and leadership of the generation that won World War II, we might have safeguarded democracy and prosperity for all. But these types of leaders were no longer around. If they had been, we could have chosen to reduce arms spending, promote demand and invest in the protection of natural resources. This would have built up the demand for the products of the industrialized nation and secured continued growth with a cleaner environment. We could have put into place farsighted immigration policies to maintain productivity and population in Europe. But instead, we had no vision and in the event we did not behave as real democrats. We did not care about the greater good of the greater number and, in this shortsightedness we missed an opportunity for our own good.

At the same time, I do not mean to idealize what is happening outside the western world. The Islamic fundamentalists slit the throats of sixteen-year-old girls on the streets of Algiers because they do not wear the chador, and from Latin America to India, the Third World seems to sink further into corruption. Hutus and Tutsis send each other to hell while singing and dancing. We have some reasons to believe that better governance in these countries would be desirable. But if we want to propose a model of democracy to the developing world, it should be credible.

WHERE WAS DEMOCRACY COMING FROM?

Perhaps we should climb a few branches on the genealogical tree of Mr. D and learn something about his genetic set up. It bothers me not to know who is taking the decisions for me.

In libraries, I found that the ancestry of Mr. D., from Aristotle to Rousseau is noble and generous. Although there were forms of democratic decision-making in various parts of the ancient world, we should travel first to ancient Athens. The concept and the word democracy was coined in Greece and glossed over by Aristotle who, in good logic, turned out to be the preceptor of one of the most flamboyant antithesis to democracy: Alexander the Great. We read these lines in Aristotle's treatise on *Politics*: "The proper application of the term 'democracy' is to a constitution in which the free born and poor control the government - being at the same time a majority; and similarly the term 'oligarchy' is properly applied in a constitution in which the rich and better born control the government - being at the same time a minority."[56]

[56] *Aristotle the Politics*, ed, tr, Ernest Baker, Oxford University Press, Oxford (1969), p. 164.

To the Greek fathers of political philosophy, democracy could only be viable in the structured system of a city *(polis)* which should not be larger than about 15,000 citizens. The scale factor was key to communicating and sharing power in ancient society. Put a wall around Babylon and you don't get a city, according to the political meaning that the Greeks gave to the *polis*. Small size lends itself to democratic rule but when the city grows too big, the key players hide their game and citizens lose touch with the complex processes that secure the democratic sharing of rights and duties. Then obscure intermediaries capture the levers of power. If that is so, what does it mean to be a citizen in today's large nations or mega-metropolises? The citizen has become a hybrid between a taxpayer, a voter and a consumer but he does not rule.

The ancient philosophers were suspicious of democracy and, like Confucius, would rather entrust matters of collective interest to a homogeneous group of competent and virtuous rulers, selected on their merits; a system called aristocracy. It could have worked if competence had been a hereditary quality.

However, it is not and democracy is safer than oligarchy. '*Aristos*' means the best. In modern times self-assertions of being 'the best', Aryan or otherwise, have often only served to pave the way to brutish stupidity. With the advent of Nazi Germany, it was said that Germans with narrow foreheads and large jaws should replace Germans with large foreheads and narrow jaws. With perhaps the possible elegant exception of Oscar Wilde, every form of modern elitism ended in blatant idiocy. Today's American followers of the late Leo Strauss, the political philosopher who held court at the University of Chicago in the 1960s, have become the apostles of predatory capitalism.

As for the modern forms of monarchy, they are best forgotten. The twentieth century expression of absolute power stretched from the clownish (Mussolini) to outright insane (Stalin and Hitler). The modern monarch turned out to be both sinister and homicidal. If this is the result of power being vested in a single person, democracy is certainly safer than monarchy.

CHECKS DO NOT BALANCE

At once, in place of the individual personality of each contracting party, this act of association creates a moral and collective body, composed of as many members as the assembly contains voters, and receiving from this act its common identity, its life and its will.

– Jean Jacques Rousseau

Rousseau is the benevolent father of Mr. D. He cloaked the legitimacy of modern democracy in abstract construction, the famed 'social contract'. This lofty language left Rousseau's students equally convinced and confused: convinced that democracy is good for us and confused as how to make it work. Hobbes, who had said "*homo homini lupus,*" that is, "man is a wolf for man," is the pessimist who got it right, trying to do the least damage in managing society, assuming people are crooks. Anglo-Saxon liberal democracies, in his footsteps, functioned reasonably well.

There is tragedy brooding in the cradle of Mr. D. Rousseau, trying to do the greatest good and assuming people are innocent, is the nice guy who it wrong: Stalin, Mussolini and Hitler deduced the foundation of the totalitarian state from his social contract. Again, thoughts and actions are diverging; our wishes fly in one direction, our deeds go off in another.

In the eighteenth century, Montesquieu proposed practical solutions to regulate the use of power. He expanded democracy from the city to the country. He insisted on the importance of rules for checks and balances such as the separation between the executive (government), legislative (parliament) and judiciary (Supreme Court) powers.

Checks and balances turned out to be a necessary but insufficient condition for democracy's stability. It cannot be said either, that checks and balances exclusively characterize democracy because such mechanisms are found in many non-democratic forms of society too. For instance, thousands of years ago, during India's Vedic age, checks and balances among the chief social players became the raison d'être of the caste system. Those who had the brainpower, the intellectuals, teachers or priests (Brahmins), were separated from those who had the administrative or military might (Kshatryas). These in turn were not to engage in commercial activities; the power of money was vested in the businessmen (Vaishyas); finally, physical work was reserved for the workers (Shudras). The castes split the cake and there was a bite for everybody. With the advent of nineteenth century capitalism, the Vaishyas (bourgeoisie) swallowed the Brahmins (clergy) and the Kshattryas (nobility) and became the sole ruling class of the industrial age. In a sense, when Marx and Lenin were exposing the necessity of the class struggle, they were reacting to the breakdown of the social equilibrium that had been maintained by former checks and balances. They did not find it healthy that one class, the bourgeoisie, would have it all.

The only remaining caste, the Shudras (working class), confronted the bourgeoisie. However, the workers lost out too. Firstly, inside the socialist camp, they lost out to a class of bureaucratic mandarins, the communist nomenklatura. Ultimately the communist block collapsed altogether. Now when I check in at Addis Ababa airport, the Marxist red star no longer watches over me. Instead, I see huge advertising boards celebrating the powers of the Vaishyas: Coca-cola, Marlborough, Rothmans; the Shudras have finally lost the battle. With only one class ruling, and quite avid at it, the healthy principle of counter power and competition among social groups is weakened. Money rules OK. As the pop song goes, "I want it, I want it all, I want it now."

The old checks and balance mechanisms based on the separation of typical socio-economic functions of the 'Ancien Régime' such as military or magisterial nobility, clergy, tradesmen and corporations lasted thousands of years on all continents. In modern democratic societies, lawyers will tell us that they are maintained by the more abstract constitutional mechanisms of Montesquieu's type. The purpose is to control power by dividing it. However, a sober observer of the scene suspects that these tricks are no match for Mr. D's considerable appetite. The legal prosecutors of 'mani pulite' in Milan, for instance, have been under fire while unearthing the corruption of the Italian political class including, of course, the Christian Democracy. But, in the endgame, the tycoon under investigation still leads the country and it is the magistrate who was the corruption buster, di Pietro, who will find himself gradually more lonely and then cast aside.

Thatcher's neo-liberalism opened the seas and perhaps a symbolic legacy from the Thatcher era is the son of the Iron lady. From failed accountant manager to multimillionaire, Mark Thatcher was reported to be the archetypal nepotist of the new era. The man made a mint on the strength of his mother's name, including a £12 million commission on the sale of British aerospace military aircraft to Saudi Arabia.[57] Sailing through the high sea of the 1990s corporate plunder, the Western ship was to lose its moorings. Thus democracy does not balance itself very well.

Corruption means only making money by other means. In a world dominated by plutocratic values, ethics does not fare well. While the more affluent countries can afford, on the whole, to stick to honesty, the poor countries cannot resist the lure of corrupt practices, a fact sadly illustrated by the Transparency International Corruption Perception Index. Even in an ancient country such as India, the home of Gandhi's ethical freedom campaign, modern democracy stinks. As the personal secretary of Prime Minister Shastri, Mr. C.P. Shrivastava, a prominent Indian civil servant, was used in those times to the highest ethical standards. He observes the Hydra like phenomenon. "The giving and taking of bribes is now commonly accepted as a way of life and a part of the well organized and well oiled graft machine. The poor, who cannot pay, groan and suffer and cannot further their cause. Those who have the resources, shrug their shoulders, pay the bribe and get on with the job. Most of the bureaucracy, the police, the judiciary and the political hierarchy is infected by what is truly a national epidemic."[58] As mentioned earlier, C.P. Shrivastava is Shri Mataji's husband.

FROM DEMO-NO-CRACY TO DEMONOCRACY?

When I am abroad, I always make it a rule never to criticize or attack the government of my own country. I make up for lost time when I come home.

– Winston Churchill

Democracy is currently the best system available as it tries to guarantee our basic freedoms and a level of opportunity and choice. But the opportunity for democracy to succeed in reaching common prosperity can be missed. The balance is fragile if we do not make the right choices. Let us recapitulate this short walk through the history of democracy.

Democracy had many roots, from the Icelandic council to the Swiss 'Landsgemeinde'. All these communities were small by today's standards. According to the Greek founding fathers, the people cannot assume power beyond the size of a relatively small city. Democracy was ushered into the modern age through a variety of experiments. Generally, they were linked to the fate of cities such as the Hanseatic or Italian trading centers. But, in fact, these cities mostly corresponded to a republican oligarchic regime. Bernese and Venetian patricians were certainly not promoting social equality. Modern democracy is a child of reason for it is the eighteenth century philosophe who drew the sketch of the modern political constitution.

[57] Paul Halloran and Mark Hollingsworth, Thatcher's Gold: The Life and Time of Mark Thatcher.

[58] C.P. Shrivastava, *Corruption: India's Enemy Within*, Macmillan (2001), p. 1.

As larger collectives grew, checks and balances were lost, leaving the modern ship without moorings. 'Demos' means the people, 'kratos' means power. Demo-no-cracy means that the people do not really have the power. People got ownership instead. This is not bad, but, perhaps, it is not enough. Democracy depends on the large dissemination of private property, seemingly bringing the materialist millennium within the reach of the middle class who can soon have that mirage fade away if those who are really at the helm of affairs take too many wrong turns.

We know now that our world is becoming in many ways a more dangerous place, plagued by a multitude of challenges and split by a growing and threatening disparity in income levels. This is partly because the neoliberal 1990s reduced the nexus desire-thought-action to a global money-grabbing proposition in which the West's collective resources were channeled and largely wasted away.

We still do not exactly know who is hiding behind the drive for power money?

Where is the one who set us on this course? Who is the taxi driver who has taken us for a ride? On the name plate there is only a first name: Adam. Is this the same old Adam, after a long journey away from home, a journey that went wrong? We do not know. No family name for there is not any family. If we had thought to be related we are sadly mistaken. We are not his offspring, we are just the people. He drives fast, looking straight ahead, without ever paying attention to the passengers. He does not talk to us and has hung a sign on the back of the front seat: "Do not talk to or otherwise disturb the driver." We did not even get a chance to tell him where we want to be dropped off.

This peculiar Adam is absorbed. He does not hear or see anyone. If he the first Adam, he does not seem to remember Eve or the Garden. He is absorbed because he is hosting a ghost, perhaps the ghost of Mr. D's dark side. Mr. D makes him drive. We cannot recognize the true face of Mr. D Of course, Marx had already decided that Mr. D is most likely to be a plutocrat. Marx and Engels tried to uncover Mr. D to describe his clothes, tricks and habits. Their attempt to catch him backfired mostly because they focused on sociology and economics and largely ignored the field of psychology.

Mr. D has his two sides: he is like the Jekyll and Hyde story. His luminous self carries an ideal of liberty, equality, and fraternity. He follows a path of growing maturity and balance between multiple interests so as to achieve the greatest good of the greatest number. His dark side is naturally binding. Let us again trust ancestral wisdom and give the floor to the medieval monk who had spotted the six dark horses, the shapes of mankind's enemy, because they are those who have crept into Mr. D. In Mr. D's groin, lust is working. Anger and fierce competition burn in his belly. Greed boils in his stomach. Attachment and possessiveness close his heart. His throat spits jealousy and vanity adorns his forehead. Mr. D. is made out of the anti-force of the chakras and is hiding, deep within modern man, for he is not pretty. If such is the ruler of our city, the chances are that democracy could turn into 'demonocracy'. For these are the old demons of our race that we were told in ancient times, would lead us to our destruction. Have we boarded a taxi for Armageddon?

213

Web sites for further information on Sahaja Yoga and related topics:

www.sahajayoga.org

www.yoganewyork.org

www.sakshi.org

www.daisyamerica.com